Praise for *A Joyful Noise*

"*A Joyful Noise* is a well-written celebration of the ways that music can surround a life and enrich it."   —*Dallas Morning News*

"Engagingly readable . . . A number of themes thread through this thoughtful memoir, intertwining to create complex harmonies."
                                        —*The Columbus Dispatch*

"This is a lovely memoir of life in the acutely functional family of a fine and learned composer. Deborah Weisgall writes of a milieu of discourse immersed in and emerging from music, and in which love and knowledge are not at odds. . . . *A Joyful Noise* is that of her own particular music of remembering."   —John Hollander

"An absorbing memoir, with music in the background and fore-ground."   —*New York Jewish Week*

"Deborah paints the picture [of life within the Jewish musical tradi-tion]—and it's almost impossible to depict music in words—charm-ingly, and evokes the vanished past of her father, as well as her mother and of her grandfather. From start to finish I identified in-timately with a milieu at once close and far."   —Ned Rorem

"A conventional chronology only tells us the facts; Weisgall, a poet, novelist, and art critic for *The New York Times,* tells about the pas-sion underlying them. . . . Highly recommended."
                                        —*Library Journal*

A Joyful
Noise

A Joyful Noise

Claiming the Songs of My Fathers

Deborah

Weisgall

Grove Press, *New York*

Excerpt from *Purgatory* by William Butler Yeats reprinted with the permission of Simon & Schuster, Inc., from THE COLLECTED PLAYS OF W. B. YEATS: A NEW EDITION. Copyright © 1940 by Georgie Yeats; copyright renewed © 1968 by Bertha Georgie Yeats, Michael Butler Yeats, and Anne Yeats.

Published simultaneously in Canada
Printed in the United States of America

FIRST GROVE PRESS EDITION

Library of Congress Cataloging-in-Publication Data

Weisgall, Deborah.
    A joyful noise : claiming the songs of my fathers / Deborah Weisgall.
      p. cm.
    ISBN 0-8021-3730-x (pbk.)
    1. Weisgall, Deborah—Childhood and youth. 2. Jewish women—Maryland—Baltimore Biography. 3. Jews—Maryland—Baltimore Biography. 4. Weisgall, Hugo. I. Title.
F189.B19J5889   1999
975.2'004924'0092—dc21
[B]   99-24263

Design by Laura Hammond Hough

Grove Press
841 Broadway
New York, NY 10003

00 01 02 03   10 9 8 7 6 5 4 3 2 1

In memory of my father,

Hugo Weisgall (1912–1997)

For my daughter,

Charlotte Wilder,

to remember

Make a joyful noise to the Lord, all the earth.

Serve the Lord with gladness,

Come before His presence with singing.

Know that the Lord He is God; He made us,

And we are His people and the flock in His pasture.

Enter into His gates with thanksgiving and into His court with praise;

Be thankful to Him and bless His name.

For the Lord is good, His mercy is everlasting

And His faith endures to all generations.

Psalm 100

One

Tell Your Son

When I was a child in Baltimore, Maryland, I imagined that from the highest point of the arc of my swing I could see the Pyramids in Egypt. I believed that when two people fell in love, they sang arias to each other. The deep green forest where fairy tales happened really existed, and history, remote and vivid as fairy tales, took place there, too. Time was measured in seasons, and it went in circles. I had been born after terrible events, but there had been a happy ending. I would grow; nothing else would ever change. In April I was just a month short of seven years old. Almost everyone I loved lived in Baltimore, and I would live there, too, forever.

My mother steered our blue Plymouth down the serpentine road through Druid Hill Park's great lawns. We sped past huge specimen beeches and maples with young, transparent leaves, and empty baseball diamonds cut into red Maryland clay, past the zoo's brick reptile house where my father took me to observe the python and the boa constrictor. The last sunlight turned the spring grass golden green. In the back seat, my younger brother, Jonathan, and I tilted with the curves; I concentrated on trying not to squash the bow of my beautiful new yellow, smocked, hand-me-down dress. Up front, my father balanced on his lap the special Passover nut torte my mother had baked for the Seder. We were late my father accused my mother. She had taken too much time brushing my hair, and, as usual, had misplaced her car keys and sunglasses. My stomach churned, and I prayed that they wouldn't start yelling.

We careened around the reservoir, its pale water reflecting the evening sky. Beyond the reservoir's ornamental iron railing, I saw the grand, square block of Chizuk Amuno, my grandfather's synagogue. We were almost there. My father turned and smiled at us. "Tonight there is a full moon. Passover begins in the middle of the Jewish month, on a full moon. It commemorates the Exodus from Egypt, when God delivered the Israelites."

My mother spun around a curve, and my father turned forward again and clutched the precious nut torte.

My brother looked at me, puzzled. "Delivered where?" he whispered.

"Not delivered. Saved," I told him. Almost two years younger than me, Jonny had turned five a month earlier; for seven weeks a year he seemed to be catching up with me. I did not mind putting him in his place. He regarded me suspiciously. I explained: "Sometimes delivered means saved."

The synagogue's copper dome swelled green and sacred in a city of gentile spires. My grandfather, Adolph J. Weisgal, whom we called Abba—Hebrew for father, had been the cantor of that synagogue forever. My father, Hugo Weisgall, wrote operas; he also conducted the synagogue's choir. When he was in his twenties, he had added an extra "l" to his name because, he said, it made the spelling more authentic. Forgetting about my sash, I sat on the edge of the seat with anticipation now, both pleasant and anxious. The sun had almost set, and Passover was beginning.

We passed in front of the synagogue and turned down Chauncey Avenue, where my grandparents lived. With the happy thrill I felt whenever I saw somebody who belonged to me, I recognized my grandfather walking to evening services, dashing and immaculate in his double-breasted gabardine suit, Borsalino hat, and his cane. He saluted us with his cane. My mother stopped the car and took the cake. My father got out and opened the back door on my brother's side. "Come with me, Jonny," he said, then looked at me and hesitated. Girls and women traditionally did not go to the short service before the Seder; they stayed home preparing for the feast.

"Daddy, I'm coming, too!" I declared, sliding across the seat.

My father glanced at my mother and smiled. She had not had time to put on her lipstick, and her beautiful face, with her brown eyes and dark hair, looked unfinished and harried. Everybody said I looked like her, but my hair was blond and naturally curly, while she relied on permanents. "Nath, do you want to go to services? Park at Papa's and walk back with Deborah."

No, I prayed. Say no.

My mother shook her head no, delivering me.

I scrambled out of the car. Abba hugged me perfunctorily, his mind already on higher things. Proudly, I took my father's hand, and with the men I went to *shul*. *Shul*—from the German for "school"— was what we called the synagogue; in Jewish tradition prayer and study are synonymous.

We almost never came in by the shul's grand front doors; we used the stage entrance, instead, a street-level side door on Chauncey Avenue, but this soft evening, my grandfather decided to walk around the corner to the front. A stately flight of white limestone steps the width of the building rose from the sidewalk to a portico with three sets of double oak doors. Abba climbed the long stairs vigorously. He was in his sixties and carried his cane for decorative purposes only.

The synagogue was practically empty, but Abba strode down the center aisle past rows of walnut pews as if he were a great tenor and the seats were filled with adoring fans. He had detached himself from us; he strode ahead like a king, conscious of his gift, and he greeted effusively the few men who had already arrived. He shook their hands and bowed and smiled, and they did adore him. We followed him, greeting the men, too; my father was only slightly less grand than Abba. I was terribly proud. As God visited his anger onto generations of children, he visited his love on generations of Abba's children, too, and adoration filtered down to me. Surosky the butcher, eyes rimmed red, big hands chapped red, smiled with his fleshy lips and murmured, "Beautiful." I smiled gently and bobbed my head.

I rarely saw the synagogue from the floor; usually, I went straight upstairs from the stage entrance to the choir loft. The choir loft was at the front, next to the balcony, set off by a small proscenium like a box in a theater overlooking the stage of the bimah, the wide, low platform, like a stage, where the rabbi and cantor stood. It was dark now. The open dome made the synagogue seem like an opera house. I gazed at the bimah. I loved the arches and columns of richly veined purple marble, the heavy blue velvet curtain, embroidered in gold, that covered the ark, the ornate brass lamp of the *ner tamid,* the eternal flame, that hung above the ark. The rabbi's lectern was of white marble, the cantor's of olive wood.

Daddy, Jonny, and I sat in one of the pews near the front. Abba mounted the steps to the bimah and disappeared through a small door that led to his study, which I thought was his dressing room. He appeared a few minutes later, having exchanged his hat for a yarmulke. At tonight's quick service, which the rabbi did not even attend, Abba did not wear his robes, and it had the air of a dress rehearsal. He stood at the rabbi's lectern and counted to be sure there was a *minyan,* a quorum of ten adult men.

My father found a prayer book, turned to the appropriate page, and handed it to me. I took it solemnly. The book was sacred; if you were careless and dropped it, you had to kiss it to apologize. In Hebrew school I was beginning to decipher the Hebrew letters and learning to read their sounds, which was considered more important than understanding their sense.

"Hugo! Move over!" Uncle Freddie, my father's brother, seven years younger, waited impatiently in the aisle until we made room for him. He was taller than my father and thinner, and he had more hair. They both had big mouths and round, pale blue eyes that got bigger and wilder when they took their glasses off. Freddie was a lawyer; he defended the poor who were accused of crimes, and he represented Negroes fighting for their civil rights. He understood injustice. He sang first bass in the choir and cracked jokes. He was

married and had children of his own, but Abba yelled at him as if he
were still a bad boy, always in trouble, always wrong. I adored Uncle
Freddie. "How are you, doll?" he asked, giving my shoulder a quick
squeeze. "You look gorgeous." Audaciously, he fanned a big vaude-
ville wave at my grandfather, who nodded haughtily in acknowledg-
ment and reproof.

Abba cleared his throat and began chanting at top speed. He
chanted faster than any man in the world, and this evening, especially,
he was in a hurry to get home and begin the real singing at the Seder,
the feast of Passover. But he could not resist a melody.

Our music was full of melody; it was unlike any other synagogue music. It was not wailing and melancholy but grand and operatic—I knew; my father had run an opera company, and I had heard
a lot of opera. In our synagogue, each season and holiday had its
special tunes. Abba had brought his music with him when he came
with his wife and two sons to this country in 1920 from Czechoslovakia. His father had been a cantor in central Europe, as had his father before him. Abba sang the music they sang and the songs they
had written. He had saved the music from destruction; it had nearly
been annihilated in the war, shot, starved, and gassed. This synagogue was one of the few places where it survived.

A tune caught Abba's fancy. He had started to skim the prayer,
but its lovely line seduced him. He tilted his head back and sang, and
my father and my uncle took his cue and joined in and harmonized
even though there was not supposed to be a choir at this service, even
though there was hardly anybody to hear their singing. Abba was a
tenor, my father a baritone, my uncle a bass. Their three strong voices
echoed in the empty building and rose up into the hemisphere of the
synagogue's dome. I could almost see them playing, dancing up there
with the seraphim and the messengers of God. Singing connected
them to each other and to the past and to the future; it was as real
and mighty and unattainable as God. Their brave, holy noise seemed
to me the most wonderful thing in the world. With all my heart, I
yearned to add my own voice to it. It was a music of men's voices,
though; men sang in the choir, men sang in my family.

"The Lord shall reign forever and ever," Abba read in his accented English at the end of the service. It was one of the few verses
we recited in English.

"The Lord shall rain forever and ever. And that's why the ball
game was canceled," Uncle Freddie leaned over and whispered to
my brother and me. That's what he always said, and each time it
seemed funnier; part of the joke was wondering whether Freddie
would come through. Jonny and I tried not to crack up. Freddie
watched the two of us trying not to laugh and began to laugh himself. Daddy glanced in our direction and attempted to disapprove,
but he couldn't help smiling. For us, even for my father, Freddie's
incorrigible irreverence in the presence of God and Abba made bear-
able their arduous requirements.

. . .

"What language does Abba speak best?" I asked Daddy—who spoke
every language with no accent: English, German, French, Hebrew,
Italian—while we waited for my grandfather to collect his hat and
cane after the service.

"None," he answered.

"Is it German, or English, or Hebrew?" I insisted. "Or all of
them?"

"None of them." He took my hand as we left the shul.

"Then what do you speak best?" I answered my own question
confidently: "All of them."

The full moon rose huge and golden through the linden trees
and over the roofs of the row houses. God, I thought, had chosen a
full moon for the night the Israelites escaped from Egypt. My brother
and I ran on ahead of the men, racing. My patent leather Mary Janes
gleamed in the streetlights and skidded on the sidewalk. My corkscrew curls, which my mother had painstakingly arranged, bounced
disheveled against my shoulders. I ran as fast as I could. I had long
legs, and I always won. Our cousins were waiting at the house; they
couldn't be trusted to behave in shul.

I felt the eagerness of an audience and the nerves of a performer, both. Tonight, for the first time, I was going to recite the *Ma Nishtana*, the Four Questions, which the youngest child at the table is supposed to ask. I was the oldest grandchild, but the youngest person who knew Hebrew. What is the difference between this night and all other nights? Why do we eat matzo, unleavened bread? Why bitter herbs? Why do we recline? The questions begin the Seder. They spark the telling of the story of the Exodus—this is the night God brought us out of Egypt; there was no time for bread to rise; the bitter taste of the herbs reminds us of the bitterness of enslavement; in olden days, only free men reclined while they ate—the story of the journey from slavery to freedom.

This was my debut. I was going to read the Hebrew; I was going to sing the words. My singing was going to join that play of voices—my voice, the first girl's voice. Ignoring my brother's pleas to wait for him, I ran, breathless, up the steps to the front porch of my grandparents' semi-detached house and pushed open the dark oak door that opened into a tiny vestibule. The glass-paned door to the living room was already ajar. Smells of chicken soup and turkey filled the house. Freddie's wife, Aunt Jeanne, sat alone in the living room. Thin and sexy, with short salt and pepper gray hair, she sat on the sofa, her skirt riding high on her thighs, displaying the dark tops of her stockings, and she swirled the ice cubes in her drink with her fingernail. Her long nails matched her lipstick in the color of the moment: a frosted apricot. The cuffs and hem and neck of her suit jacket were trimmed in marabou feathers dyed the taupe of the fine, light wool. She dragged on her cigarette, which she smoked in an ebony holder. "So where's my husband?" she asked in her throaty, provocative voice and thick Baltimore accent.

"He's coming," I said and asked: "Where's Mommy?" though I knew the answer. I heard her aggravated voice coming from the kitchen.

Jeanne glanced toward the back of the house. "Do you like my suit?"

I nodded. I did, very much. I reached out and stroked the marabou down on her jacket hem; I appreciated my aunt's finery. The front door opened again. Jeanne stood and twirled in her taupe high-heeled pumps. "I made it myself," she said. "I finished it this morning. Fabulous, isn't it?" The men came in, with my brother, who was pouting because he'd lost our race. Jeanne patted her flat stomach and flat rear end. My father looked away. Abba smiled. "*Gut yontif,*" he said. "*Gut yontif,* pontiff," Freddie said as he kissed his wife. I had just figured out that Yiddish expression. "Yom tov," literally good day, meant holiday in Hebrew. So, good good day, I said to myself. Despite her glamorous clothes, I thought, Jeanne could never be as beautiful as Mommy, or as good a cook, but I wished that my mother could have new clothes, too.

In the kitchen, my three cousins crowded around the icebox clamoring for Pepsi. My grandmother, Aranka, whom we called Lady, regarded them as if she didn't recognize them. She wore a plain, navy blue dress and black shoes with thick heels. Her graying hair was parted in the middle and pulled back into a bun, and her strong features crowded into narrow bones. She had deep-set anxious eyes ringed with shadows; when she saw me, she smiled, like a pale sun behind clouds. I went to kiss her, but, distracted by the turkey, which needed basting, she turned her back on me. I took her affection on trust and loved her from a distance. Like a sea anemone, she shriveled with a reticence beyond her control.

"Deborah! Get those kids out of here!" My mother's angry voice cut through the clatter. She had tied an apron over her old tweed suit; it was not sleek like Jeanne's; it pulled across her stomach, round after two babies and no exercises. Her cheeks were flushed from the heat, from the effort of helping, and from frustration. Her hair was coming loose from her barrettes, but she had put on lipstick. She charged around the kitchen, circling Ozelia Potter, Lady's languid, mahogany maid. Ozelia walked with a calm that drove my mother crazy. Ozelia cut tomatoes and iceberg lettuce into wedges as if she had all the time in the world, while my mother impatiently thrust the salad platter under her chin. There was so much to do. On the counter I noticed another tinfoil-shrouded cake beside Mommy's wrapped nut torte. "Who brought that?" I asked.

"Jeanne," Mommy muttered. "She wasn't supposed to. We don't need it."

Quickly, I poured myself a tumbler of Pepsi and hustled my brother and cousins out of the kitchen. I whispered to myself the words of the Four Questions. We raced through the narrow passageways between grownups and heavy furniture. The oak dining room table had been extended with two folding tables borrowed from the synagogue. They stretched into the living room, each covered with a white damask cloth, each place set with a silver wine cup. We circled the tables hunting for our favorite cups and moved them to where we guessed we would sit.

Guests were arriving. I hugged my father's cousin, Klari, and her husband and sons. Klari's father, Lady's brother, had been killed in the war. I thought of her as my father's only cousin, but there were others, in Budapest, whom I would never see because they were locked behind the Iron Curtain. Klari's husband, Fred Kaufman, had been a pianist. To escape the Nazis, he fled to Panama and worked in a laundry, where an explosion burned and scarred his hands. He was a scientist now. Klari brought a nut torte.

Mrs. Werner brought a nut torte. Tiny and Viennese, packed like a knish into her blue serge dress, polka dots of rouge on her cheeks and on her thin lips an inaccurate filament of lipstick, Mrs. Werner was one of the Germans, as my mother called them, one of the refugees Lady had taken in during the war. Mrs. Werner came with Mr. and Mrs. Hirschler, a gentle couple with wounded, gracious manners, who had owned a kitchen supply house in Vienna. They all smiled at me, but I was shy with them. They carried with them shreds of a different life: severe and formal clothes, hesitant English, and a sadness that frightened me.

Abba had stowed his hat and cane and inspected the preparations in the kitchen. Then he returned to the dining room and sat himself in his armchair big as a throne placed at the center of one side of the table and cleared his throat. "Come on!" he commanded.

"Where is everybody?" We children stood around waiting to take our places.

Freddie sauntered into the dining room and considered us. "You sit on my right hand, and you sit on my left hand," he intoned, pointing to Jonny and me. "And—" he paused, making sure of his audience "—I'll eat through a straw!" I laughed until I got hiccups. I was in college before I learned that Freddie got his seating plan from Groucho Marx.

"Freddie, enough!" Abba scolded. "Now, sit down. Everybody sit down."

We scuttled to the seats we had staked out, worried that somebody would usurp them. It was an aspect of our general fear and trembling; Abba could decree that we should be arranged differently. Stealthily, we shuffled the wine cups one last time. I sat to my father's left at the Seder table and Jonny sat to his right. We faced Abba. Freddie's children sat near the ends of the table, removed from Abba's direct line of vision.

Lawrence, Freddie's oldest son, spilled Jeanne's cup of wine; it puddled a purple sea on the white cloth. "Goddammit!" bellowed Abba. Lady came in from the kitchen and looked pained and disappointed. Ozelia sponged up the mess. "I need more wine," Jeanne announced, waving the empty cup.

"Nath!" my father called. "Nathalie! We're starting. Nath!"

Reluctantly, my mother emerged from the kitchen and sat beside Jonny. "Nothing's ready!" she whispered loudly to my father over my brother's head. "You should see what's going on out there. It's appalling. Ozelia isn't doing a thing."

"Don't worry about it," my father begged.

"If I don't, who will? Your sister-in-law and your cousin certainly couldn't care less."

I shivered with embarrassment, but Jeanne and Klari, who were talking hard to each other, hadn't heard. Abba cleared his throat again and opened his Haggadah, the text read at the Seder. I turned the pages of my Haggadah to the Four Questions. The Haggadah was illustrated. I turned past a picture of a family, a father, a son, and a grandson, reading from a book; their mouths were open. The mouths of the women were shut.

The Germans sat quietly. Freddie's children squirmed. Abba closed his eyes. He began to chant the Kiddush, the opening blessing over wine. He began softly. Aunt Jeanne kept talking, to Mommy now. Abba opened his eyes and glared at her. I wished I had the authority to reprimand her; I hated that he was interrupted. Halfway through the Kiddush, the chant blossomed into melody. His sons joined in. Abba had tears in his eyes. The Germans listened in sad wonder. Then we all sang the Shehecheyanu, the prayer thanking God for bringing us to that time, that season, in our lives. Our voices clung to the heroic voices of the three men. Crowded around my grandparents' table in Baltimore, Maryland, nine years after the end of the Second World War, our family was lucky beyond measure and blessed. It was almost my turn.

Abba got up and washed his hands, as was prescribed in the Haggadah. I heard the water run in the sink; I hoped his hands were really dirty and he would take a long time. He sat back down. How beautiful the Hebrew letters looked, like drops of black water. I stared at them. They began to run and blur. I put my finger on the first word, to hold the letters still. "So?" Abba asked, surveying the children.

"I'm going to say the Ma Nishtana," I said.

"Deborah will say the Ma Nishtana," my father announced at the same time. Abba smiled and raised one eyebrow. His pale blue eyes widened.

My face grew hot, and I tucked my hair behind my ear even though it was already caught with barrettes.

"*Ma—*" Abba prompted.

"Papa!" my father admonished.

"*Ma nishtana,*" I began to sing. The table fell silent. I heard my voice, high and piping and wavering: a trickle of sound. "*Ha leila hazeh mikol halaylos.*" There. The first question finished. I took a deep breath.

"*Sheb'chol,*" Abba said impatiently: the first word of the next sentence.

I glared at him, furious. I knew that word. I was just breathing. "*Sheb'chol*," I repeated. The note was wrong. Vaguely, I heard my father humming. "*Sheb'chol halaylos*—" My voice shook. I hurried the rest of the words, but I could not get the tune. I couldn't even try to sing. I had to get the words out before Abba corrected me again. I wanted everybody to know that I knew all the words. I didn't need help. I could do it.

"Louder," Daddy urged.

I could speak no louder. I finished, shaking and dizzy with disappointment. I had not sung; my voice had failed. Lady smiled sadly. Mommy smiled with pride, but she knew nothing about this business. My mother could neither read Hebrew nor sing. Abba nodded briefly at me and launched into the first answering paragraph of the Haggadah. The Hebrew spilled from his mouth in a glorious rapid river, words and music inseparable. Haggadah means "telling." I knew that, but I had no idea what Abba was singing; I tried to read the English translation, but much of it had to do with numbers and times of day and night and the names of ancient rabbis. The telling was rushing past me, and I tried to catch what I could of it.

But my father pointed out one passage. His strong, stubby pianist's finger touched the English: "You shall tell your son this story. Tell him—"

"What about your daughter?" I interrupted him. "Why doesn't it say 'Tell your daughter,' too?"

"'Son' is a general term for a child, the way we say 'he' to refer to an individual. It's a convention, just a way of speaking." My father answered my questions with great seriousness, although I did not always understand his explanations. When I had asked him, recently, how babies were made, he had told me: "Naturally, it's very pleasant."

"It should say daughters, too," I insisted.

My father shrugged. "It implies daughters," he said.

I wanted to believe him, but I could not. Doubt and failure pulled at my brain. It was a physical sensation, a painful angry buzzing that brought me close to tears.

Daddy went on: "Tell your child that on Passover we eat no leavened bread for seven days because of what the Lord did for me when I came out of Egypt." Each father, my father explained gravely, must tell this story as if it had happened to him, as if he himself had gone out from Egypt. That was memory. The Jews must never forget. I heard the changed word: "son" to "child," and I was almost comforted.

I asked: "Did you? Did this happen to you?"

"I know what it felt like," my father answered, and I believed that.

. . .

Abba and my father and Uncle Freddie sang every Hebrew word of the Haggadah (and the few paragraphs in Aramaic, too). They took off their suit jackets and loosened their ties. Every few paragraphs, Abba would let Daddy chant for a while; Freddie, who wasn't even a year old when he arrived in this country, couldn't read Hebrew as well as my father. My father was eight when he immigrated, and in Czechoslovakia—the name itself, thick with consonants, was interior and mysterious—he had already been studying music for four years and Hebrew for three. I had been born in Czechoslovakia, too, and I proudly attached to myself its dark magic. But compared to my father I knew about as much Hebrew as a *goy*. I was like Freddie, brushed by the place. Freddie had had an American education, too, but Freddie sang.

I would, too. I would not give up. I would learn. Abba began a song. I stopped up my ears with my hands so that I could hear my own voice, but the other voices intruded. I heard them too well; I did not know which line to follow. I got confused. Not that it mattered; nobody could hear me.

"Jonathan! Sing!" Abba commanded my brother. Jonny sang— not words; he did not know the Hebrew words, but Abba listened attentively and smiled approval nonetheless.

I waited for my grandfather to command me.

"Lawrence!" he ordered. "Sammy!" He glared at my boy cousins. Bad like their father, they lowered their eyes. My face burned with eagerness, but Abba did not ask me. I had had my chance to sing alone.

Abba washed his hands again, according to the ritual prescribed in the Haggadah, and the feast began. We all had to swallow bits of bitter horseradish before we gobbled up matzo and *charoset*—chopped nuts, apples, cinnamon, and wine, symbolizing the mortar the Hebrews used to build the pyramids—and eggs, symbols of springtime, that had been boiled for twenty-four hours until the whites turned brown. Then gefilte fish—pike and carp my grandmother had chopped into quenelles, which my father loathed; he would eat nothing that swam. Then we had *knedlach*, matzo balls, in soup, then turkey—Freddie and I vied to grab the drumsticks off the platter; in my family you fought for everything—and sweet potatoes and string beans and cranberry sauce and salad. It was the same every year.

The women, except for Jeanne, who believed in being a guest, scuttled back and forth between the dining room and the kitchen. They frowned, concentrating on dirty dishes and food. "Deborah!" my mother, who believed in chores, called. "Help clear the table!" I pretended not to hear.

Finally, Jeanne got up and headed toward the kitchen, not to help, but to supervise the serving of her dessert. A few minutes later, the women unveiled their nut tortes and placed them on the oak sideboard. The cakes were their voices. Lady put her sponge cake at the head of the parade. Everybody was careful to eat Lady's cake plus the cake his or her closest relative had baked. Aunt Jeanne shamelessly told everybody that her nut torte was the best and served it even to those who hadn't requested it. I tried one crumbly bite and left the rest. People asked for my mother's. Sedulously, I took a piece of Klari's cake, too.

After dinner, the Hebrew in the Haggadah stretched in long blocks. Abba chanted at top speed, but he stopped often and sang ravishing, tender tunes, melodies garlanded on two or three lines of text, before he rushed on. Other verses came with vigorous music, and he banged the flat of his hand on the table to mark the syncopation. Matzo crumbs danced. Abba pounded the beat, and then he raised his hand and stretched out his arm, bringing into his song my father and my uncle. They did not so much sing as unleash their voices, straining to be let loose. Their voices were different; my grandfather's was high and clarion, Freddie's bass was rough, my father's baritone was mellow and expressive, but they blended so naturally that together they sounded like one being. Singing was their peace and their connection, their love, their combat: their life.

Abba sent the children to open the door for Elijah. According to legend, the prophet Elijah flew around the world to visit every Seder; we poured a big, ornate silver cup of wine for him, and as the adults sang the song beseeching him to come and redeem us, we crowded into the vestibule. I, the eldest cousin, held open the screen door and watched for the spirit. I stood on the threshold, the heat of the house at my back, the cool spring night air on my face. Here, the voices weren't so loud. The moon had risen, distant now, white and full. I stood at the boundary between two mysteries: the bright urgent noise and a dark restoring silence. The song ended, and I closed the door and went back to the table.

For some of the psalms and songs, we had three or four different melodies, and we sang them all, one after the other. Each expressed a different mood; usually we sang the slow ones first, and usually we saved the melodies written by our family for last. As we finished those songs, Daddy said to me: "This was by your great-grandfather," or "Your great-great grandfather wrote this." The songs formed a golden chain dangling in front of me, out of my reach. The men with their big voices sang for the sake of the past; it had all happened to them, terrible and wonderful things, thousands of years of memory. Armed with their voices and music, they were our warriors.

We sang a few traditional tunes, too, but not very many. Freddie had made up lyrics to one of them, the tune to "Adir Hu," a hymn listing God's virtues. First we sang the hymn straight, then Freddie went around the table substituting our names: Jonny, too, Deborah, too, Hugo, too, Nathalie, too, Klari, too, all around the table. Finally we sang Freddie's verse:

Adir Hu went to the zoo,
Saw a monkey and a kangaroo.
Said Adir Hu to the kangaroo,
"Why do you stay in the zoo?"
The monkey said, "We get fed.
That's why we stay in the zoo."

Freddie and his children and my brother and I shouted the words. My father joined us; my grandfather smiled. Lady, despite herself, smiled, too. This wasn't in the script; nowhere was it written in the Haggadah, but it stayed. Every year we sang it. Even when we were all adults, not a child at the table, we sang it, thrilling again to childish insurrection.

We ended with "Chad Gadya," which translates from Aramaic into "One Kid." Father bought the goat, the cat ate the goat, the dog ate the cat, all the way through the butcher to the Angel of Death and finally to God. Tired, I sat in Daddy's lap. My brother dozed against Mommy's shoulder. We sang all twelve verses, my father, my uncle, and my grandfather in turn taking the solos. I leaned my head against my father's chest, and his voice reverberated in my skull, loud and hard and wonderful.

Lady sang "Chad Gadya." Mrs. Werner and the Hirschlers sang, tears in their eyes, remembering the Seders of their childhood, the voices of their dead families. My father got Fred Kaufman to sing an inner line of harmony. One Kid; the kid was Israel, the Jews. We got to the last verse, the last chord, and the Seder was over. We sat, dismayed and unwilling to end, and so we began the last verse again. My father took the solo. *"And the Holy One, Blessed be He, came and conquered the Angel of Death."* My father conducted; his arms waved on either side of me. We hummed as he repeated the chain: the Angel of Death, the Butcher, the Ox, the Water. One Kid, persecuted, suffering, redeemed. Everybody sang now. *Chad gadya.* It wasn't exactly singing. Our voices grew louder and louder; the minor chord blossomed into major. We each found a note, any note, and we shouted it out—I heard my mother, piercing and hopeless—in one discordant, triumphant, and joyful noise.

. . .

During the ride home, I pressed my face against the car window. The moon lit the park's lawns blue, and stagy little blue-white clouds floated in the sky. My grandparents' house condensed to a dark, magnetic place, a place of arcane secrets and fresh yearning. Beside me, Jonny slept. My parents must have thought me asleep, too.

"Jonny sings rather well," I heard my father say to my mother in the front seat.

"What about me?" I protested.

"Deborah, you don't sing in tune."

"You're like me," my mother said.

I hummed the songs as quietly as I could, aching to get them right, afraid that my father would hear my wrong notes and correct me. They ran perfectly through my head but not from my mouth. I loved them. I wanted them.

"Jeanne's cake was too dry," my mother said.

"I didn't have any," my father answered.

My breath fogged the window. I drew a Star of David in it. The illustrations in the Haggadah of the Egyptians drowned by the closing waves of the Red Sea showed bodies and chariots and horses tumbled like clothes in a washing machine. I wished God had spared the innocent horses. Almost home, we passed the Pimlico Race Track. God had shielded his Chosen People, the Israelites, with pillars of clouds, pillars of fire. I loved that history. I, in Baltimore, in the United States of America, in the world, in the universe, yearned to experience those miracles as my father had, and his father and his father's father had, too. My desire was as strong as theirs; my voice was not. My breath stalled against my vocal cords, and the back of my throat throbbed from stopped-up songs and angry tears. I wanted to sing. I wanted to be heard.

Two

A New Dress

It was early May, two days before my birthday. The school bus dropped me off in front of the ragged hedge bordering our front lawn. Luxuriant shoots wrecked the wall of greenery. All the other hedges in the neighborhood were neat, but my mother pruned haphazardly, when she couldn't stand looking at stubble anymore. Our car was gone. There was no telling when she would come back. I hoped she hadn't locked me out. Sometimes she left the door open, but sometimes I had to wait.

Sycamores, their bark mottled like camouflage, lined our street. I heard a car engine a block away and hoped for the sky blue of our Plymouth turning the corner. No. I started up the cement walk to the porch. A blue spruce stood to the left of the path and a big maple to the right; the red Baltimore clay was bald beneath their shade. I walked as slowly as I could, scuffing. Dust filmed my shoes. Maybe, please, she would drive up before I got to the porch steps.

A crashing chord blasted from our house. My father's voice boomed: "*Anthony's Pig!*" I hadn't expected him to be home. Greatly relieved, I ran up the stairs. Anthony's Pig. He'd been singing about that pig for weeks. The window of his piano room opened onto the porch. My father was composing an opera, a commissioned work, that was to be produced by The New York City Opera at Center. *Six Characters in Search of an Author,* based on the play by Luigi Pirandello: It was the first opera he'd written that his own company, the Hilltop Opera, would not perform. I sat on the top step and lis-

18

tened. He played the same progression of dissonant chords again and again. The notes fell, high and jarring, like shards of glass. He began to sing over the chords, first in his baritone and then in falsetto, repeating a jagged line that approached melody, then veered away. "*Anthony's Pig!*" he sang. "*Anthony's Pig!*" He stamped out the beat with his heel. Anthony's Pig. I had no idea why he was singing about an animal, a pig, especially. Pigs were not kosher.

The sound of his work, anxious and relentless, not-yet-music, was as much a part of him as his smell or his glasses or the cambric handkerchief he knotted around his neck to catch his sweat when the weather got hot. His sound permeated our house, and on the days when he was not at home the silence of his absence was as loud as his noise. On Tuesdays he took the sleeper train to New York to teach at the Juilliard School of Music and the Cantors Institute of the Jewish Theological Seminary. He spent Wednesday nights at the Hotel Paris in Manhattan, returned to Baltimore Thursday evening, and went straight to a rehearsal of the Chizuk Amuno chorus. He finally got home after my brother and I were asleep. Wednesday and Thursday were the silent days.

He sat at the piano in a T-shirt and shorts. Sheets of music paper spilled out of a black loose-leaf binder and spread across the piano's music stand. A boxy metronome stood at the bass end of the piano; sharp yellow pencils and a pink eraser were arrayed at the treble end. My father held a pencil in his mouth as he played. He stopped to erase some notes and write down a few others. He did not notice me looking through the window.

It was a soft, sunny day. I loved the warming certainty of springtime. The grass, where it grew in our yard, wasn't mowed. The house had once had beautiful gardens: there was a holly tree in the front, and in the back there were three apple trees and a cherry tree and a long, wooden arbor covered with red climbing roses. The hairy stems of gone-by poppies marked an overgrown perennial bed. Mittens, our marmalade cat, trotted up the steps and brushed against my legs. I lowered my head, and he nuzzled my nose. His white nose was gray from dirt, but his fur smelled sweet from the long grass. He was young and new and skittery. I patted him, and he arched back and forth. Encouraged, I tried to pull him onto my lap. He tensed and wriggled from my arms and shivered off my touch. I scratched, pleading, at the fabric of my skirt. "Here, kitty!" I whispered, but he compacted into a crouch and purred at me from a distance.

I waited on the porch, half inside, half out, still in the easy world. From the outside, our house was ordinary, too plain, I thought, for what went on inside. It was white clapboard with an L-shaped porch; not even a turret gave it romance. But inside it was filled with things my parents had brought home with them from Prague, marvelous things, fragile and irreplaceable.

Opening the door, I felt, as always, half a stranger to the European splendor of our house. Mittens slithered past me. I slammed the screen door for my father to hear.

He played a ribbon of high fast notes. "Hello!" he shouted.

"Hi, Daddy. It's me. I'm home." I waited at the door to his piano room.

He played a chromatic scale ending on an unresolved, unsatisfied tone. "Where's your mother?"

"How should I know?"

"She was supposed to pick up your brother half an hour ago. Doris Rogers called looking for her." Not knowing where my mother was always upset him, left him incomplete.

"She'll be back soon." I assuaged my own anxiety.

My father banged a loud, distressing chord. "Close that door, will you, darling?" he said.

I shut his door, keeping myself out. I threw down my book bag and the jacket my mother insisted I wear against the brief morning chill. The room—it must have once been the parlor, but my parents called it the hall—was lit a dim yellowy green. My mother kept the blinds closed to prevent sunlight from fading upholstery. "*Anthony's Pig!*" Daddy sang softly, aware of me. His noise built a wall around him that I could not breach.

For comfort, I gave myself over to the room's pleasures. My father had bought the art and furniture during the war, in London and in Prague; its arrangement was my mother's work. She had a sense of a room's rhythms. She knew how to beguile the eye. Here, beauty counted; Prague's enchantment held. A disappointing stained-glass window in a geometric pattern of amber and brown was set high in one wall, but she couldn't help that. Lozenges of topaz light tinted the underwater blues of the oriental rug a springtime green. Silks and damasks picked up the colors in the rug. The cabriole legs of our tables and chairs danced around the edges of the room. When it was clean and perfect like this, like a setting for high drama, I hesitated to sit down and dent the sofa pillows. This was not a room in which to enact my small stories.

Little bronze Roman gods sat on a shelf; beside them a carved ivory St. Sebastian six inches high was propped like an archery target against a lightning-struck ivory tree trunk. On the mantel a pair of turquoise porcelain Ming ducks nested in ormolu candlesticks cast in the shape of reeds. Between the ducks hung a painting of a writhing naked man: St. Anthony. St. Anthony, my father had told me, in the desert tortured by the temptations of the flesh; the temptations, however, were so dark I could barely make them out.

Temptations of the flesh. St. Anthony's flesh glowed lunar white. He lay across the foreground of the painting. His arms and legs knotted behind his back. A dull, faint halo hovered behind his head. Why is he twisted? I had asked my father. He answered: The artist lived in Italy in the sixteenth century, when it was the fashion to paint people in impossible positions. That kind of painting was called mannerism. Did they have bad manners? I asked, and he laughed. He loved this painting, its languorous, seductive torment.

St. Anthony's flesh was firm and muscled, but his skin was painted as delicately as a girl's. His neck seemed pressed against the earth by an invisible boot. His tormented eyes searched past the picture and found me. Usually I avoided his eyes. This time I stared back, repulsed and fascinated, drawn by his pain and desire. His luminous fingers reached from the canvas. I closed my eyes against him and turned away. I looked back over my shoulder. He was still staring. I faced him and stuck out my tongue. He receded, like a nightmare, into the murky varnish of his trials.

I picked up a silver condiment holder from Prague. It was an open-work cylinder, about four inches high, meant to contain a liner of cobalt glass. My mother stacked cigarettes in it when she gave parties. Stray flakes of tobacco, aromatic and glamorous, clung to the bottom. The basket's silver sides were worked in low relief into a landscape traversed by a path. I traced the path with my finger. It bordered hedges, crossed an arching bridge over a silver brook where trolls might have hidden, then, ever diminishing, it wound up to a castle tower on top of a mountain, near the rim. I pushed at the tower's arched door, but it was only carved into the silver and did not open.

. . .

The Hilltop Opera Company survived for four summers, until 1951. My mother worked in the box office and kept the books; my father was music director. The company put on his operas, *The Tenor* and *The Stronger*, as well as *Albert Herring* by Benjamin Britten, Smetana's *The Bartered Bride*, Gilbert and Sullivan. I knew them all; I saw them all. My father often held rehearsals at our house. After a rehearsal of his opera *The Tenor*, based on a play by the Viennese playwright Frank Wedekind, my parents and the stage director had loaded our furniture into a truck and driven to the theater, a converted barn on a working dairy farm in the rolling hills west of Baltimore. The next day I discovered, amidst the weathered, unfinished posts and beams of the barn, our brocaded sofa, side tables, lamps whose shades my mother had sewn from the parchment leaves of illuminated medieval manuscripts, a couple of chairs. Up on the stage, under lights, they seemed two-dimensional and not quite ours. I wanted them returned. "Will they ever come back?" I asked my mother.

"Of course," she answered, her voice sharp with mistrust. "They'll come back. They'll come back. They'll be wrecked, but they'll come back."

Some careless singer who did not appreciate good things was going to scratch an inlaid surface or dislodge a sliver of veneer. I winced from the table's pain as its skin was flayed. Or jostle a delicate table leg; or get makeup on damask upholstery. During the action of the opera, the Tenor was supposed to overturn one of the chairs.

"Tell him to be careful," Mommy warned my father. "Tell him to knock it over gently, with both hands. He can't let it drop. You have to keep an eye on our furniture."

"I'm worried enough about whether he can sing the notes," my father retorted.

At *The Tenor*'s first performance, I sat with my mother. I didn't understand the story. The loud, angry singing frightened me. At the end of the opera the Tenor shot his wife. The shot, a brutal crack, happened in almost our living room. I jumped and clutched my mother. "It's not real," she whispered. "It's not a real gun." I started to cry and hid my head in her lap. "Shh," she whispered. "Shh. It's almost over."

A few moments later, there were the dead wife and the Tenor standing on stage smiling and bowing and holding hands. The audience applauded. My father came out, too, and bowed, beaming; his glasses flashed with reflected spotlights. But I held my ears, fearing the next shot.

Our furniture came back. "Look at this!" My mother rocked the overturned chair. One of the back legs wobbled. "I told you this would happen." She ran her fingers over the top of a little table. "It's scratched. What could they have done to this? How could this have happened? I told you it would. You shouldn't have given them our things. This is ridiculous! Hugo, you're going to have to tell them to get this repaired."

"With what?" my father retorted. "There isn't enough money to pay me, let alone fix your furniture."

"It's not my furniture. It's ours. It's all we've got. And it's ruined. Absolutely ruined." Mommy caressed the top of the table as if it were a wounded pet. "Never again. They can't have anything of ours ever again."

"Don't worry about that. We won't do *The Tenor* ever again, either."

I waited for the next volley, fearful and fascinated. I never had the sense to leave them alone.

The scratch cut like a moral failure across the table. Daddy put the table back where it belonged and arranged a lamp to hide the scar. "In Europe," he said, "we wouldn't have to lend our furniture."

"In Europe," my mother said, "you could earn a living writing operas." Her tone was vehement, still, but I could hear that her anger had shifted. "And your operas would be done in opera houses, not barns." She sniffed the back of their settee. "This smells like hay, and—" she glanced at me. "Manure."

My father smiled ruefully. "Maybe that's only fitting."

. . .

Mittens meowed and arched against me as I headed into the kitchen. It was a dark sliver of a room painted yellow to try to make it bright; my mother had turned the original kitchen into our dining room and jammed a sink and a stove and a refrigerator into what had been the pantry. She desired public grandeur, not domestic convenience. Accidentally, I kicked the cat's dish across the floor. It was empty. Dried bits of food stuck to its sides. It was supposed to be my job to feed him, but I hated the smell of cat food. It was too early for his dinner, I decided.

I checked the refrigerator. Mommy had made custard: six glass ramekins, each topped with a drift of meringue; she knew I loved it. I ate two cups and went back into the hall. I pulled up the blind over the front window and waited, suspended in a cottony white anxiety, imagining my mother in a car crash, in a bank robbery. I sat on the radiator's cold coils. In his piano room, my father crashed to a crescendo. "*Of all creatures both little and big, /There is none with the remarkable features/Of Anthony's Pig!*" My father sang a whole line, ending with a triumphant cacophony on the piano. He laughed out loud.

With *Six Characters,* everything would change. "*Today we shall rehearse our novelty again,*" my father sang in falsetto. "*Weis-*

gall's Temptation of Saint Anthony." Sharp little high notes minced after him.

Blue metal flashed through the leaves of the hedge. My mother swooped to a stop at the curb in front of the walk and hurried up the path, clutching her purse, her keys, and two department store boxes. She wore a dress and pumps and bright lipstick; her heels rapped on the wooden porch floor. As she came inside, her forehead furrowed, and she bit her lower lip.

She dropped her bundles in a heap beside the front door.

"What's in the boxes?" I asked.

She smiled mysteriously and put her finger to her red lips. "Shh. Your father's working. Don't disturb him."

"Are they for me?"

Her brown, almond-shaped eyes narrowed. "Maybe."

"Can I open them? Can I?"

"Darling, don't you want to wait?" she teased. She didn't want to. I snatched the boxes and followed her into the dining room and put them on the table, which was covered with a plastic cloth printed to look like damask. The cloth was sticky with spots of red jelly from my brother's breakfast.

"Deborah, be careful!" she admonished and pushed the boxes to the clean part of the table. She spotted the empty ramekins on the kitchen counter. "I see you found the custard. I can't hide anything from you, can I?"

I shook my head.

"Do you want another?"

"I already had two. Are both boxes for me?"

"Isn't one enough?" She pushed one toward me and glanced at the closed doors of the piano room; my father was worrying a cluster of high notes.

"Now, this is from Lady, too, and Nanny." Nanny was my mother's mother. "We all bought it together. For your birthday."

I unlatched the cardboard clasps, unfolded the crisp white tissue and lifted out a dress made of fine, almost transparent voile printed with a pattern of tiny yellow rosebuds that hung over a creamy cambric underskirt. A black velvet ribbon was sewn around the waist, and its streamers were tied in a precise symmetrical bow.

"Isn't it beautiful!" Mommy exclaimed.

I nodded. It was taking me a while to comprehend it. I did not remember ever having a brand-new dress, one that wasn't a hand-me-down from Eddie Shalowitz's daughters. Mr. Shalowitz owned an insurance company and was a member of the congregation. His wife had beautiful taste; even my critical mother thought so. The only drawback was that the Shalowitz girls were much larger than I was, but those clothes delighted me, especially in their abundance. This new dress seemed as precious and as difficult as a work of art.

"I wish it had a ruffle," I said.

"A ruffle? Deborah! This dress is classic. It doesn't need ruffles. Ruffles would be too much. They would ruin the whole thing." She was almost shouting. "I shouldn't have bought it." Her voice had quieted. "I saw it the other day with Bess." She called her mother by her first name, as if they were friends. "I couldn't get over it. I thought how beautiful you would look in it, and I had to have it. That's why I'm late. I went all the way downtown." She looked pleased and doubtful and guilty over her extravagance. "I have to pick up your brother. I was supposed to be at the Rogers's ages ago. It takes so long to get everything done. I never have a moment to sit down. Look! I haven't even cleaned up the breakfast dishes." Her smile narrowed to a harried frown.

I sniffed the dress's new smell and touched its hanging tags and the gauzy material. I rubbed my fingers over the nap of the velvet.

"Are your hands clean?"

I nodded.

"No, they're not. Go wash them."

I went into the kitchen and ran my fingers under the cold water.

"Nath!" my father called.

I came back into the dining room as my father emerged from his piano room. His hair, balding on top, curled over his ears. "Nath! Where have you been? My God, I thought something terrible had happened to you. Doris Rogers called an hour ago. You have to go pick up your son." My mother tried to hide the unopened box on a chair. Daddy took off his glasses and rubbed his eyes. He looked lost and unfocused. He put back his glasses and saw the packages. "What are those?"

"Deborah's birthday present. The dress. The dress that Bess and Aranka bought for her."

"And what's in that?" He pointed to the box on the chair.

"Just something I picked up. Nothing, really. Just a dress."

"What do you need that for?"

She stared at him. Her eyes and mouth narrowed. "Because I don't have anything to wear. Because I haven't bought anything in years." She pushed my dress box aside, and it toppled onto the floor. Tissue wafted across the black and white vinyl tiles. At night, with the candles lit, that floor looked just like marble. Now it was flecked with crumbs. I scrambled to rescue the paper. "Where are my keys?" my mother yelled. "Deborah! What happened to my keys?"

"How should I know?" I spoke with my father's voice. The keys were on the floor, under the dress box.

I handed them to her. My mother glared at me. My father retreated to his piano room, slammed the door, and banged out angry chords.

. . .

The holy smell of roasting chicken rose through the house. We had chicken for dinner every Friday night. I came downstairs and wandered into the kitchen. "I'm starving!" I announced.

"If I didn't have so much to do, we could eat at a decent hour." My mother sipped from a tumbler she kept beside the sink. The counters were cluttered with preparation. She had taken a long time to fetch my brother from the Rogers's house. The laugh track of a television show drifted into the kitchen. Jonny loved television.

I opened the refrigerator.

"Don't eat anything, now. You'll spoil your appetite." Mommy thrust a handful of heavy silverware at me. "Here. Go set the table."

A capital "G" surmounted by a crown was engraved on the handle of each piece. The service had been made for a Bohemian prince. It amused my mother that we, in suburban Baltimore, ate on a plastic tablecloth with this silver and Meissen plates. We had more sets of Meissen porcelain in the basement, packed in barrels and cushioned by wood shavings. With the curtains closed, blocking the lights of the neighbors' houses, and candlelight enhancing the illusion that our checkered vinyl was marble, it was easy to pretend that we still lived in the hills of Bohemia.

My mother's eyes were red. She had changed out of her dress and wore denim pedal-pushers and a plaid shirt. Her stomach bulged slightly. Her lustrous dark hair, frizzed at the ends by a permanent, was coming loose from her barrette. The heat of her dissatisfaction filled the narrow kitchen. The Shabbos candles, short, white, and quick burning, stood ready in their candlesticks. I arranged knives and forks, pointing the knife blades inward, sure I would miss some detail and do the job wrong. From my father's piano room, a long, lyrical melody flickered like a smile over the house. I stopped still and smiled back. Afterward, there was silence, and then the melody repeated, twisted and disguised in dissonance.

"What else do I need?" I went back into the kitchen.

My mother opened the oven and pulled the rack halfway out to baste the chicken.

"It looks done to me," I said.

"It's not brown enough," she growled. She squeezed the bulb of the baster fiercely. Juice bubbled like molten lava. "Ouch!" she shouted and dropped the baster to clutch her forearm. A blob of fat spattered onto the floor.

My father came out of his room. "Nath! Did you hear that? Nath!" he exclaimed. "That quote—that tune from Strauss?" My mother held her arm under the faucet. "What happened?" he asked. "Can I help?"

"It's a little late for help." With her free hand, Mommy thrust a wad of paper towels at him. "Close the oven and wipe the floor. There's grease all over it."

My father did as he was told. My mother reached over his head
to stir the rice on the stove. "Excuse me," she said sarcastically. She
took another sip from her glass. Dinner was far away.

Finally, she called us in. Jonny sat down. The food was on the
table; my mother lingered in the kitchen. Jonny watched her warily,
ready to run back to television land if a fight started. "Nath, come
here," Daddy called. "Deborah's lighting the candles." We waited.
"Nathalie! Come say the B'racha with Deborah." He lit the match
and handed it to me. "*Baruch atah adonai, eloheinu melech ha'olam,*"
I recited quickly in a quavering voice: blessed art Thou, our Lord,
our God, King of the world. I never sang the blessing. Out of the
corner of my eye, I saw my mother standing in the doorway. "*Asher
kidishanu bimitzvosav vitzivanu lihadlik ner shel Shabbos.*" Who made
us holy with His commandments and commanded us to light the
Shabbos candle. Hesitantly, Mommy accompanied me in the Hebrew
syllables. I wanted to shake off her voice riding mine. This moment
belonged to me. I lit the candles.

"Can I light one?" my brother asked.

"This is for women to do, Jonny," Daddy told him. "And, believe me, the Jewish religion doesn't give women very much to do."

It was all we did for the Sabbath at our house, lighting the
candles and eating roast chicken and rice. At home we never said
Kiddush; my father never poured wine into a silver cup and sang
the long blessing. We never had *challah,* egg bread braided and
sprinkled with poppy seeds and eaten after a prayer. I had the sense
that those ceremonies did not belong here, that by marrying my
non-observant mother, my father had forsaken the daily practice
of Judaism. Daddy never spoke to me about prayer; he never talked
to me about God. He left ritual to Abba, as if it lost meaning when
it was not performed by a man who could fulfill the ancient commandment to love God with all one's heart and soul and with all
one's might. Our lapses bothered me; although I sensed my father's
ambivalence, I blamed my mother. It was somehow her fault that
my father felt constrained in his own house, that he separated us
from his faith.

"Nath, come sit!"

"Mommy!" I echoed.

She didn't come to the table until I had almost finished what was on my plate. She put her sweating tumbler on the table; she had refilled it with fresh ice. She regarded my empty dish. "See?" she exclaimed. "If I sit down, I'll only have to jump up again."

"Then if the kids want something, they'll just have to wait," said my father, and, mustering a Sabbath peace, he softened his voice and added: "This is delicious."

"It's the same thing we have every week. It's your mother's recipe. Ginger and paprika on the chicken."

"But you're the one who cooks it."

She bent her head over her plate, resisting him. Picking every bit of flesh from the chicken bones, she took forever to eat.

"Can I be excused?" I asked.

"Not until your mother's finished," my father said.

I sighed angrily. Her glass left a ring of water on the tablecloth. She sipped from it and cut a small, precise morsel of chicken and chewed slowly.

"Can I go?" Jonny asked.

My mother glanced at him. "You haven't eaten anything. Look at all that rice, and you haven't touched your string beans. Finish your string beans. You'll sit there until you do."

Jonny blinked and looked hopelessly at the beans. He hated green food.

"Denis Johnston's libretto is absolutely wonderful," my father said. "Denis is a very funny man."

My mother shook her head. "Given the way singers enunciate—or don't—nobody will ever be able to understand the words. So who cares if the libretto's funny?"

"I do. The libretto's not for the audience, it's for me—for the composer."

My mother was mixing salad and didn't answer at first. I snatched the string beans from Jonny's plate and stuffed them into my mouth. Jonny pushed his rice around, spilling most of it onto the tablecloth. Mommy said: "Maybe you should care more about the audience."

"Maybe you should care more about the composer. Maybe you should criticize things you know something about."

She flushed and stiffened and gulped from her glass. Its rim bore the imprint of her red lipstick.

I spoke quickly. "Daddy, I thought your opera was about six characters. But you were singing that it was about the temptation of Saint Anthony."

He smiled, diverted. "No, darling, that's the name of the opera within the opera. It's still about six characters who walk into the middle of that opera and take over."

"Well, what about Anthony's pig?"

"'Anthony's Pig' is a pretend aria. It's supposed to be silly; it makes fun of operas."

"But what's it about? Is it about the Anthony on our wall?"

This time, he laughed. "Why, yes, I suppose it is. I never thought of that. Good for you, Deborah!"

"Can we be excused now?"

"Of course," he said. Jonny and I jumped up. As I passed by Daddy's chair, he reached for me and pulled me close to him. "You're a very smart little girl," he whispered as he hugged me. As he let me go, I saw my mother's look: lost, angry, between tears and fury. "Jonny!" she called, but he had fled.

. . .

My bedroom was full of precious things. The headboard and foot-board of the sleigh bed were carved with garlands, the dresser was veneered with a pattern of vines, and its ormolu drawer pulls had been cast in the shape of leaves. The mirror had a gilded gesso frame. My walls were papered a pale, grown-up green to set off the draw-ings: there were putti, and a red chalk madonna and child without haloes, so they could almost be a generic pair. Over the bed hung a colored pencil study of animals, crouching rabbits surrounding a sitting greyhound. It was by Oskar Kokoshka, a Czech expressionist artist who had been a friend of my father, and Kokoshka had in-scribed it to him.

I picked up books of fairy tales, Andersen and Grimm. In the illustrations, Hansel got stuffed into an oven behind the gingerbread house, dogs had eyes as big as saucers, a witch gloated over a golden cage imprisoning a bird that was once a princess. Princes were trans-formed into swans. I loved that story, "The Wild Swans," Andersen's tale of a princess who wove twelve shirts from nettles to change her twelve enchanted brothers back from swans into men. She did not have time to finish all the shirts, and the youngest was left with the wing of a swan. I thought of my brother deformed with a wing and shivered with delicious pain.

Downstairs, my mother clattered the pots and pans, danger-ously loud. I heard my father coming up the steps. "Daddy," I called. "Would you come read to me?"

"I have to put your brother to bed."

"Please!"

He called Jonny into my room, and the three of us sat across my bed and leaned against the wall under two drawings of putti. I handed my father Andersen, open to "The Wild Swans," and snuggled against him. Reading, he threw himself into the characters. His stepmother voice and his witch voice, his shrill little princess voice: I heard in them a half-intentional mockery that shut me out of the story. "Read with your own voice," I begged.

"I don't like that story," my brother announced.

"I would have finished that sleeve," I reassured him, guiltily. "I would have saved you. I wouldn't have let you walk around like half a bird."

My father looked at me doubtfully.

"Yes, you would have," Jonny declared. "You would have been glad."

"I would not!"

Daddy said: "It's a better story if it doesn't have a happy ending."

"I like happy endings, though."

"There are not many of those. Jonny, brush your teeth and put on your pajamas. Go on. Your mother will be furious."

I had my father to myself. I leaned against his sturdy chest. "What's your favorite story?" I asked.

"I don't have one." He always said that.

"Daddy, come on! Choose."

"Well, if I had to, if I had to pick just one, I suppose it would be "The Elder Tree Woman.""

"Why that one?" I didn't know what an elder tree was. My father had been a child in a place so foreign that even the trees were unknowable.

"Because my Uncle Baci used to read it to me when I was a little boy."

"Tell me about Uncle Baci."

My father closed the book. Through his glasses his pale blue eyes looked out over my head. "He wasn't really my uncle. He was my great uncle, my mother's uncle. He was the cantor in Ivančice. When Lady was sixteen, she ran away from home, which was in the city of Budapest, in Hungary, and she went to live with Uncle Baci and Rosa Neni."

"Why did she run away?"

"Because her mother treated her like a maid. She made Lady wait on her three younger sisters."

"Like Cinderella."

"Except that they were her real sisters."

"And then what happened?"

"She met Abba and married him. He had come to Ivančice to be the assistant cantor, to be Uncle Baci's assistant. But when the First World War broke out, Papa was drafted into the army."

"Ivančice," I said. "*Ee*vansheetsheh." The town where my father was born. Its consonants clogged my mouth. I imagined it a place of tiny, poor, misshapen houses under a gray sky, a shtetl in a perpetual winter twilight. "Abba fought in the army just like you did."

"Not quite. I joined the United States Army. Abba fought in the Austrian army. He fought against the United States. He was gone four years. Uncle Baci took care of me. He was like a father to me. His son Victor was a soldier, too. Victor was declared missing in action, but his mother never believed that he was dead. For the rest of her life, and she lived to be over a hundred, she sat at her window waiting for him to march back home, wearing the uniform of the Austro-Hungarian empire."

Daddy smelled clean and slightly spicy from shaving lotion. His life in Europe seemed fantastic as a fairy tale. Rosa Neni was a witch peering from a crooked, cobwebbed window.

"I thought Ivančice was in Czechoslovakia."

"There was no such thing as Czechoslovakia when I was born. Ivančice was in Moravia."

I nodded, not understanding the treacherous fluidity of European geography. "Did Abba ever kill anybody?"

"I don't think so."

"Did you?"

He shook his head.

"What about the soldier you got your gun from?" My father had a German pistol that he kept in his night table, a Luger. Even the name sounded sinister.

"He was already dead."

Dead to me happened in a story; it was the fate of enemies, of the wicked. "I'm glad we were born in the same country," I said.

"We weren't. I was born in Austria. And Prague is in Bohemia, not Moravia. Your mother didn't like the idea of your being born in Prague at all. She wanted you born in Switzerland. It was all an accident, anyway. The army could have sent me anywhere they wanted. And you were born an American citizen."

My father had tossed me to the other side of a divide.

"But they sent you to Prague because you knew about it, and you spoke Czech." It was no accident. It was a marvelous coincidence. My mother and brother had both been born in Baltimore, bad luck for them.

"I didn't speak much Czech. At home we spoke German. Jews in that part of the world spoke German." My father nudged me away from his side. I sat up, fearful of distance. His full lips trembled. "And Jews don't have countries. Or, to be more accurate, countries don't have Jews."

"What do you mean?" He was making me cry.

"Jews are Jews. They don't belong to countries. Abba was born in Poland. Lady was born in Budapest. I was born in Austria, Uncle Freddie was born in Czechoslovakia, but we were both born in the same town."

"Hugo!" my mother called from downstairs. Her voice rasped in her throat.

He stood and left the room. "Jonathan, don't you have your pajamas on yet?"

If I tilted my head backwards, I could see the drawing of the little animals above my bed. The greyhound sat with its head cocked, alert and listening. I listened for my father to come out of my brother's room, to waylay him before he went back to my mother. "Daddy," I whispered when I heard his footsteps. "Daddy!"

"Shh!" he warned. "Your brother's trying to sleep." He stood beside my bed. A percussion of dishes sounded downstairs. He turned to leave.

I kept him with a question. "Daddy, why did Kokoshka give us that drawing?"

"I have to go help your mother." But he stopped at the doorway. "Kokoshka had a Jewish wife. I tried to find her after the war."

"Where was she? Was she lost?"

"The Nazis had put her in a concentration camp. She was dead."

Concentration camp. I'd heard those words. I did not understand them. "How did she die?"

"Starvation. Tetanus. Or she was shot. Or gassed. I don't know. She died."

"Did you see one? A concentration camp?"

He bowed his head. He swallowed. He took off his glasses. His eyes without lenses were suddenly large and unprotected. He stared at me as if I, too, were unprotected and he could do nothing for me. I watched him, afraid and fascinated, as if I might see in his pale bleak eyes what he had seen. My stomach lurched. I was terrified that he would answer me. But he blinked and put his glasses back on and crossed the room to my bed and kissed me, turned out the light, and left.

I lay with my eyes open until they had become used to the dimness and got up and kneeled on my bed, against the headboard, and looked at my animals. They seemed enchanted, sweet and in danger, aware of some shadow just past the edge of the paper. Silently I moved my lips over the syllables of the Shema, the central declaration of Judaism: "*Shema Yisrael:* Hear, O Israel, the Lord is our God, the Lord is One," and I prayed to God to let me live forever.

The fight began in whispers. There was a crash, ringing and metallic: the rice pot. Her voice spilled curdled and viscous, words propelled in a motorized rhythm. Her cadences began softly and grew louder and louder; his harsh and guttural interruptions only fueled the engine of her speech. "Don't be so stupid!" he exploded. She hushed him with a hiss and kept at him. "Who's stupid here? Who? Who? Who? Don't you dare talk to me like that! Don't you dare!" They had moved to the living room now. There was no door between the living room and the hall. I slept with my door open. Nothing buffered their battle.

Money, my dress, her dress, his opera, his ambition. "Idiot!" "Don't you talk to me like that!" Each outburst tightened a knot between them and could not be undone. They growled. They roared. They screeched like animals. My heart pounded. I lay in bed hearing, watching the angles of light in the hall, dreading their shadows cast by the lamps with the manuscript shades, helpless even to close my door. This would devour me. This was the bass ground to our lives, the dark contradiction, the anti-music.

I rolled onto my stomach and burrowed into the huge, thick, square, down pillow my mother had brought back from Prague. My heart thudded in my ears, until, clinging to its beat, I slept.

. . .

I dreamed that a wolf chased me through a house with no doors and no windows, only wooden stairs that I climbed up and up to nowhere. I could not scream. Nobody would hear my voice. I opened my mouth and choked. The wolf wore shiny black leather boots and a uniform. It pounded behind me and reached to grab me by the ankle. It was going to catch me, and I was going to die. I woke up. The house was dark and silent. The blue night showed through the slats in my window blind. My throat ached from my stopped voice beating against it. I pushed back the covers and got up and ran down the hall to my parents' bedroom. Their door was shut. I pushed it open. They were both there, asleep, huddled against each other, back to back. Their room was chilly. I got into bed beside my mother. "I had a bad dream," I said. "Shh . . ." she whispered and smiled and raised her arm to encircle me. I pressed against her heat and slept.

Three

Distances

I awoke back in my own bed. Bright sun slithered through my blinds. Nightmare faded, flimsy as the moon in the morning. I heard my father hurry up the steps; his slippers swished on the wood as he went into the bathroom beside my room. "Nath!" he called. "Shh . . ." she hushed him in her stage whisper. "You'll wake Deborah." No trace of battle; like nightmare, it had faded, too. Water ran in the sink; my father shaving. He ran downstairs again; leather-soled shoes tapped on the wood. A horn honked outside. The front door opened and shut. Daddy left for shul, to conduct the choir. He sometimes got a ride with Marty Willen, who sang second tenor. Only on holidays did he insist that my brother and I go to shul.

This was another way my father kept Judaism to himself. I saw these mornings as a reprieve, and my father must have felt that they were a reprieve, too. He retreated to the synagogue and to its music. They were his constant home: a refuge from doubt, from his life with my mother, from the burden of loving her, and us.

From the guest room, I heard chase music and a crash: Saturday morning cartoons. My brother sat on the floor for hours in front of our tiny table-model television set. I stretched and slid low in the bed until my feet butted against the footboard. I was supposed to be asleep. Nobody would bother me. This was luxury. Despite the television noise, the house seemed silent, as if each of us—me, my brother, my mother—was wadded in cotton, insulated and separate. I picked up my book; I sensed the world still in the dark dream colors of fairy tales, pulling me into their mysteries and evil, thrilling, not frightening, in the morning.

My feet burned from the nettles the princess in "The Wild Swans" trampled to soften the fibers so she could spin them, and my fingers burned from weaving them into cloth, and my heart ached for the smallest boy. I touched my arm and let it hang useless and feathered. I shivered.

I climbed out of bed and pulled up the blinds and opened the window. A warm breeze came into the room, but I remained in the princess's cold cell; robins on the rose arbor in the back yard seemed less real than the enchanted swans. I started downstairs. The house seemed unfamiliar, skewed. The stairs in my dream had been stained dark like these, and the dream had been lit mustard like the light shining through the yellow stained-glass window.

The phone rang. My mother scraped her chair against the dining room floor as she jumped up to answer it. "Hello! Bess?" My grandmother. "No. No. Hugo's gone to shul. Deb's still asleep. Hold on . . ."

I slipped down the stairs and peered around the corner.

"Bess . . . hold on. Just a sec." My mother sounded impatient. She put the phone down and rushed into the dining room and grabbed her coffee. She didn't notice me.

"Hi, Bess. We're fine, I told you, we're all fine. I was just having a cup of coffee, reading the paper. I have to get going. No. What? Tell me." She was going to be on for a while. She and her mother spoke every day. We lived only three miles from Nanny. She came to our house all the time; she cruised the city in an ancient black Packard with her two cocker spaniels sitting like sentries beside her. Lady didn't drive, but my mother didn't think that was the reason she avoided our house. Mommy did not keep kosher; Lady feared contamination.

"Why don't you get another plumber, then?" My mother's voice rose in irritation, and I backed into the hall. "If a plumber had made a mess like that in *my* house, I'd give them hell. I wouldn't let them leave until they'd cleaned it up. And then I'd get somebody else! . . . Umm. Oh. How did they cheat? I don't understand."

Then she was silent for a long time, murmuring: "Uh huh. Mmm." In conversations with Nanny, Mommy mostly listened.

. . .

I tiptoed back upstairs. In the hallway to my parents' room hung a second drawing Kokoshka had given my father. This was a charcoal sketch of his wife, the Jewish wife. I saw in the lines of the woman's austere head the shape of a skull, her death. I turned my back, but her eyes, hollow as a skull's, wouldn't leave me alone. I hated her for being Jewish and dead; I hated her fate.

My parents' bed was unmade, half the spread spilled on the floor. My father's pajamas sprawled on the chaise longue along with the dress and underclothes my mother had worn yesterday. Their blinds were still closed. It was cool in there and damp and smelled slightly sour, like a raw day. I was drawn to their room, to search it for signs of war or reconciliation. They—my mother and father— were a singular noun; they and their marriage were a source of unsettling mystery.

Their wedding portrait stood on the dresser, my mother, nine years younger than my father, serene and perfect as a movie star with dark wavy hair and ebony lips. My father's face was round and youthful, and he had exuberant curly hair. A pair of miniature crossed rifles decorated the points of the collar of his army uniform. A few months after they were married, he sailed to England, where he spent the war.

He still had those brass crossed rifles. I fished them out of a little Limoges box—I knew the difference between French Limoges and German Meissen—on his dresser. He kept his military ribbons in that box, too. A little disc with a spring-loaded clasp fit over a pin soldered to the back at the point where the rifles joined. I attached the rifles to my pajamas and laid the decorations out in rows along the top of his dresser. I arranged them one way and another. On television the music changed.

I opened the drawers of the little chest where Mommy kept her jewelry and gazed at the lacy necklace of golden flowers studded with seed pearls, the long, gold, linked chain that closed with a clasp in the shape of a hand, and the array of garnet bangle bracelets; these were all presents from my father. Some he had sent home to her from London during the war. They were all delicate and finely wrought. Occasionally, through the open window I heard the swish of a car passing through the morning, marking ordinary time.

I was dawdling; my dawdling drove my mother crazy. She would be furious if she found me in here. I closed her jewelry box and wandered around the bed and sat on my father's side. His night table was a low cabinet that stood on cabriole legs. Its doors were inlaid with a pair of marquetry figures in oriental costume. I opened one of the doors. The bright cover of the Baltimore Yellow Pages glowed in the dim room. I reached behind the telephone books and felt around the back of the cabinet for the Luger. I lifted it out. It was heavy, with cross-hatched metal plates screwed into its thick, squared-off grip and a long, narrow barrel. It was a dense greenish brown, the color of frozen mud. It felt greasy, and it smelled bitter in my hand. It was an evil thing; it bore no connection to my shiny cap guns with their ivory plastic handles. I looked up the barrel with its small flange to sight with, to aim. Why hadn't the Jews shot back? Why hadn't they fought their way out of those concentration camps?

The floor in the upstairs hall creaked. I panicked and stowed the Luger in the night table and shoved the telephone books against it and backed away from the bed. I waited, but nobody came in. It must have been Jonny going downstairs for something to eat. I took a deep breath in the peace of the house. I was safe here, safe in Baltimore, Maryland, where there was no war and never had been, except once at Fort McHenry, and there never would be again.

Beside the chaise longue there was a bookcase where my mother kept the books she was reading and the photograph album of her year in Prague. I sat on top of the pile of clothes and pulled the album onto my lap. It was bound in red; a large black-and-white photograph in a celluloid sleeve formed the cover. The photograph was of a bridge at twilight. Fog gave the lamps lighting the bridge luminous haloes that reflected in the water below it. Behind the bridge rose the dark magical mass of a castle that seemed to grow out of the mountain, rock and wall intertwined. Twin gothic towers crowned the mountain. Kings and queens inhabited those spires; it did not occur to me that they really were attached to a cathedral.

"Deborah! What are you doing here? You surprised me. I thought you were still asleep." My mother stood in the doorway. She had snuck up on me. I was angry, then afraid. She was still in her bathrobe; she hadn't combed her hair, and she looked low, as if she were trying to hide from the morning. She did not like spring, but she had not been born in springtime, as I had. Her birthday was in November; she was going to turn thirty-three six months and a day after I turned seven.

I yanked her mashed clothes out from under me, sure that she was going to yell at me for crushing them and for looking at the photographs without her permission. I tightened my stomach against her onslaught.

She said: "You had a bad dream last night. What was it? Tell me about it."

I shook my head no.

She looked at me. Her brown eyes matched mine. Sometimes she would force me to do what she wanted, though I could be as willful as she was. Sometimes she backed down, as if she understood the pain she was causing. I was never sure what she was going to do. Now she lowered her eyes and reached for her clothes. I started to put the album back, but she pushed away the clothes and sat down beside me. "Wait," she said. "What were you looking at?"

"Nothing," I answered.

"Here, let me see," she said with her eager, irresistible smile. "Just a minute!" She opened the blinds and sat down beside me and drew the album into both of our laps. She smelled coffeeish. I moved close against her. She laid her palm on the cover. "This is the Charles Bridge," she said dreamily. "It crosses the Moldau, the river that runs through Prague." She began humming off-key. I knew the tune; it was "The Moldau," by Smetana. I'd heard it for the first time a year earlier, at a concert my father had conducted. When my mother took me backstage afterward, I begged him to play it again, and everybody laughed at me. But my father played it for me at home; he thundered a bass of great, rippling waves and sang the melody in rolling vowels. It embarrassed me to hear my mother sing. I nudged her. She bit her bottom lip and touched the dark mountain. "And that is the Hradčany. The castle." She stumbled over the thick Czech consonants; she couldn't roll her r's. "We could see it from your bedroom."

She opened the album. She had glued black-and-white snapshots to its dark gray pages; each page was carefully laid out. Before and after this year in Prague she tossed photographs haphazardly into shoe boxes, cardboard cartons, whatever was available. But this year she had preserved.

Here she was in Prague in the summer of 1946. She stood beside an ornamental pool, in front of a rock garden that climbed a steep hill. Two barrettes held her hair back at her temples; then it fell in waves to her shoulders. She was twenty-four years old and had perfect skin, shining lips, high cheekbones, and her wide-set almond-shaped eyes tilted upward in eagerness and delight under precisely arched brows. A belt cinched her small waist, and the bias cut of her dress draped close over her narrow hips. She wore platform pumps with open toes, and she crossed her ankles in third position, assuming a formal pose.

My mother looked old-fashioned, separated from her present self by more than time. In this picture, she was more complete than she seemed now. She was jaunty, on top of the world. I doubted that I would ever be that beautiful. She was laughing there, and her face was clear and happy. I studied her beside me. An anxious frown pulled at her face. Her hair seemed not so clean. The wings of her nostrils were red—raw from crying?—and she had tired shadows under her eyes.

"You are so beautiful," I marveled.

She covered the photograph with her hand. "My cheekbones are too wide. My hair is too straight. I'm not beautiful."

"*I* think you are."

"Well, darling, *I* think *you* are." Her bare knee showed where her bathrobe fell open. She had beautiful slender legs, tiny ankles, and high-arched feet. My feet were like hers, but Jonny had inherited my father's flat ones.

She turned the page and pointed to a snapshot of two women. They had plain peasant faces and wore hesitant, abashed smiles and babushkas over their heads. "Joshka and Maria took care of you just as if you were a princess," my mother said. "They washed you and dressed you just like a little doll."

I snuggled closer to her. "And that's what you were," she cooed, her arm around me. "You were our little princess."

There were photographs of parties and of my father; there were not so many of my mother. She had been the photographer. She still had the camera she'd brought with her, an imposing German box camera, its metal frame protected by a brown leather case. You held it at waist level and looked down into the view-finder. Her father, my Grandpa David, had given it to her. He was a doctor and lived in Hartford, Connecticut. He also played the viola and was an amateur photographer who carried with him everywhere a leather camera bag fitted with the latest equipment.

My mother had recorded strange people in rooms furnished with our possessions. "These were the downstairs rooms in Prague," she said. "We had two living rooms and a big entrance hall, perfect for entertaining." There was the inlaid secretary, there St. Anthony, there the gilded Italian sofa with green and gold cut-velvet upholstery that we weren't allowed to sit on, there the marble relief of Adam and Eve. Everything was rearranged, as if my parents themselves had lived in an opera.

The pair of Ming turquoise ducks perched on a sideboard I had never seen. "Where is that?" I asked.

"In storage. It's too big for this house. And that chandelier," my mother sighed, pointing to a cascade of glass. "It's in pieces in the basement, packed in sawdust in a barrel. I don't know if we'll ever take it out. You can't imagine how beautiful it is."

She turned the page. Another party. My mother smiled. "There's the ambassador and his wife. Ambassador Steinhardt. And the doctor who delivered you."

"What was I like when I was a baby?"

She squeezed me. "You were very sweet, and you were so good. You never cried. You just looked around, you stared at the world with your big brown eyes."

"What was it like having me?"

She loosened her hold on me and didn't answer.

"What was it like?" I repeated.

"What do you mean?"

"When I came out of your tummy."

She paused and frowned. "Well, you were born with your umbilical cord wrapped around your neck. It could have choked you. I was frantic. And there were no anesthetics. There were hardly any medicines in Prague after the war."

"What are anesthetics?"

"Pain killers. Drugs like phenobarbital." My mother spoke with authority about medical matters, because of her father. In college, she had studied biology, and she had worked in a laboratory during the war while my father was gone.

"Did having me hurt?"

"Believe me, it did."

She turned the page and pointed to a picture. My father sat at the piano beside another man; in the background people were standing around and listening. "That is Jan Masaryk." My mother pointed. Her hand was slender, her fingers beautiful and long, her cuticle ragged. "He was the foreign minister of Czechoslovakia after the war. He was a musician, too; he and Daddy used to play together. Then the Communists got rid of him."

"How did they do that?"

"They defenestrated him. They pushed him out of a window, and then they said that he fell." She blushed with fury. "But by then we had already gone home." Vertical frown lines dented the skin between her eyebrows. "They took music seriously in Prague. Here, nobody cares. Nobody knows anything about music here. On Joshka and Maria's nights off they went to the opera. They went to hear Daddy, when he conducted at the opera. I saw them there, at *Traviata*. They'd spent all their money on better seats than I had."

"What window? What window did they throw him out of?"

"How should I know? I suppose one of the castle windows on top of the hill."

"What do you mean?"

She closed the album, keeping our place with her finger. "Here." She touched a tiny rectangle near the top of the photograph on the cover. "That's a window. It could have been one of those windows. It's a long way down from there."

"You'd smash on the rocks."

"That was the idea."

I bent over to look more closely, but my mother opened the album again.

"Did you ever see anybody dead?" I asked.

"Why do you want to know?"

"In a concentration camp?"

"What are you talking about?" she exploded. She sat up straight. The album slid off our laps. She caught it and shut it. "But I helped displaced persons."

"What were they?"

"People with no place to go after the war, with no homes and no families. Children who had been separated from their parents."

"Were they Jewish?"

"Yes."

"That won't happen to us, will it?"

"Of course not. Don't you even think such things." Her voice rose. "What on earth makes you think a thing like that? Nothing is ever going to happen to you!" She opened the album again and flipped through several pages. "Look. Here you are." My mother sat in a garden, and she held up for the camera a baby, swaddled in blankets, whose face was hidden inside an eyelet cap. Me. "You couldn't get baby clothes in Prague, so Joshka made you this hat out of a ruffle on a skirt. Even though it was May, it was still freezing cold. It even snowed a couple of days before you were born. I've never been so cold as I was in Prague. There wasn't any heat, even in the hospital. I thought your father was going to freeze, waiting for you to be born." She laughed and glanced back at their closet. "Do you see those stadium boots? I wore them every day, from November to the middle of May. I can't remember the last time I needed them in Baltimore."

But I looked at myself, tiny and swaddled. In the picture, my mother regarded me gravely, a half-hearted, anxious smile on her lips. I recognized that smile. Her chin was thrust forward proudly, but she looked as if she were trying not to cry. My father stood beside us. He wore voluminous pleated trousers and a gleeful, immoderate grin. Behind our heads, the two spires of the Hradčany rose like cypress trees.

"You were our princess, our little girl," my mother crooned.

"Mommy, why did we come back from Prague?"

"Oh, because of you." She looked up, into a distance. I looked up, too. We were sitting opposite the mirror that hung over my father's dresser. We looked at each other in the mirror. It was true what everybody said; we looked alike. We had the same dark eyes inherited from Nanny, the same expression, maybe even the same nose; mine already had a little bump at the end of it, like hers. But her lips were sharply delineated, whereas mine were full like my father's. And my forehead was high and round, while hers was heart-shaped, with a widow's peak. Her hair had turned dark when she was five, and she expected mine to do the same; so far it was holding light.

"Because of you," my mother repeated. I heard the devotion in her voice, and the resignation and discontent. "We came back because you couldn't get anything in Prague after the war. There was nothing to eat. No fruit, no oranges; we once got sent a bunch of bananas in the diplomatic pouch. They were almost rotten, but we ate them anyway. And then the State Department wanted to send your father to Yugoslavia. That was too much. It was so primitive, and I didn't want you growing up speaking Serbo-Croatian. So we came home." She smiled out the window. "As soon as we got to Baltimore, Nanny gave you orange juice, and you drank it all up. And you still love fruit." Her arm was around me, but she was talking to the infant I had been. "We came home because I wanted my baby to grow up healthy."

She looked at her watch. "Oh, my goodness! It's after eleven! Hurry, Deborah, get dressed! I promised your father I'd get you and Jonny to shul. I just don't know where the time goes. But we're supposed to have lunch at Abba and Lady's, and then Daddy wants to take us to the museum for your birthday. Go on! Hurry! I have to get your brother ready." I resisted; I wanted to stay in her past. She took her arm away from me and pushed me up.

"Can I wear my new dress? Please?"

She winced. "No. Not today. It's not your birthday yet. Save it, Deb. Save it for tomorrow. Wear the yellow one from the Shalowitz girls instead."

"Please! It's too big. All their dresses are too big."

"No! Not today."

My mother was right. That dress was too precious to wear. Just having it was enough. I started down the hall.

"Deborah," she called me back. "All right, go ahead, put the dress on. Then Lady can see you in it. She won't come to your party tomorrow, and it's her present, too."

I laid it across my bed and gently pulled loose its perfect bow. As I lifted it over my head, it felt as if I were putting on wings. Its waist fit mine; the hem just brushed my knees. I trailed the sash into Jonny's room.

"Mommy, look!"

My mother smiled. "Oh, darling, it's beautiful. It's exquisite. Here, I'll tie the bow for you." Her expert fingers cinched the velvet ribbons. She glanced at her watch and bit her lip. "Where's your brush? Bring me your brush and I'll do your hair."

We stood at the bathroom sink while my mother dampened sections of my hair, brushed them around her forefinger, and let them fall into corkscrew curls. With a barrette, she caught the curl that hung over my eye and clipped it behind my ear. She kissed my head, where my part was.

"Now you look just like a princess. Go downstairs; I'll just be a minute."

I waited in the living room. I pushed against the door of the tower on the little silver basket, but I was stuck outside. I wished that door to open onto tiny thrones and tapestries, a story illuminated with miniature candles, and I could go home and inhabit the castle where I was born. My parents had fallen from that castle, they had been defenestrated into America. My mother and father had been happy in Prague. They left because of me; my life began with their expulsion. Prague had been their Eden.

. . .

We pulled up in front of Abba and Lady's house just as the men were climbing the steps to the porch. My father was happy to see us; he wasn't angry that we had missed shul. He kissed my brother and me, and after a tiny hesitation, he kissed my mother, too. Nothing would change.

"Turn, Deborah," Lady asked. "Turn around so I can see your beautiful dress."

In my grandparents' dark living room, I whirled as fast as I could, testing the flare of the skirt.

"Slowly, slowly," Lady admonished. "You make me dizzy."

She was tall, two inches taller than Abba. She bent and touched my shoulder. I stopped still. She stroked the material and nodded. "Very good," she said, pronouncing the "d" like a "t." Lunch was the usual: chicken soup with noodles, boiled chicken. No cake, no "Happy Birthday," but I didn't expect anything like that. The only events observed in this house were Jewish holidays.

After lunch, Mommy, Daddy, Jonny, and I drove to the Baltimore Museum of Art for my birthday outing; going to a museum was my father's idea of a celebration. Holding hands, we proudly climbed its front steps. We came here to visit our most prized possession, a statue carved from wood, far too grand for our house, and far too fragile to be in the company of children playing. It occupied a niche on one side of the museum's entrance hall, opposite a bronze Degas ballerina. My father read out loud what was written on the brass label under our statue: "St. Margaret, polychrome wood, Tilman Riemenschneider, South German, late fifteenth century. Lent by Mr. and Mrs. Hugo Weisgall."

"You'd think we were rich," he said with some satisfaction, his hand on my shoulder.

"Then you'd look at us and know we weren't," said my mother.

"What about me?" I asked. "Would everybody think that you didn't get this dress for me?"

My father laughed. "They'd guess we'd borrowed you for the day."

"But you didn't!"

"Of course we didn't," Mommy said. "You belong to us."

They had bought St. Margaret from a Jewish doctor in Prague who had hidden her along with himself during the war. We talked about her as if she were a person, not a piece of wood. My father held my hand as we admired her. Jonny was trying to slide across the marble floor, but his rubber-soled shoes frustrated him. My mother had put on a sundress, silk printed in a stylized floral pattern. Its crimson flowers matched her lipstick, and its skirt swished against her thighs. I had seen that dress in the photograph album. She'd had it in Prague, before I was born. She wandered a few steps away to look at the ballerina in her dingy tulle tutu. I stayed with my father. "Your mother's very beautiful," he whispered.

So was St. Margaret. She stepped lightly on a dragon coiled underfoot, and she cradled a little tower in her upturned palm. Her dress swung as if she were measuring a stately dance, a saraband. Traces of color clung to her skirt. I spun. My smooth-soled party shoes slid perfectly on this floor, but my dress did not open out into as wide a circle as I would have wished.

My father said: "We bought her for a hundred dollars."

"And a carton of American cigarettes," my mother added. She glowered at the little ballerina and announced: "I don't like her attitude."

"Why did the doctor sell her?"

"His son didn't want her," my father told me, "after the doctor risked his life to save her. He had a special coffin built for storing her, but when the war was over and he found his son, his son had no interest in her."

"Where's your son?" my mother asked my father.

"I thought you were keeping an eye on him."

"I thought you were."

I thought they were going to blow up again.

"Jonny!" my mother called. We heard slapping footsteps in one of the corridors. My mother in her high heels ran after him. My father started after her. I pulled on his hand. "Daddy!" I said. "Daddy, why don't we have any art that is Jewish?"

He smiled; it was a particular small, sad smile that came over his face when I said something that touched him. He touched my head and explained in his serious way. "Well, darling, Jews traditionally didn't make very many statues or paintings of people. Because of the Second Commandment: 'Thou shalt not make any graven image.' That means a painting or a statue of anything that is alive, because people are tempted to worship images. But God is invisible. You can't see Him and you can't hear Him."

"Except sometimes. Except in olden days."

"Well, yes. In olden days, it used to happen with much greater frequency, that's true."

"But I wouldn't worship our paintings."

"Christians worship images of saints, like St. Margaret."

I turned my back on her, lest I be tempted. "Then maybe we shouldn't have her, or have any pictures. What if somebody came and tried to worship them?"

My father smiled. "We have them because they're beautiful."

I turned back around and gazed at St. Margaret's delicate, wooden face and wished that she were Jewish, too. At least she'd belonged to a Jewish doctor.

"Daddy, why did we leave Prague?"

"Why did we leave? After you were born your mother wanted to go home." His tone of patient explanation hardened. "I sometimes think we should have stayed. I sometimes wonder exactly what she wanted to come home for. If we'd stayed in Europe, my life certainly would have been different."

"But what would be different? Why do you want anything different? You have us."

"Yes, I do have you, sweet, and I wish things were always that simple."

"Daddy—" I squeezed his hand to divert him. "Daddy, tell me about when I was born."

"Not now." He scanned the room and the corridors we could see. "Where's your mother?"

"I don't know."

"We should go find her and Jonny."

"Tell me! Tell me about when I was born." I pulled at his hand.

He looked at me. "Well, it was very cold in the hospital, and I had been in the waiting room for hours. Waiting. Waiting for you. Let me tell you, my dear, you kept me waiting. We'd been at a party the night before, and Mother's doctor was there, too, so that when you started to be born, we all went to the hospital together." He had been speaking quickly, but now his voice softened.

"How long did you have to wait?"

"It was the next morning, but it seemed like forever. Finally the door opened, and the nurse brought you out for me to see. You were all wrapped up, swaddled, in a blanket. All I could see were your eyes."

"Was I crying?" I knew I wasn't. I loved this story.

"No, you were quiet." He looked at me tenderly, holding me in his smile. "And you looked at me with your big eyes, and you recognized me."

Four

The End of Summer

Waves with little whitecaps foamed on the lake. I walked out against them until the water lapped over my chin, then I floated on my back. The northwest wind shot gray cumulus puffs, late summer clouds, over my head and across the sun. The white wooden cross marking Maiden's Cliff on Mt. Megunticook stood out against the sky. Seventy years earlier a girl chasing her hat had fallen from that rock to her death. The mountain rose almost vertically beside the lake, and the tops of the maples were already turning red, patches of sunset colors flaring among the firs and pine. Fall came to Maine at the end of August.

The lake stayed shallow in this cove at its southern tip. Waves rocked me toward land. I inhaled water and stood, snorting, and ducked again up to my neck. Compared to the air, the water was warm. On shore, my mother sat up and shaded her eyes. She beckoned, but I pretended not to see and plunged back in and opened my eyes to the green blur. When I surfaced, she was standing up, frowning and beckoning. I dogpaddled toward shore. As soon as I could touch bottom with my hands, I stopped and braced myself against the waves and bobbed up and down with them like a moored dinghy.

"I don't want to leave," I protested.

"Deborah, we have to go into Camden. And I have to start packing the house." But she loved the lake as much as I did. All summer, brown and glistening, basted with baby oil, she cooked in the sun on the little beach while my brother and I played in the water.

Our house was seven miles inland, and sometimes she took us to ocean beaches, to Camden or to Lincolnville, claiming that you got a better tan at the ocean than at the lake. But the ocean water was frigid; I preferred the lake. My mother reveled in these indolent days, and while she dozed, she was accomplishing something—keeping us out of the house so my father could work. She said: "Maybe, if we leave now, Daddy will come back with you later. And your lips are blue. You're freezing."

"I am not. Did he say he'd come?"

"He said maybe." I raced out of the water, and she wrapped me in a towel, white with a blue stripe down the middle into which was woven the word "Pullman": one of the many towels that my father had removed from the New York train. I crouched on our blanket to get as much of me covered as I could. Jonny, his back toasted from two months of castle construction work, kneeled nearby, scooping a moat out of the muddy sand.

"Deb, come here! Come help me," he called.

"In a minute."

"But then it'll be too late," he protested.

I shrugged. Everything was too late now; everything was almost over. All summer long, time had stopped. One day followed another like the clouds scudding across the sky. But we were leaving Maine on Labor Day, in less than a week. If my brother and I didn't have school, my father said, he wouldn't have to return to Baltimore until the High Holy Days. This year, though, they came early, so it didn't make much difference.

I stared out over the lake to memorize the scene: the granite loaf of Mt. Megunticook, the tongue of blue lake, and across the horizon, the low ridge of Moody Mountain. All winter long I drew crayon pictures of this view. North of Moody Mountain, out of sight behind Megunticook, rose the twin peaks of Levensellar Mountain, and in front of Levensellar was our house. At its highest point, Megunticook's spine lifted only thirteen hundred feet above sea level; it seemed taller because the waters of Penobscot Bay lapped almost at its base. This eroded coastal range was called the Camden Hills. For me it was the most beautiful place on earth.

The summer of 1954 was our third summer in Maine. In 1952, Grandpa David had told Mommy about a cottage for rent in Camden. It had a piano, and my parents found Camden on a map, saw that it was on the coast, and took the cottage, sight unseen, for the summer. After a two-day journey, we drove up to a tiny, brown-shingled cabin hardly better than a shack set into a clearing just off the road. It was raining, fog hid the mountains; the cabin was sheathed in gloomy shingles, brown and curled like tree fungus. We continued up the road, but there was nothing else. We turned around. This had to be it. We sat in the car for a long time, absorbing our bad luck. I burst into tears, but we had come too far to go home. The next day the sun came out, and we saw the hills, the lake, and the bay.

The following summer, we rented the cottage again, and just a week before we had to return to Baltimore, my parents looked at a house with a ramshackle barn and one hundred acres. The same day, they offered three thousand dollars for it. Abba gave them the money for a down payment and co-signed the long-term mortgage. When the mortgage went through, they laughed, giddy at the thought of their recklessness; they couldn't afford the place, but they wanted it.

It was a white Cape Cod farmhouse with bedrooms under the eaves on the second floor and no indoor plumbing. A month later, the barn blew down in a hurricane, which my mother said saved her the trouble of knocking it down herself. It had blocked the view of Megunticook and Bald Rock Mountain. Before we arrived this summer, a plumber had installed bathroom fixtures and a kitchen sink. The bathroom still had a plywood floor, and the well threatened to run dry, but the sun rose behind the mountains, and its last deep yellow light fell on their forests and blueberry fields at sunset. The cat's fur smelled of hay; his dingy suburban belly turned country white. Beside the house there was an old cedar hedge that had grown into an arc of seven tall trees, and between two of them, our carpenter screwed hooks for a hammock. Jonny and I fought over posses-sion of it. When I succeeded in tipping him out, he ran inside. I lay rigid and swung, staring at the sky between the lace of the cedar needles and listening to the wind, waiting guiltily for my mother to yell at me to yield the hammock to my brother.

. . .

By the time Mommy, Jonny, and I drove by the lake on the way back from our errands in Camden, the wind had subsided, and the waves had flattened. Only a few long wisps of clouds hovered over Moody Mountain. When we arrived home, our house was silent; usually we heard the repetitive, anxious noise of my father's piano. I bolted from the car, through the unfinished kitchen littered with boxes half-filled with the utensils Mommy carted back and forth between Baltimore and Maine. The lackadaisical carpenter had achieved far less than my mother had hoped; just a week ago, as a show of good faith, he began building the kitchen cabinets. The house smelled of new wood, and sawdust filmed the floor and sifted into our cereal bowls in the morning.

I found Daddy in his piano room stacking his scores into card-board liquor cartons. Every summer he brought his editions of Bach, Beethoven, Brahms: his favorite composers, and in the evenings, he made music for us. He sang Schubert lieder and Gilbert and Sullivan and Czech folksongs. His big voice filled the house, tying us together. I watched him arrange his Schubert in the bottom of a box.

"Daddy," I said. "Mommy says you promised to come swim-ming with us. Now."

He looked outside at the apple tree heavy with ripening fruit. "I didn't promise."

"Please."

"How was the lake?"

"Perfect. Warm. And there are no waves anymore."

Daddy shrugged. "Well, why not? It's too late to get any work done." He dropped *Mikado* into the carton. "Nath, come with us, too."

We tossed our towels on a big rock that had been half submerged at the beginning of the summer and now rose dry a foot from the water's edge. When he took off his T-shirt, my father's sturdy body was white compared to ours. He ran into the water, each step splashing, and plunged in, exuberant and furry as a seal. He swam straight out, arms thrashing, legs kicking up a roiling wake, shoulders out of the water from the force of his stroke; he swam into the metallic swath the lowering sun cast across the lake. I ran in after him.

"Don't go out so deep!" my mother shouted. "Hugo, Deborah's behind you. Deb, stay where you are!"

I ignored her.

"Deborah!" Mommy warned.

"It's not even over my head," my father called.

"It's over hers."

But I was in his arms. He carried me, buoyant, out deeper than I had ever dared. When he let go, I paddled around him and then circled my arms around his shoulders and clung to his back.

"I don't want to go back to Baltimore," I said. "I want to stay here."

"Where? Here? Out here in the middle of the lake?" He loosened my arms. I floated on my back, and he floated beside me. His stomach broke the water's surface like an island. "How would you eat?"

"Mommy could row out and give us food."

"Not a bad idea," he agreed. "My belly could be our table. Do you think she'd mind?"

"Maybe," I admitted.

We floated for a while. It wouldn't be fair. Jonny could row, too. The air was cooling, and I was waterlogged and growing tired. "Come on," I said, "let's go back."

"I thought you wanted to live here forever."

"Not here. In Maine."

"Oh," he said. "Now I understand."

I reached for his arm and tugged him underwater.

He emerged, spluttering.

"I'm cold," I said.

"Swim to shore, if you want. I'll keep an eye on you."

"Come with me."

"In a minute." He was treading water.

"What are you doing?"

"Looking, just looking."

"But you don't have your glasses on."

He laughed. "I was thinking of a tune."

"What is it? Sing it to me."

He shook his head. "It's nothing."

"Daddy, sing it."

"It's late." He sighed. "The end of summer is so sad."

. . .

Saturday, my mother lingered at breakfast, writing lists, delaying the labor of packing. My father sat with her and read an old New York *Times;* we couldn't get the Baltimore *Sun* in Maine. As I passed by on my way outside he looked up. "Deb, what do you want to do today? Where should we go for a hike? What about Mt. Battie?" he hesitated. "Do you think Jonny can make it?"

We had never attempted Mt. Battie. The trail was short, but we'd heard that it was steep and parts of it could be slippery. "Sure," I answered, wanting very much to try it myself.

"Nath, what about you?"

"Don't ask me," Mommy said. "You know how I hate to walk."

"But there's supposed to be a good view."

"I already have a view, right here." My mother shook her head. "If I have to climb something, I'd rather climb the Empire State Building. Anyway, I could use some peace and quiet." My mother, whose own mother cultivated an exquisite garden, claimed that she preferred civilization to nature. We went to Maine for my father.

Daddy stood. "Well, tell your brother what we're doing. I just have to find my hiking boots, and I'm ready." On Saturdays, on Shabbos, he didn't work. He took us for rides, or for hikes in the Camden Hills. These were his summer services. He loved being outdoors. I did not understand this. I imagined that he had been a city boy who had grown up playing in the alley behind Abba and Lady's house, between back fences and the car barn, a brick shed where streetcars were parked overnight. Once, he told us, he had tried to fly and jumped off the roof of their garage using two garbage can lids as wings.

He came downstairs wearing shorts and his steel-toed army boots and a handkerchief tied around his neck. We drove into Camden, the three of us in the front seat, and parked at the end of Mountain Street. As we started up the trail, my father found himself a walking stick, a thick fallen branch. Jonny and I followed him through the trees at the base of the mountain. "Keep an eye out for snakes," he warned, although he had assured us that there were no poisonous snakes in Maine. There were snakes in western Maryland, where he had been a camp counselor and later trained for the war; once, he told us, he had marched into a nest of copperheads. I hoped to have a similar adventure one day.

Soon we emerged onto bare granite ledges. My father leapt from rock to rock like a rotund mountain goat, while I clambered after him. "Wait for me!" Jonny called from about fifty feet back. His voice trembled. "I'm stuck."

Daddy turned and retraced his path, taking small steps down the steep, smooth ledge. "Deborah, going down is always more difficult," he instructed. "This is where you have to be careful. Jonny, give me your hand." He braced himself and pulled my brother up beside him. Jonny clung to his hand. "Jonathan, you go first, and I'll push you. It's not very far, now. You can see the top."

A stone observation turret about thirty feet high marked Mt. Battie's summit. When the trail leveled off, Jonny raced across the bald ledges and ran up its iron steps. He emerged at the top and waved. "How did they get that tower up here?" I asked Daddy.

"There used to be a road up the other side, which isn't as steep, a carriage road, for horses. And there used to be a hotel here, too, but it burned down." I assumed my father knew everything, and he never disappointed me.

All I could see from where I stood
Was three long mountains and a wood;
I turned and looked another way
And saw three islands in a bay.

He recited those lines. "That is the opening of 'Renascence,' by Edna St. Vincent Millay," he said. "She wrote it when she was nineteen." Millay had grown up in Camden. We stood where she had stood on the hill overlooking the town and the bay; islands, many more than three, speckled the water. The cabin where we spent our first summers had belonged to Edna St. Vincent Millay's sister, who knew somebody who knew Grandpa David. The truth was that my parents rented it as much for its name—the "Millay Cottage"—as for anything else, and my mother never said the word "cottage" without a little twist of irony in her voice.

In Camden, cottage usually meant a grand summer house. Mary Louise Curtis Bok Zimbalist, who founded the Curtis Institute of Music in Philadelphia, had a cottage in Rockport, just south of Camden, and several teachers from that school also summered nearby. My father had studied composition and conducting at Curtis, and although my parents discussed the Curtis musicians, we never saw them. Possibly they ignored us, as my mother claimed, but I suspect that my father hesitated to get in touch with them. He conducted only a choir, and he wrote esoteric operas; he had not become famous. His name did not decorate concert posters.

In Maine, though, there remained room for possibility. Sitting at his piano with the sound of the wind through high grass outside his window, my father believed in his work, in the hours of concentration spent trying out harmonies and lines of tones, in the slowly thickening stack of manuscript pages accumulating on the piano. In Maine, he was peaceful.

"Deb, Daddy, come up here with me!" Jonny called, and we stamped up the echoing iron stairs that spiraled inside the tower. The parapet looked down on the tableland below the summit of Mt. Megunticook, a tangle of boulders, swamp, and forest.

One Saturday at the end of July, climbing Maiden's Cliff on a still, cloudy afternoon, my father had stopped short. "Over there!" he whispered, pointing uphill. "There! A mountain lion!" My mother didn't believe him when we came home and told her the story, but though I never saw it, I knew that it had been there, camouflaged like the dappled forest, lurking behind a gray rock.

. . .

Our last night in Maine, my father cooked hamburgers outdoors. He nursed the fire and carefully timed the grilling according to our separate requirements. We ate from paper plates; my mother had packed away our dishes. "Let's go for a ride," Daddy said after we'd tossed our plates into the garbage.

"I'm still in my bathing suit," my mother protested.

"Put on a skirt over it. Nobody will know."

We piled into the car. It was chilly; we needed jackets. My father wanted to drive west over the Appleton Ridge to see the sunset; Jonny and I wanted to look for deer on Howe Hill and then go to Dougherty's drug store for ice cream cones; my mother asked to go to the dump so we wouldn't have to stop in the morning. Without starting the engine, Daddy released the emergency brake and we rolled around the driveway. At the road, he slowed just enough to be sure no car was coming and turned right, down the long hill—toward Camden. We cheered and coasted in the car, faster and faster. "Ten, twelve, fifteen, twenty, twenty-five, thirty," Jonny and I shouted out the numbers on the speedometer. "Forty-two!" The hill bottomed out in a little hollow, but we had enough momentum to climb a short hill to the stop sign at Lincolnville Center.

On the sidewalk in Camden, we shivered licking our ice cream. "It's almost dark," my mother said. "A month ago, it was still afternoon."

"Well—" my father began to contradict her.

"I wasn't being exact," she said. "It just seems like it was afternoon. Let's get to the dump before we can't see a thing."

Mittens was waiting for us at the back door when we returned home. My mother scooped him into her arms and held him on his back. His white stomach gleamed in the dusk. The Big Dipper hung upside down above the field across the road, and over the ridge of Megunticook, the sky was cobalt. In the house, only the overhead fixtures worked; lamps with their warm light had been packed for the winter. "It looks so bleak," my mother said anxiously, standing in the dining room piled with boxes. Jonny and I worried that we'd be sent to bed. Mittens arched back and forth in front of his empty bowl. "Who's going to feed the cat?" my mother asked. My father went into his piano room. "I guess I am," she answered herself.

Daddy played two or three chords and then began a bouncing accompaniment.

"*I am the very model of a modern major general; I have information vegetable, animal, and mineral.*" The Gilbert and Sullivan patter song spilled from my father's mouth. He banged the accompanying chords, left hand, right hand. His big voice filled the house and tied us together. Jonny and I marched into the middle of the piano room, erect and pompous, and shouted out as many of the Major General's words as we could remember. "*About binomial theorems I'm teeming with a lot of news* . . . *Hmmm* . . . (slowing down) . . . *lot of news, lot of news* . . . *aha!* (speeding up) *With many cheerful facts about the square of the hypotenuse! With many cheerful facts about the square of the hypote-pote-nuse!*" We belted out the chorus. Between verses we strode importantly back and forth, stomachs puffed, until my father segued into Buttercup's song. "*I'm called little Buttercup, sweet little Buttercup, though I could never tell why.*" Then we simpered and swayed, and tried to suppress spurts of laughter.

"Deborah," Daddy said, "find *The Mikado*. It should be in that box, there, in front of the bookcase."

I rummaged until I found the worn score.

Jonny and I were the three little maids from *Mikado*. We minced and tiptoed, we tittered on cue, we pretended to fan ourselves. "Nath! Where are you?" my father called.

My mother stood in the doorway. She had taken off her skirt and put on her threadbare yellow terrycloth bathrobe.

"Come here!"

She stood beside him, tentative, reluctant to rely on music for tenderness.

"*A wandering minstrel I— / A thing of shreds and patches, / Of ballad songs and snatches, / And dreamy lullaby! / Through every passion ranging / And to your humours changing / I tune my supple song!*" Smiling up at her, my father crooned the words of Nanki-Poo, the heartsick musician. Then he thundered into the final chorus. "*For he's going to marry Yum-Yum!*"

And Mommy stepped into the center of the floor and danced. Arms akimbo, eyes half-closed, mouth mock serious, she hopped from leg to leg, knees bent, ankles flexed, in a vaguely Japanese quadrille. The bathrobe, risqué kimono, fell away from her long, tanned legs as she spun and skipped. Jonny and I were doubled over. We tried to imitate her, but we laughed so hard that we tripped over each other. "Be careful!" My mother shifted out of character for an instant, then she cocked her head to one side and continued her dance. Daddy could no longer sing. Tears of laughter rolled down his cheeks as he played for her dance. He played Pooh-Bah's song, and Mommy stuffed a sofa cushion under her belt and mimed the Lord High Everything Else.

Finally, we recognized the gently rocking introduction to Jack Point's last song from *Yeomen of the Guard*. Daddy's voice grew tender. "*I have a song to sing, oh!*" We sang the chorus: "*Sing me your song, oh!*"

"*It is sung to the moon by a lovelorn loon, who fled from the mocking throng, oh! It's the song of a merry man moping mum, whose soul was sad, and whose glance was glum, who sipped no sup and who craved no crumb, as he sighed for the love of a lady.*"

We couldn't laugh during this song's chorus. "*Hey dee, hey dee, misery me, lack-a-day dee! He sipped no sup and he craved no crumb, as he sighed for the love of a lady!*"

We sang it all the way through, every verse until the last: "*And he died for the love of a lady!*"

My father looked tenderly at my mother. "Do you remember?"

She nodded.

"What?" we clamored. "Remember what? Tell! Tell!"

"Oh, your father," my mother began. "Your father at Camp Airy. When he was a counselor there, he put on the Gilbert and Sullivan operettas every summer. He did everything, the musical arrangements, the conducting; he even played the lead. And I used to go; I'd come over from Camp Louise, all the girls would. He was Pooh-Bah, he was Jack Point. Jack Point was my favorite." She smiled wistfully.

"Yes," my father agreed.

"It was your finest role," my mother said.

My father went on: "Jack Point dies, right here, right at the end of this song—"

"And everybody applauded so much that your father got up and sang it and died all over again!"

My brother and I hooted and laughed.

"It wasn't funny!" protested my father, trying not to laugh himself. But it was.

"Sing it again, Daddy," I begged.

"Sing it!" Jonny echoed. And my father did. At the close of the last verse my brother and I collapsed on the floor in a heap.

"Bravi! Bravissimi!" shouted my mother in her most correct Italian. "Now, my darlings, it's getting late. Brush your teeth and wash your faces. Time for bed. Daddy and I have to finish packing."

We protested, of course, and as we straggled out of the piano room, my father started to play again.

"Go on! Go on!" my mother urged and marched my brother into the bathroom.

My father played a lullaby, lilting and sweet, with German words. "*Schlafe, schlafe,*" he sang. Sleep, I knew that much. The piano chimed soft as bells. I lingered at the door. When he had finished, my father looked up and saw me. "Come here," he beckoned.

"Come here, sweetness." Sitting on his piano chair, he took me into his arms.

"Do you know what that song means?" he asked.

Against his chest, I shook my head, no.

"It means: 'May you sleep wrapped in the pure sounds of love.'"

I listened to the sweet vibration of his voice against my ear.

"That is the most beautiful lullaby, the most beautiful of all, prettier than the Brahms," he said. I nodded, and he kissed the top of my head. "It's by Schubert. I used to sing that to you when you were tiny, when we were still in Prague."

"Deborah!" my mother threatened.

My father pushed me off his lap.

Later that night, when I was supposed to be asleep and my father was supposed to be packing, I heard him singing, through the closed doors of his piano room: "*Sleep, sleep, wrapped in the pure sounds of love.*"

The next morning, we loaded the car and bolted the farm's storm door against the winter. We coasted down the hill one last time. As we drove south, it became greener and hotter, the air thickened with exhaust fumes and humidity, and my father grew more and more withdrawn. His mood affected us all. We were sullen and silent as we turned onto our street in Baltimore, and the heat in our closed-up house mashed us flat with misery.

Five

Days of Awe

None of us was ready for Yom Kippur. This stale September morning, the leaves of our sycamores hung limp as we hurried into the car. The road downtown ran parallel to a creek for a while; Jones Falls was a diminishing strip of wilderness within Baltimore city limits. Like dusty snakes, vines circled the trunks of trees along the banks. I looked with longing at the tired trees and parched vines and yearned for Maine's woods and emptiness.

"I don't ever remember its being so beastly hot in Ivančice on Yom Kippur," my father complained. The wind through the open window tangled my hair but cooled my face and lifted my prickly woolen skirt off my legs. It was a pleated skirt, tailored, very grown up, from my new box of hand-me-downs. Yom Kippur, no matter the temperature, required wool. We pulled up at the curb by the side entrance to the shul. Chauncey Avenue was already lined with Buicks and Cadillacs; chrome and bright paint shone in front of the shabby row houses, which the members of the congregation, had abandoned for the suburbs.

"When will I see you?" my father asked my mother. He was keyed-up and anxious; he had been fasting since the night before. I was on edge, too, in wary anticipation of the beautiful performance of holiness, and of boredom.

Harried, my mother glanced at my father. She had thrown a raincoat over her cotton bathrobe. "I haven't been able to finish unpacking from Maine," she began. "I—" She stopped and bit her

66

lip; she wanted to please him, but pleasing him made her angry. "I'll be back as soon as I have a chance to get dressed. And have a cup of coffee. I can't survive without a cup of coffee." My father winced, but he leaned across the seat and kissed her. Yom Kippur was the holiest day of the year; he hated that she violated it. I already dreaded the day six years hence when I would be required to fast.

Daddy took our hands for the few steps to the entrance. He pulled open the heavy oak door, and my brother and I passed under his arm into the cool stairwell. Dark varnished steps fitted with rubber mats angled around the stairwell; the wood creaked under our feet, announcing our arrival. Up half a flight a small door opened onto the bimah. We peered around it. Abba sat in his chair, his head bowed in pain, and listened to the *shamas,* or the beadle, the devout man who chanted the secondary parts of the service. The shamas was middle-aged, red-faced, scrawny, and bent. He swayed, entranced by the prayers, and he had a terrible voice, rasping and loud as a fire siren.

Abba looked up when he heard our footsteps. He wore a white cambric gown, a white velvet onion-domed hat trimmed in gold braid, and rubber-soled casual shoes with cloth uppers. On Yom Kippur observant Jews did not wear leather because leather was deemed too comfortable, and a fast was a day of deprivation. I was learning these specks of Jewish law glinting in the dark passages of faith. Abba sat up and nodded at us. We nodded back but dared not cross the few feet of marble to his seat. The bimah was his stage, and even when he was not singing, Abba held that stage. We continued up another flight of stairs to the choir loft.

The stairs led to an antechamber; here, it was as hot as outside. To the left was a bathroom, a men's room—it never occurred to me to use it. Its door had a frosted glass panel. Straight ahead was a window, glazed, like all the synagogue's windows, with small panes of watery green and blue glass: a reminder that even this room, furnished with a couple of wooden chairs and a cast-off desk from the days when the Hebrew school was held in the synagogue itself, was a holy place. But the profane butted up against the sacred; an old, folded newspaper littered the windowsill, along with a few bumper stickers and an empty pack of Lucky Strikes. "Fred E. Weisgal for Representative," the bumper stickers read. Uncle Freddie had run in the primary elections for Congress. The window was open. The hot breeze fluttered the paper. There was no screen, and the buildings outside, seen through no wire mesh, seemed very close.

Freddie stood in front of the window. Marty Willen, the second tenor, sat at the old desk. "Negroes complain about Jewish landlords," Freddie was saying. "But these houses don't belong to Jews anymore. They sold them all, to Negroes. Negroes are ripping themselves off, but they blame the Jews anyway!"

"So why are you always defending Negroes?" Marty Willen asked.

"Because they're human beings like the rest of us!" Freddie thundered. "Because they've had a rotten deal, worse than the Jews in this country, believe me. Because if somebody gives them a fair shake, maybe they won't have to keep each other down. And maybe then they'll stop blaming the Jews!"

"Shh!" my father hissed. "Freddie, keep it down!"

"But Hugo, it's true!" Freddie protested without turning around.

"I know it's true. You don't have to convince me. Maybe you should go downstairs and give the sermon."

Marty Willen rubbed his fingers over his smooth pink jowls. "You know, Freddie, white people think you're too liberal, and Negroes don't like what you tell them. So how the hell did you think you were going to win the primary?"

Freddie roared with laughter. "Who said I thought I was going to win?"

"Christ, it's hot!" my father said.

"Christ, I'm hungry, and it's not even ten o'clock in the morning." Freddie laughed and turned around and saw my brother and me. "Hi, doll. How are you, handsome?" His pale blue eyes gleamed, and he gave us each a sudden, enthusiastic hug and just as quickly let us go. "Hugo," he said. "I have a story for you."

"Later, Freddie! We're going to start any minute. Where is everybody?"

"They're all inside listening to the shamas," Freddie answered. "Trying to learn something."

My father glared at his brother.

"Come on, Hugo, laugh."

My father shook his head. "Call the boys, Freddie. Stop fooling around."

Downstairs, the shamas finished up with a distressing cadence. The congregation squirmed and resettled themselves. My father hurried down the two steps into the choir loft itself; it was like a big box in a theater, and it had two levels, the back one raised by a step from the floor in front; on the top level there was an arched opening into the balcony. The choir loft was situated just above the edge of the bimah and the wide aisle in front of it. The other members of the choir entered the loft now through the arch.

"What were you doing out there?" my father asked. "Praying?"

"Hugo," Marty Oberman answered, "don't look so shocked." He was a tall, florid man with a square face who worked for the National Brewing Company, makers of National Bohemian Beer and sponsors of the city's new baseball team, the Baltimore Orioles. Marty Oberman sang second bass and contributed to the choir loft's clutter pressed-paper coasters printed with the National Bo beer mascot, a round cartoon man with a monocle and a mustache, swinging a baseball bat.

A black iron music stand stood in the center of the floor, and my father's music was spread out on it. I slithered behind the men gathering around the music stand and reached my perch, the marble sill that formed the base of the proscenium overlooking the bimah. I sat in the corner behind the first tenor, a slight man with wispy white hair named Paul Nachlas, and nudged open the short blue velvet curtain that hung from a brass rail about eighteen inches above the marble sill. From there, I could see my grandfather, and I could also look out into the audience.

"The house is sold out," Freddie said. He stood opposite me and braced himself against the thick ledge to lean out into the space of the synagogue. "Even the balcony."

My father glanced over his shoulder. "Not bad," he nodded. "They must have a lot to repent for."

I peered out. Downstairs the pews were full of women in tweeds and pumps with matching pocketbooks and thin leather gloves and men in sober suits. They were elegant and assured. Some men, the most German members of the congregation, wore hats instead of yarmulkes. Their names were the names of department stores: Hutzler, Hecht. They were doctors and lawyers. They were descendents of families that had settled in Baltimore over a century earlier. It was cooler down there than it was up in the choir loft.

"They should atone for not giving Papa a raise," said Freddie.

My father shrugged and shuffled his sheaves of music. "What about me? I've sung in this choir for more than thirty years."

"So have I. What about me?" asked Freddie.

"If they give you a raise, will you promise to stay away?" asked Marty Oberman.

Daddy took out a round pitch pipe and laid it on the ledge of the music stand. The men formed a semicircle around him. Opposite the choir loft there was another box that remained empty most of the time; under it, in an alcove, were a few rows of seats. My grandmother Lady sat there, where she could see her husband and her sons. In Chizuk Amuno, men and women sat together; in orthodox congregations, women sat in a gallery separate from men. Lady set herself apart from the rest of the congregation, and nobody ever presumed to join her in her solitude. She wore a navy suit, in an old-fashioned cut with an elaborately seamed and buttoned jacket and a skirt that hung away from her hips and thighs as if it dared not touch her body. She parted her graying hair in the middle and pulled it into a bun, subduing its natural curl. I could barely differentiate her dark eyes from the brown rings surrounding them. I made a tiny gesture and waved at her. She frowned and motioned to me to pull the curtain shut. Stung, I closed it, almost.

The rabbi strode to his marble podium and surveyed the congregation. He was younger than Abba and wore a satin robe pleated across the shoulders so the material fell in heavy gathers like drapes, more imposing than Abba's cotton one, and much hotter. His wife and teenaged daughters sat trim and impeccable in their fall suits and neat hairdos in the front row. The rabbi greeted the members of the congregation and exhorted them to remember the solemnity and holiness of the day. His sentences had a slow, beseeching, monotonous cadence.

"All right, all right," muttered my father. "We know why we're here. Let's get going."

Abba had taken up his position at his lectern. He stood back to back with the rabbi. The rabbi faced the congregation; Abba faced God.

After a moment, Abba glanced over his shoulder. The rabbi kept talking. Abba cleared his throat, with great resonance. The rabbi paused. Over his shoulder, Abba said something to the rabbi in a guttural whisper. I could not make out the words, but the impatience carried. With a pained look, the rabbi announced to the congregation the page number where the service began and retreated to his chair.

Abba pressed his hands against the white velvet cloth of his lectern until the rustle of paper subsided. Then he glanced up quickly at my father, his pale eyes lit with anticipation. He threw back his head and opened his mouth and began to sing the first words of the Kaddish, the prayer that began the service. His voice reverberated against the marble walls beside the ark and rolled back over his head into the empty space of the dome. The choir echoed his words, softly at first, then louder and louder. The men's voices surrounded me; they rang into my ears and reverberated in my bones. I tried to sing along; this music was as familiar as my heartbeat, and as mysterious. My voice came out small and thin. I couldn't hear myself, so I stopped up my ears against the men's voices. In the small, interior space of my skull, I sang, I hummed, I pronounced whatever words I knew.

I followed the service by matching the shape of the Hebrew paragraphs in Abba's prayer book with my own. It proceeded in slow majesty and seemed as long as an unknown road, a distance I measured by the thickness of the pages left to turn. Abba skipped nothing. He repeated every word. The scrolls of the Torah were taken out. As the shamas read the day's portion, the choir took a small break, but they had to be ready to sing when the reading finished and the scrolls, swaddled in silk and dressed again in their silver breastplates and crowns, were carried around the aisles of the synagogue. My grandfather led the procession, carrying his prayer book, his voice growing louder and softer as he progressed around the building. He passed in front of my grandmother's pew. She touched each Torah with her white handkerchief and kissed the handkerchief. I watched for a smile or a wink, some current, to pass between my grandparents, but I could see none. Holiness took precedence.

The Torahs were replaced in the ark, and the rabbi approached his marble lectern and spread out the notes for his sermon. Abba sat down heavily with a little groan. "Why doesn't Abba just leave?" I asked. "Why doesn't he go off?"

My father didn't answer. In shul, in Baltimore for that matter, he was preoccupied. "Why?" I pressed.

"He can't. This isn't a theater."

Abba rummaged in the pocket of his robe and pulled out a handkerchief to wipe his forehead. I stood and loosened my skirt from the backs of my sweaty knees. In the congregation, a few people left, more came in. I could not understand why people would choose to arrive now; for me, the sermon was the low point of the services, and I was offended that they would choose the rabbi over Abba.

The members of the choir hurried to the antechamber. I loved this intermission, this flowering of irreverence. But my father stayed behind.

"Come on, Daddy," I urged. My brother had followed Freddie out of the choir loft, but my father stood with one foot propped up on the marble sill at the front of the choir loft. "Daddy!" I stood at the door.

"I want to hear what he has to say."

I was annoying him. I returned to my perch, the good daughter.

The rabbi was speaking in his tremulous voice: "On this most solemn day, we examine the innermost recesses of our hearts. It is difficult to do so surrounded by our families, in the midst of plenty, in the midst of God's blessings. . . ." He did not sound as if he felt at all blessed.

"What the hell?" my father exclaimed. "Who does he think he's talking to? Not the Hirschlers, not Mrs. Werner! Where are their families?"

I peered out from behind the blue velvet curtain. The Hirschlers and Mrs. Werner sat where they always did, at the back of the congregation. They wore heavy suits, severe like Lady's, but sadder. They had worn them before the war, when those clothes were new, when the Hirschlers and Mrs. Werner had been prosperous and went to shul in Vienna blessed with their families. My father turned his back on the rabbi and left the choir loft for the antechamber. I scurried after him. "Deborah, close the door!" he said. My cousin Margit was sitting in the old school desk beside the window; she had walked the three blocks from Abba and Lady's house.

Freddie pushed against the door between the antechamber and the choir loft to make sure I'd closed it all the way. "Hey, Hugo," he grinned and grabbed my father by his arm, "did you hear about the inmate who comes into the prison dining room? A group of guys . . ."

"Yes, Freddie, I've heard this joke before."

But Freddie kept going. "A group of guys are sitting at a table, and one of them shouts: 'Thirty-four.' Everybody cracks up . . ."

"Freddie!"

"'Thirty-four? What's so funny about that?' the new inmate asks the guy sitting next to him.

"'Thirty-four's a great joke,' the guy says.

"'Thirty-four, nothing else, just thirty-four? I don't get it.'

"'Listen,' says the guy, 'it's like this. We're in here for life, so we don't hear new jokes very often. We give numbers to the old ones. It's more efficient.'

"Just then a little guy at the end of the table yells, 'Fifty-six.' Nobody even cracks a smile. 'So now what's going on?' the new prisoner asks." Freddie stopped. He was laughing so hard that he could barely get the words out. "The guy next to him shakes his head." Marty Willen was laughing, too. "'That's Rabinowitz,'" Freddie sputtered and gasped. "'That's Rabinowitz,' the guy says. 'Rabinowitz! He never could tell a joke!'"

My father tried not to laugh. He squeezed his mouth shut, he turned his head so he wasn't looking at Freddie, but nothing helped. His face got red. "Thirty-four!" he blurted. "Thirty-four! Christ, Freddie, I feel like one of those prisoners!"

Freddie howled. Daddy roared. Marty Oberman chortled. I laughed until I got hiccups, and so did my brother and Margit, or they pretended to have them, too. We'd all heard the story a hundred times, but it didn't make any difference. Freddie could tell a joke.

A hat arose behind the stair railing, a black homburg, like a walking Magritte. It belonged to Efrem Potts, who was the son of the president of the synagogue. Efrem was a decent, gentle man; he loved Abba. "Hey, boys, please, keep it down," he warned, flushing red with embarrassment. "Please, we can hear you downstairs."

"Efrem," Freddie said. "Efrem, don't you want to know why we're laughing? Did you hear the one about the new prisoner?"

"Freddie . . ." Efrem Potts protested. "Not today. Some other time, but not today!" He hurried downstairs with his round chin tucked against his chest, biting his lip, trying not to explode with laughter himself.

Tears streamed from Freddie's eyes. He was the bad boy, still. Many of his jokes erupted as regularly as geysers; like the prayers and melodies, each joke had its season, but each time we laughed as if we were hearing it for the first time. Freddie sighed, sobered up, and broke out laughing again. It was wonderful, this laughter; it burst through dams of righteousness and poured over us like love.

I tried to catch my father's eye, but he was watching his brother. Freddie shook his head, as if he were trying to get rid of a thought. It wouldn't leave him alone. "Hugo," he said, helpless, "Hugo, Marty, Paul, come inside." He nodded toward the men's room. Everybody followed him, leaving the children out in the antechamber. Jonny pulled out the checkers set from under the desk.

"Don't play," I said, righteously. "You can't play. It's Yom Kippur."

"It doesn't matter," Jonny said.

"It does. You can't."

He looked at Margit, but she shrugged. "I don't want to play. You'll beat me."

He began setting up the board, anyway. Margit pretended not to watch him. I felt sorry for her; he'd make her play. She was soft. There was in my family a hardness, a sometimes merciless edge. We were not always kind; it seemed that our cruelty was in proportion to our love. I sat on the windowsill in the hot breeze, listening to the city's din, the swish of cars, the clatter of trucks around the corner on Eutaw Place, voices shouting from the street. I felt city grime land on my face, black particles of dust borne on the wind. In Maine the air was clean. I wished we were back in Maine. The air had a clarity there, bright as laughter. In Maine my father was peaceful.

Back in Baltimore he was distant again. He held our hands as we walked into shul, but once inside he abandoned us for the music. The voices of the men penetrated my bones, vibrated in my skull, hurt my ears. To me they were beautiful. But my father had higher standards. He heard the rough blend of timbres and the false notes. He had sung in the choir since he was a little boy in Ivančice, when his great Uncle Baci was the cantor and Abba was in the Austro-Hungarian army fighting on the Italian front.

. . .

From inside the men's room, there was an explosive noise. The door opened, and the choir spilled out, choking, weeping, from laughter.

"What's so funny!" I demanded, but nobody answered. "What's so funny?"

"Nothing," said my father, wiping his eyes. "Never mind."

"Tell me! Tell me the joke!"

He shook his head, turned to Paul Nachlas, and pointed into the choir loft. "Is the rabbi still talking?"

"Hugo, he's not all that bad," Paul ventured.

"I'm sure he's not."

"The congregation likes him." Paul Nachlas opened the door to the choir loft.

"And what is that supposed to mean? What do they know?" my father whispered.

"Well, they hired you," said Marty Oberman.

"That's exactly what I mean." My father grinned. He followd Paul Nachlas into the choir loft to gauge how much longer the rabbi would talk.

"Hugo." Freddie, chuckling with another joke, started to call my father back when he noticed the checkerboard, but not my brother. "Margit!" he bellowed. "What in hell do you think you're doing? Put that away. It's Yom Kippur."

Margit looked stricken. "But . . ." she began.

"I said put it away!" Freddie interrupted.

Margit turned her back and bent over the board. The sun cast red highlights in her dark hair. Her shoulders shook as she piled the checkers back into the box. Freddie didn't notice. He called my brother over to him. "Jonny, listen, hon, could you do me a favor?"

"Sure," Jonny said innocently.

"I'll give you some money, and could you go down to Mann-heimer's and get Abba a cheeseburger? It's almost lunch time." He spoke earnestly with an encouraging smile.

I listened, breathless. Adults fasted on Yom Kippur. Lunch was out of the question. And a cheeseburger—milk melted on top of meat; you never ate dairy products with animal flesh—was blatantly not kosher any day of the week. The rest of the choir, trying not to laugh, gathered behind Freddie.

"I can't go alone," Jonny said.

"Margit will go with you. Won't you, doll?"

Margit blinked away tears. I wished Freddie had asked me to go, too, although I knew his request was blasphemous. I yearned to be included in his prank.

"I don't like cheeseburgers," Jonny said.

"You don't have to. It's not for you, hon. It's for Abba."

Jonny nodded. "Okay."

"Here." Freddie reached into his pocket. Another blasphemy. On the Sabbath, and Yom Kippur was the Sabbath of Sabbaths, you did not even touch money. He fished around for a long time. My father came back to the antechamber.

Jonny said: "Daddy, can I go to Mannheimer's? Freddie wants me to go."

"For what?"

"To get Abba a cheeseburger. It's lunchtime."

"What in the world is he trying to do?" My father exploded. He glared at Freddie, who seemed relieved at the excuse to take his hand out of his pocket. "Freddie, this is not funny!"

But it was. Freddie cracked up. The choir snickered. Jonny looked bewildered; Margit looked like she was going to start crying again. My father turned his back, in disgust, I imagined, but his shoulders were shaking and not from sobs. Paul Nachlas stuck his head around the door. "He's finished!" he said.

"Quick! Come on boys!" my father hissed in a stage whisper. "Musaf." He hurried to his music stand and began handing out parts. "Come on! Get down here!"

The Musaf service was the most beautiful of the day. Musaf meant "additional," but it was only additional in the sense that it repeated the central prayers. On Yom Kippur it was much longer than usual. Abba had set much of this service; he had lavished his most beautiful melodies on it and turned it into an oratorio, with solos for his tenor and his sons' baritone and bass.

On Yom Kippur, Jews were supposed to spend the entire day in the synagogue. In Europe before the war, my father told me, this had meant that men arrived at sundown for Kol Nidre, the solemn ceremony dissolving all unfulfilled vows human beings made to God during the year. They spent the twenty-four hours until the next sunset at prayer, neither sleeping nor eating nor drinking. In Baltimore, everybody went home to bed after Kol Nidre, and my father and grandfather sometimes took a short break in the afternoon to walk around the reservoir. When I said that I thought it was much better that way, my father replied that it wasn't necessarily better. Making life easier did not make it better.

As the rabbi gathered his sheaf of papers, people got up to leave, women, mostly, their excuse the need to give their children lunch. Even the rabbi's wife left, although her daughters were over thirteen and adults. I wanted lunch, too. Ozelia was at home, and she would feed me, but my father would never let me go now. The light inside the synagogue was changing as the afternoon sun progressed from window to window. Slowly, gravely, Abba returned to his lectern. These prayers were sung only on Rosh Hashanah and Yom Kippur.

My father and Uncle Freddie leaned over the choir loft curtain. Abba began. "*Hineni*"—"Here I am"—he prayed that his singing might be acceptable to God. Most cantors treated this as their big aria, a chance to show off all their vocal tricks. Not Abba. When he first came to this country, he had wanted to be an opera singer, but Chizuk Amuno needed a cantor to lead the High Holy Day services. The congregation heard him and offered him a permanent job. Now my father was an opera composer. He could have been a singer, too.

Abba knew that the greatest trick of all was to sing a simple, unadorned line. His hands hung straight at his sides. His white hair sprung luxuriantly from under his onion-domed hat. He was not tall, but he stood straight, and in his white cotton robe he was regal. History, my father told me; the Jews have history. But Abba standing there facing the holy ark erased time. He sang like David. David, the sweet singer of Israel. Abba sang, and the tune of his song, the long, operatic melody, caught my heart. He sang with absolute conviction, and with fervor that resonated with doubt. How could he presume to sing to God? How could he keep silent?

Abba finished. My father turned back to his music stand. I had a glimpse of his expression: awe and doubt—doubt of a different, secular nature—mingled with stubbornness in the set of his full lips: his mind, his intellect beating against faith, against what he loved. He took off his glasses and wiped his eyes. His solo and Uncle Freddie's solo were coming next. I looked out through the curtain at my grandmother. She sat still and straight as if she had been touched with lightning. On the bimah, Abba cleared his throat.

Again, Abba led. *Unesane tokef*, a medieval prayer: a prayer for life. This time he began loud, announcing the prayer like a trumpet; he was cajoling God, pleading for mercy. *"You remember, God, all that has been forgotten."*

My father frowned. He reached for the round, black and chrome pitch pipe on the ledge of his music stand and blew into it, two notes. He shook his head in frustration. "He's gone up a tone." He leaned over the railing. "Psst! Papa!" he hissed. "F!"

But Abba paid no attention. *"You open the Book of Remembrance, you judge who shall live and who shall die, who shall be at peace and who tormented."* My father blew defiantly on his pitch pipe and brought the choir in on the original key. Abba glared at the choir loft. He shook his fist. The congregation thought he was imploring God; we knew that he was threatening my father.

Uselessly. My father paused before his solo, giving the congregation time to forget his father's unrepentant pitch. My father sang in the correct key. He and Freddie each sang a verse of this prayer; each voice sang, full of beauty, ripe with the need to be heard, to differ from their father's voice, to bloom from the same root. Then Abba sang: *"The great shofar is sounded."* The choir answered, in a whisper: *"And a still, small voice is heard."*

My hands gripped the prayer book. I could barely breathe under this noise, this ravishing noise. A still, small voice: my own. I would be heard.

. . .

At the end of Musaf, Abba paused. Seats thudded against the backs of pews as more people left. Abba glanced balefully over his shoulder, then looked up at my father and shrugged. Jonny and Margit went back to Abba and Lady's.

"Can I go, too?" I begged.

"Not yet," my father admonished. "Not yet. Stay, sweet. Stay for the Avodah. I'd like you to stay." Downstairs, the congregation had seriously diminished. This part of the service consisted of passages from the Talmud recounting the ancient rituals at the temple in Jerusalem, when the high priest entered the Holy of Holies on Yom Kippur and pronounced the forbidden name of God. The ceremony seemed to me barbaric and thrilling, frightening, antithetical to this religion of the intellect, this tradition of the People of the Book. The high priest, I read in English, dipped his hand into the blood of a sacrificed bull and sprinkled the blood in the air and on the ground. Once, twice, three times; the choir counted, singing modal music, ancient and rigorous, harshly different from the melodies that had come before. As he spoke the terrible Name, the priest's hand would have been crimson and sticky; his clean white linen garments, like Abba's cambric robe, would have been splattered with blood.

My father sang and conducted and watched. I listened with growing nervousness. I read: The high priest uttered the name of the Lord. And he bowed down three times, once for himself, once for the other priests, and once for his people, Israel.

"Deborah! Come here!" my father whispered. I came and stood beside him.

Abba bowed down. He lay prone on the worn, brown rug on the bimah. He prostrated himself before God. My father placed his hand on my head like a benediction. The hairs on the back of my neck prickled.

"This is how I want you to remember your grandfather," he charged me. His voice was thick; he was close to tears. I trembled under the honor and burden of his injunction; I stared at Abba, in order to remember. Abba, face down, singing into the carpet. It was hard for me to look, hard to see him drop to his knees and press his face against the rug. It was hard for him to get up; he grimaced as the rabbi and the president of the congregation lifted him under his arms. I remembered the wrinkles in his white robe, his bare neck under his white hair, his canvas shoes with their red soles. I remembered his awful humility and the triumph in his voice when he stood straight again.

. . .

Finally, the sun shone low through the western windows of the synagogue. It shone onto the bimah and washed the limestone golden, turned the white velvet curtain covering the ark gold, gleamed pale gold on Abba's hair. After the Avodah service, I had walked down to Abba's and played with Jonny and Margit until my father collected us and brought us back to shul. We were approaching the end. We had repeated lists and lists of sins, the men had beaten their breasts. They were lightheaded, dizzy from fasting and singing all day. Now they sang Ne'ilah, the closing service, the most solemn. The ark remained open. The congregation stood. Abba sang the Ne'ilah theme, four notes, a minor second, tonic and a minor third, haunting, small, suggestive, hopeful. "Deborah," my father whispered as he passed out the parts. "We sing this tune only for Ne'ilah, only once a year, never any other time." My father kept his High Holy Day music in folders, one folder for each service. The music was old, stained brown, some was photocopied. The Hebrew, in many of the pieces, was transliterated into German. Downstairs, I saw Mrs. Werner take her place; she had come back after leaving for a while; her legs were swollen and hurting, I'd heard her tell Lady. I tried to catch Lady's eye now, but she bent her head close over her prayer book. When I had sought her out before I left in the afternoon, just to see her, just to say hello and cheer her up, she looked so sad, but she had not wanted to talk. "Shh," she had whispered, although only the shamas was chanting. The day was too solemn for children, I thought, wishing I hadn't bothered her.

The sun was setting; the light inside dimmed and grew blue. "How long?" I asked.

"Only a few more minutes," my father answered, but I could see that he had lost track of time, that he was suspended in the music, in the slow murmur of Ne'ilah. The gates are closing, I read, the gates of righteousness, the gates of return. God has sealed the fate of every creature for the coming year.

I measured the pages. We were almost done, almost there. The shamas shuffled off the bimah and returned with the shofar. The exhausted choir sang the final prayers with fresh energy. Their faces shone with sweat, and their eyes shone with accomplishment. Then Abba threw back his head. "*Shema Yisrael,*" he proclaimed. "Hear, O Israel." It was almost over. He proclaimed the Shema once, and the choir echoed, "*Blessed be His Name, the honor of His Kingship for ever and ever.*" Three times Abba and the choir repeated that sentence, half a chant and half a shout. "*The Lord is our God,*" Abba sang. His voice rang out rich and clear, the melody as ancient and primitive as the call of the shofar. Seven times Abba proclaimed, "*The Lord is our God*"; seven times the choir echoed. Abba and my father each kept count on their fingers. My ears rang with the sound; I shivered; I sang with my own small voice the ancient formulas echoing back thousands of years to the temple in Jerusalem, echoing and repeating.

"*Tikiah gedolah!*" Abba commanded. The shamas blew a long, triumphant blast on the shofar. Yom Kippur was over.

"Not bad," said Uncle Freddie, judging the blast as he did every year. "Not bad. If that guy wants another job, I know a band that needs a good horn." He had worked his way through the University of Baltimore Law School playing piano in nightclubs.

"Good *yom tov, gute yar.*" My father kissed me and kissed my brother. He embraced his brother, too.

"Let's eat," said Freddie. "I'm starving."

We had done it, we had prayed, searched our hearts, and now we had achieved an ordinary evening, we had returned to the world.

. . .

In early October, when the nights were cold and we wore jackets to school, I woke up on a Saturday morning and found my brother dressed and standing on the landing with my father.

"What are you doing?" I asked.

"Jonny's going to shul with me," my father answered.

"What about me?"

"You don't have to come if you don't want to."

"Why? What's Jonny going to do?"

"He's going to sing in the choir."

My father started downstairs, and my brother followed him. In my pajamas, I waited, unsuspicious, deciding whether I wanted to go, too, until they had reached the hall, and then I slid down the banister railing. "Can I sing, too?" I asked.

My father looked upset. He already had his hat on. He reached for the handle of the front door.

My brother grinned at me. He was missing both his front teeth. "I'm getting paid," he announced. "I'm getting five dollars a month."

"Who's paying you?"

"The shul."

"Then I want to sing, too!" I said, hot with jealousy and fury. "I'm coming. I'm joining the choir, too. Wait for me!"

My father shook his head. "The choir is just for men. For boys. Only men sing in the choir."

"But that isn't fair!" I yelled. "I know Hebrew. I know the prayers. I know them better than Jonny. And I'm older. He doesn't know them at all!"

My father kept shaking his head, miserably and helplessly.

Outside, a horn honked. He pushed aside the filmy white curtain covering the window, then he opened the door. "Okay!" he shouted. "We hear you."

We.

"Bye," Jonny said and hustled outside.

The door shut. I watched in the dead silence of the house as Marty Willen's car pulled away from the curb and the men went off to sing.

Six

A Rhine Journey

Halfway up the stairs in Abba and Lady's house there hung a water-color of Abba that was painted when he was a young man. The metal band of a radio headset crossed his forehead like the strap of *tefillin:* phylacteries—little wooden boxes, containing scrolls upon which the Shema was written, which devout Jews bound to their foreheads and left arm while reciting morning prayers. But in this little portrait, Abba looked anything but devout. The headset flattened his wavy hair, and he had a thick blond mustache. He wore a gray jacket with chest pockets and epaulets: the uniform of the army of the Austro-Hungarian empire. His lush lips curled in a musing, mischievous smile, and his cleft chin was rounded and young. The sketch was dated 1917; it had been painted in the trenches.

I dawdled, studying it, disturbed by its connection to my white-haired grandfather. "Deborah! Go on up! Go see your grandmother! Go, please." My father watched me climb the rest of the narrow, angled steps. Her room through its open door seemed close and eerie as a cavern. The blinds were shut, and the lavender curtains, drawn over the blinds, glowed a twilight purple. I stopped still at the threshold. Lady's thigh, exposed by her hiked-up nightgown, shone bone white.

"Go away!" the nurse in her white uniform hissed as she hoisted Lady onto the white enamel commode that stood by her bed. Lady, her hair sprung into a disheveled, wiry halo, opened her mouth in embarrassment and glared at me with eyes that gleamed from deep, brown-shadowed caves.

I fled down the stairs, through the dining room, into the hall leading to the kitchen. Abba and Freddie and my father were sitting at the table. The brightness there startled me; it seemed cold and without mercy. The counter was bare and desolate; nothing simmered on the stove. There was no cloth on the table. This was a weekday. I could not remember being in this house on an ordinary weekday before. Abba sat with his fingers interlocked, his hands resting on the wood and scattered bread crumbs. His hands were like my father's, compact and muscled from playing the piano.

Suddenly Abba banged the table with his palm. "I built this shul with my own hands!" Bread crumbs jumped in fury. "Brick by brick I built it! I went from house to house begging for money, to build a beautiful shul. Even if they had next to nothing, still they gave! So now, now for no reason, now they want to abandon it? Abandon me? They cannot do this." He shook his head. "What is there in Stevenson? Nothing, no community, only new houses. And this, whatever they call it, this sanctuary!"

"Sanctuary much," said Uncle Freddie.

"You're welcome," my father answered.

Abba glared at them both.

Stevenson was a suburb beyond the Baltimore city limits, past our own suburb of Mt. Washington. The congregation, along with many of its members, had bought land there to build a new synagogue. Jews had left the city, preferring new houses on shaved ground to Eutaw Place with its view of the reservoir and Druid Hill Park. Surosky had just closed his butcher shop on Whitelock Street. It was the last of the Jewish businesses in the neighborhood. On Friday afternoons, Lady used to march along Whitelock Street shopping for Shabbos; she went from Surosky to Silber's bakery to the fish store. Now all these establishments were boarded up, their buildings worthless. And Lady went from her house to the hospital.

"The president of the shul says that downtown is not safe," Abba went on. "He tells me, 'Look around. Look at your street. Look at Chauncey Avenue: rundown, a disgrace. Look at your neighbors. Negroes. They don't take care of their property. Not one Jew is living on Chauncey Avenue anymore.' So I tell him, 'Jew, shmew. I live here. I am safe. White, black. Why does color matter? I walk up and down this street every day of my life, in the morning, after dark. I walk around the reservoir. Nobody interferes with me.'"

Abba banged his hand again and the crumbs danced. "But what can I say? What can I do? Who listens to me? 'People won't come downtown,' the president says. 'They'll join another congregation. Every synagogue has moved.' And what does he want me to do? Where will I live? How will I live? And your mother?"

His hand with its sturdy, gnarled fingers lay flat and helpless on the table. His wedding ring on his left hand had grown so tight it seemed part of his flesh. His eyes, pale and red-rimmed from exhaustion, gazed bleakly into the space between his sons.

I walked in. "Why so quick?" my father asked. I shook my head. I didn't look at him; I avoided his sorrow, afraid that it would make me cry. As I started to explain, Lady's nurse called me back upstairs.

Lady sat in bed, propped up by pillows. She and Abba slept in twin beds pushed together; each had a shiny black headboard. Abba's bed was neatly made and covered with a lavender spread. Since her illness, he had slept downstairs on a daybed wedged in a corner of the dining room. Lady's night table was packed with medicines; that awful commode took up the space between the bed and the wall. The nurse retreated to a chair in the far corner.

Lady held out her arms. Her legs were well hidden under the sheets now, and a crocheted bed jacket warmed her shoulders. Her hair was neatened, pulled back into a wiry bun. Slowly I walked around the beds and slid past the commode to stand beside her. Her opened arms followed me. She had never cuddled much. When I was little, she bounced me on her knees and sang, "*Hop, hop, hop, galopp, galopp, galopp!*" But she loved me, my mother said, and I took that on faith.

Awkwardly, I leaned into her embrace. My thighs pressed against the corded edge of the mattress. Lady held me lightly and did not press my head against her, as if she feared I would hurt her, or that her pressure would make me pull away. I closed my eyes. I braced myself as best I could, but I was afraid that the rug I stood on would slip and I would pitch into her or shift backwards and knock over all her pills. I did not know why she was sick. Until I saw her helpless thigh, white and smooth and exposed, too weak to support her, I had no idea how sick she was. Now, in her arms, I felt her mortal fear, and I became afraid for myself.

She released me. She looked at me and smiled, and it seemed that she was trying not to weep. "Are you going to Hebrew school?" she asked.

"Yes," I said, impatiently. "Three times a week."

"Are you learning the prayers?"

"Yes."

"Say the Shema."

"Hear, O Israel, the Lord is our God, the Lord is One." Embarrassed, I repeated the Hebrew words to her.

She nodded.

I waited for sadness to wash over me, but I felt only discomfort. I moved to the foot of Lady's high bed and looked at her eyes. There was not very much light, and her eyes gathered it into a great distance; they did not give it out. Their darkness was contagious. I wanted to go. And I wanted to tell her that I loved her. That was not something I said; that was not something that we said in my family. But I thought it might help. I was too uneasy and too shy, though, and so I said nothing at all. I went back to the side of her bed, and I kissed her, through that terrifying distance, and I went back downstairs.

In the kitchen, Abba and Freddie and my father sat without speaking. Abba drank tea from a glass cup. I asked him if there were any cookies in the big copper pot on top of the ice box, but there were none.

. . .

It was a Wednesday, a day my father was usually away in New York. But he came home late in the afternoon. I met him at the threshold of the dining room. He said: "My mother died," and he sat on an extra dining room chair, one that stood against the wall. "Deborah, come here." He opened his arms to me and wrapped them around my waist and pressed his head against my stomach. He wailed, one loud, hollow, awful moan. I flinched, but he held me close to him. I stood stiffly, bracing myself for another cry, for grief that would unmoor me, but none came. My father just held on to me. I never heard him cry after that. I did not miss Lady. But that cry of my father's cut into my mind like music, the start of dissonance, the unresolved discord of death.

The house on Chauncey Avenue did not change much. Abba kept his daybed and covered it with a brown chenille spread. He had a shower installed in the powder room in the hall between the dining room and the kitchen, so that he never had to go upstairs again. Sometimes we, the children, would venture up. In the bedroom to the left of the landing and in the back study, everything was covered with dust; in Lady's bedroom the shiny ebony furniture remained preternaturally dust free. We peered into her room and clattered downstairs as fast as we could.

Abba had learned Lady's recipes. He roasted turkey, simmered soup, shaped matzo balls, and marinated herring. He chopped carp for gefilte fish. He did not bake, but Silber's Bakery, which had moved to Park Heights Avenue, delivered challah and cookies, and my mother and all the rest of the women continued to supply him with Passover cakes. In her lazy way, Ozelia presided over the kitchen and kept the house as clean as she had to, which, according to my mother, was filthy. Mommy was the only one who minded.

At shul, nobody ever took Lady's seat in her secluded alcove, but that spring, at Passover, Klari, Lady's niece, sat in her place. Abba wept at Passover that year, and every year after that, when it came time to sing the psalm "Shir Hama'alot," a psalm about the Exodus, the redemption from Egypt. We had four different tunes for that psalm, and Lady's grandfather, Klari's great-grandfather, had written one of them, a beautiful melody in a minor key, a slow march that ended in lyrical arpeggios, triumph mindful of pain: a treasure that we took out and held in our voices once a year, a tune that more than a decade later, my father used in one of his operas. Abba banged the flat of his hand on the table to mark the rhythm, and his eyes filled with tears. That was his mourning: music. And music was his joy.

Music opened his heart; music opened my father's heart. Did they weep from music or from the memory music invoked? Was there— is there—any separation between music and the memories it holds?

. . .

The following Passover, in the spring of 1956, Mrs. Werner sat at the head of the Seder table. Klari and her husband, Fred, were spending the year at Cambridge University in England, where he was a visiting professor. The Hirschlers were not there, either; Mr. Hirschler had decided to return to Vienna and reclaim the housewares factory the Nazis had confiscated from his family. Just after Passover my family, too, was going to Europe. For months, my parents had been planning. My father had won a Guggenheim grant. He was using it to take us to live in Florence, Italy, in the midst of what he told us was indescribable beauty. He was still working on *Six Characters,* an opera based on an Italian play, and he was sure that he would finish it on Italian soil.

On April 4, 1956, we sailed to England from New York on the *Queen Elizabeth,* all four of us crammed into one dark cabin on the lowest deck, well below the water line. We also took our car, a blue Plymouth sedan, loaded with trunks and suitcases and even a few rolls of toilet paper. We were going to be away for six months. Eight and a half years earlier, my parents had left a continent where you could not get anything, not baby clothes, not a banana. Now, leaving nothing to chance, they packed as if they were returning to a wilderness.

As soon as we emerged from our cabin, we indulged in the romance of passage: the ritual of setting our watches ahead one hour every day, the ship's costume party, the wagering on miles traversed. I was seasick every morning, but every afternoon I recovered, and Jonny and I, almost the only children on board, played shuffleboard and deck tennis. We visited pets in the kennels, and I moped thinking about our cat Mittens; Nanny had taken charge of him while we were away. My parents sat side by side in deck chairs; wrapped in blankets, they drank bouillon in the morning and tea in the afternoon. My mother, who never read fiction, had become immersed in *Mem-*

oirs of Hadrian, by Marguerite Yourcenar; it read like history, she explained to my father, like intimate, detailed history. In the afternoons before tea, Daddy worked at a piano in one of the first-class lounges, then, while my mother drifted back into imperial Rome, he and Jonny and I wandered up to the bow to watch the ship splinter the ocean into spray.

We docked in Southampton on a gray, chill April day. In our American car, our turquoise exaggeration, we sped down the wrong side of English roads toward Cambridge to visit Klari and Fred in their cold flat. "It was so cold, I thought that Jonathan and Deborah were going to stick to the toilet seat," my mother would say for years afterward. From Cambridge, we took a day trip to London. Our first stop was the British Museum, to see the Rosetta stone and the Elgin marbles. My father was our guide, beside himself with excitement at seeing these relics, these proofs of history; during the war, they had been packed away for safekeeping. He ushered us into the big oblong room rimmed with the frieze from the Parthenon and nodded approval as I tried to stroke, surreptitiously, the rearing forelegs of the horses.

In London, my father expanded. He recovered the optimism, the sense of his own potential, that had faltered when he returned to America. He became excited, confident, he brimmed with energy. He told us about the concerts he conducted during the war, the time he did Brahms's Fourth Symphony, whose slow movement opened with four horns. One of the musicians hadn't shown up; he had been caught in an air raid. Undaunted, my father sang his part. He demonstrated how he had done it; he pursed his lips, and his voice emerged through this mouthpiece mellow as a French horn. He told us about conducting the army's Negro chorus in spirituals, with Paul Robeson. "Oh, I would be very happy living in London!" he exclaimed as we headed toward the Victoria and Albert Museum in Kensington to view its collection of Renaissance bronzes. He sang in the street. "*Oh, I walk down Piccadilly with a poppy or a lily in my medieval hand,*" he pattered from *Patience.*

In Europe the sky stretched beyond the horizon; it opened into the past. We saw back hundreds of years, thousands of years. At

Stonehenge we wandered through the rings of rocks eager to decipher their magic and their mysteries. We climbed the cathedral towers of Salisbury and Ely, their interiors still monochromatic because
the stained-glass windows had been bombed or remained in storage.
We strolled through Grosvenor Square where my father had passed
every day during the war and dodged V-2 rockets. Blocks of buildings remained wreckage, part of the thrilling rubble, the jumbled
syllables of time.

My father had business, too. He was thinking ahead to the next
opera. Denis Johnston, the librettist for *Six Characters,* was Irish, and
my father, in love with Irish words, sought out Sean O'Casey in his
home in Torquay, in the south of England, to negotiate for rights to
a play. Despite the palm trees that lined the beaches, the wind was
cold, too cold to play outside. While the composer and the playwright
conferred, Mrs. Casey gave the rest of us tea, and, when I admired
them, she gave me the little blown-glass menagerie—swans, pen-
guins, a monkey—that had belonged to her own daughter, who was
now grown and living, Mrs. Casey said, far away. I wrapped the fragile figurines in cotton wool and nestled them into my traveling bag.
My father emerged from the meeting satisfied; in Europe, comforted
with his past, his future was bright.

The next evening, we sailed across the North Sea to Holland. My
mother exclaimed rapturously over the landscape. The earth stretched
like a tiny green ribbon under shifting cloud mountains. She recognized Rembrandt in the gray slanting light, and Ruisdael and van de
Velde. In the Rijksmuseum she rapturously pointed out the similari-
ties between landscape and canvas. That was important evidence for
her, evidence of beauty's reality; my mother did not trust fiction. Fresh
from *Hans Brinker,* I scanned the green for dykes—stone barricades
against the sea—and canals. I was disappointed when low, grassy
berms turned out to be the mighty retaining walls.

In Holland, my father began, reluctantly, to speak German.
"Please speak German," I urged, already loath to be considered
American and brash and uncultured and vulgar. Proud of how many
languages my father knew, I wanted him to show off.

"The Dutch hate speaking German," my father answered. "They hate the Germans."

"Why?"

"Because of what the Nazis did to them during the war."

"What did they do?"

"Terrible things. They invaded the country. They killed people. They took the Jews to concentration camps."

One afternoon we got lost. We were looking for the famous Portuguese synagogue. My father had never seen it, but he knew it from pictures. He stopped a man on the street, a man his age, in his forties, wearing baggy work pants and a smock, a laborer, a man whom my father did not expect to speak English. "*Bitte*," my father said. "*Bitte*." The man did not answer. He considered us with exhausted bitterness and turned away.

"Please," my father called in English. "We are American."

The man stopped. "Do not speak German to me," he growled in Dutch, and even I understood him.

"The synagogue?" my father asked.

In slow, patient Dutch, the man gave us directions.

After a week of English cathedrals, of Salisbury, Ely, King's Chapel, Westminster Abbey, monuments whose spires marked the political geography of Christendom, we approached a plain wooden doorway in a block of ordinary facades. My father rang the bell, and a gray old man in a yarmulke opened the door. The old man led us through another set of doors into the great synagogue in Amsterdam. It was square; the bimah, ringed by an elaborately carved wooden railing, stood in the center of the room. Great brass chandeliers hung over the pews. Only the Hebrew inscriptions on the walls connected it to my idea of Judaism. The synagogue was different from ours, my father said, because it was founded by Sephardic Jews who fled to the Netherlands when they were expelled from Spain in 1492. It was exotic and alien, and all but abandoned. There were no prayer books, no stray things, no evidence of a congregation. The building was cold, the light inside gray and hopeless.

My father addressed the man, who was the caretaker, in English, but he did not understand. "I am sorry," my father apologized. "But may I speak German?" The old man nodded and shrugged. Why not? They conversed for a long time. My father nodded. His lips pushed outward, his face flushed. He nodded grimly; he shook his head. He knew the stories he was being told.

. . .

Before we left Baltimore, my parents had obtained a map from the American Automobile Association marked with a route, a translucent red line, that wiggled south down the center of Europe to Italy. We followed the Rhine from Holland into Germany. It did not seem unusual to me then that we were driving through Germany in 1956, eleven years after the end of the war. I was eight years old and trusted in my parents' wisdom; I did not wonder why we drove that route through enemy territory. The war, to me, was only a story, its horrors as distant as those of Grimm.

With every bend of the road another fairy tale relic appeared: a gray and crenellated castle perched like a stone falcon on the edge of a crag overlooking the black river. Jonny and I watched from the car windows as each castle approached and receded, emerging from rock and vanishing back into dense forest and bare outcropping. We kept a tally and competed to be the first to spot each tower and village. From a distance we spied the towns stuck against the steep sides of the valley; then the road wound and rose up to the town's medieval gates. Our wide car squeezed between ancient facades.

In almost every town there remained evidence of the war. In a collapsed house, its crumbled plaster still strangely white and fresh after eleven years, we saw the peeling floral wallpaper of half a room. Or a new building rose jarring, sleek and bright, pastel and temporary as a Popsicle. The names of the towns were familiar; they sounded Jewish. Bachrach: that was the name of a photography studio in Baltimore. Coblenz: that was Chizuk Amuno's first rabbi, Adolph Coblenz, whose name was carved into the white marble lectern that faced the congregation.

"There were ancient Jewish communities in these towns," my father said. He spoke in his instructional tone. His pronunciation was precise; each sentence emerged complete. But his throat thickened around the words, and we heard his emotion. "The Jews first came into the Rhine valley with the Roman armies, with Julius Caesar. You know the prayer, Unesane tokef, that we sing on Rosh Hashanah and Yom Kippur? Well, that was written by somebody who lived in one of these towns. The Jews were massacred periodically. In the eighteenth century, after their emancipation—yes, like the slaves in America—thanks to Moses Mendelsohn, they took the names of their towns as their last names." Our tires jiggled on the cobblestones that paved a town square. "Moses Mendelsohn. He was the grandfather of Felix Mendelsohn, who wrote *A Midsummer Night's Dream*," Daddy added, "who converted to Christianity." He shook his head over the sad irony.

People stood in their doorways to watch our turquoise chariot pass. "There are no Jews anymore. The Jews in these towns were wiped out, early, at the beginning of the war; they were the first to go. Nothing is left of them. No synagogues, nothing."

"But their names," I said.

Daddy turned in his seat and looked at me. He nodded and bit his lower lip.

The towns seemed full, their inhabitants busy and prosperous. In our American car, I felt secure, immune from history. We had won. And I wonder if my father hadn't intended this journey to be in some way a triumph, a victory passage through town after town, with their Jewish names.

Downstream, the valley widened on one side and great black boulders spilled into the river. "Slow down! Slow down!" my father commanded my mother, who was driving. "That is the Lorelei!"

Lorelei. Even the word lilted. My mother pulled over to the side of the road. Waves from a passing tanker splashed against the rocks. Daddy told us the story of the Rhine maidens who lived underwater and guarded the treasure of the Niebelung in Wagner's operas. He told us the story of the Lorelei, the beautiful water sprite whose song lured sailors to their death. It was late afternoon, and the river was in shadow. Just ahead, on the river side of the road, was an inn. This early in the spring, we were the only guests. The rooms had painted bedsteads with thick white quilts. The inn was like the house of elves, toasty brown and spotless; it could have been carved from gingerbread, and there was a piano in the dining room. The innkeepers, a husband and wife, were pleased that an American family was staying with them, and they tried out some slang learned from American soldiers. The public rooms opened onto a terrace, and just upstream loomed the Lorelei. The white noise of the river's rushing whispered up at us. "What would they do if they knew we were Jewish?" my mother asked. I was afraid: maybe she would start a fight. But she went inside, warning us not to pitch ourselves over the railing into the Rhine.

My father asked the innkeeper if he could play the piano. He sounded a few majestic chords, then stopped and shook his head. "No," he said. "Not Wagner." He closed his eyes and began a lilting, haunting tune, and he sang. His rich, sweet voice resonated in the empty room. It was a song I had never heard. He sang the first verse and the second; he knew the words by heart. When he forgot the accompaniment, he added his own harmonies. I stood beside the piano. His sound rang in my ears, hurting, but I stayed where I was.

"What was that song?" I asked.

He smiled. When he played, he wore a smile like the music he loved, grief and yearning and happiness mixed.

"Schuman," he answered me. "The song is called 'Die Lorelei.' Isn't it beautiful? Schuman set this poem by Heine. Schubert set Heine, too. Heinrich Heine. He was one of the greatest of all German poets, and he was Jewish. Everybody learned his poetry; everybody knew it by heart. The Nazis couldn't get rid of his words, but they removed his name from his poems. They tried to pretend that he had not written his own poems."

He shook his head again. "This is what the words mean: The air grows cool in the twilight, and softly the Rhine flows. The mountaintop shines under the setting sun. . . ." He played and sang, then paused again. "In the end the boatman wrecks his boat on the rocks. These are the last lines: '*She did this with her singing, the golden Lorelei.*'" He paused and swallowed. "My father sang this song."

Outside it was almost dark. The river reflected a wavering light or two. Daddy sang, full of tenderness. German had been his first language; he had learned that Jewish poem, that song, when he was a boy. If the Lorelei had been a baritone, she would have sounded like that, urging, beckoning, promising sweetness, promising disaster. Just downstream from the treacherous rock, my father played, reclaiming the song, giving it back its name.

The innkeeper and his wife turned on the lamps and then stood shyly at the door to the kitchen and listened. Then two more figures appeared, bulky and square, one slightly smaller than the other. They both had cropped, straight, dirty-blond hair. They were teenagers; they must have been the innkeepers' children. When my father paused after singing the song again, the larger figure approached him and spoke in a low voice; I could not tell if it was male or female. I heard the word "*musik.*" Music. My father nodded.

They hurried away through the kitchen door and returned with a portable record player housed in a suitcase. I had a similar, smaller one at home. They plugged it in and put on a record, a forty-five, I could tell from the large hole. American rock and roll—Bill Haley, I think it was—blasted through the room, frantic with energy. The two teenagers began to dance. They jumped up and down with both feet, they held each other's hands and alternately pulled back and yanked themselves together and bounced like great clumsy animals in an uncouth Lindy. Their stomping feet drowned out the record, and they stopped and turned it louder. I watched; they were Valkyrie; they could have been wearing breastplates and horned helmets; they could have been wearing caps with death's heads over the visors. But they meant no harm. They frightened me with their trampling dancing; yet at the same time I believed its innocence. My father's face was grim.

When the song was over, they stood panting and grinning. I smiled back; I wanted to be friends. My father nodded at them, but he did not smile. They unplugged their record player and took it away. My father closed the piano. The innkeepers wished us good night. My father stood at the window gazing at the black river and the dark place where the magic rock must have been.

"Do you remember . . ." he said to my mother as we drove off the next morning.

Her nod cut him short.

"Remember what?" I asked.

My parents looked at each other. "He came from the Rhineland."

"Who? Tell me," I insisted.

"A man came to see me one day in Prague."

"Daddy, what did you do in Prague?" I interrupted.

"I worked for the army and for the State Department. I did all sorts of things."

"You gave orders to keep the borders open," Mommy said.

"What do you mean?"

"I let people come into Czechoslovakia. And I got into trouble for it. This man was still dressed in the concentration camp uniform."

"What was that?"

"Stripes. Stripes like a prisoner. But he was arrogant. He stood in front of my desk with his hands behind his back and demanded that I give him papers so that he could leave the country. That's what everybody wanted, papers to leave the country. His attitude irritated me. 'What did you do that makes you so special?' I asked. 'I was a pianist,' he told me. And he held out his arms. His hands had been cut off."

"What did you do?" I asked, to say something.

He choked out the words: "I gave him his papers."

. . .

In Frankfurt, my father promised me elephants at the opera, and if not elephants, then horses. He held my hand while we climbed the steps of the opera house to see *Aida*. He sang Verdi's triumphal march to me, blowing through his lips to imitate the trumpets, and I was as excited as if we were going to the circus. It turned out that in this production there were neither elephants nor horses, but a horde of Ethiopian slaves dressed in gray and green tattered rags pulling the chariot with victorious Radames in it; they doubled as the chorus.

I was disappointed, but only briefly. Opera itself was a circus of sound and light and improbable action. Daddy provided a thrilling play-by-play, and I loved every minute of it, even the ending in which Radames is buried alive and Aida sneaks into his tomb and dies with him. "Why does it have to end that way?" I whispered, close to tears. He put his arm around my shoulder, and he whispered back that sometimes it didn't, that there was a happy ending, too. I maintained faith in happy endings.

At every sad opera and every tragic ballet, my father told me the same thing; these works possessed an alternative, ending that had been tacked on when people couldn't stomach the real one. In *Swan Lake*, the Prince triumphed over von Rothbart, and the Swan Queen did not die. In *Aida*, Radames and his true love escaped to sing another day, but they didn't perform that version very often, he told me, especially not in Germany.

. . .

In Vienna, we saw *Orfeo ed Eurydice* by Gluck at the State Opera. We could not get four seats together, so my father sat with me in the orchestra, and my mother took my brother, who was very sleepy, up to the balcony. In Vienna, we had been busy. We toured the Hirschlers' housewares factory, and Mr. Hirschler invited my mother to choose whatever she wanted from the shelves of gleaming domestic machines. We went to the Kunsthistorische Museum with its Breughels, to the Prater, the amusement park, with its giant Ferris wheel. My father's cousin Latzi, who had managed to travel from Budapest, from behind the Iron Curtain, came along that day. Daddy and Latzi had not seen each other since before the war, since 1938, when my father had gone to Budapest hoping to study composition with Béla Bartók. Latzi was small and wiry; he had a mustache and wore a rakish hat and a tight plaid sport coat. He laughed often, nervously and quickly, as if the humor was going to fade before he captured it.

He spoke English, but he and my father spoke German with each other. Latzi had insisted on taking Jonny and me with him on the Ferris wheel. As the wheel lifted us into the chilly gray air, Latzi laughed and held us close to him on either side. He smelled like tobacco, and the tips of his mustache were stained ochre. "So far!" he exclaimed. "So far! You can see so far!" He was as excited as a child. He stayed for only a day; it was enough that he had been able to come. Things were loosening up in Budapest, he told us, but he dared not take any more time, or he would be suspect and his family would suffer.

I loved Vienna, I loved the teeming Breughels in the museum, and the Prater, and the pale rococo elegance of the palace at Schoenbrun. I saw delight everywhere; my parents remembered war.

"During the war, the Allies bombed the opera house. It was completely destroyed," my father told me as we waited for the usher. "Leveled. And it was one of the first things the Viennese rebuilt," he added ruefully. We found our seats. Daddy could barely contain his excitement. "Abba took me here when I was a little boy. He wanted to be an opera singer, you know. I saw my first opera in this house. My father took me; it was *Tosca*."

We sat close to the stage. This opera, with its small, androgynous cast—Orpheus was sung by an alto—was tender and intimate. Orpheus sang of his love for Eurydice. "Where will I go? What will I do?" he sang. "Without Eurydice, what am I?" My father translated for me. Flutes played the dance of the spirits, Orpheus descended into the underworld. I watched fervently, caught in the delicate, heartrending web of the music. "What happens?" I whispered. "What happens?" Daddy squeezed my hand. In the darkness, he shook his head. "Orpheus can only bring Eurydice back to life if he doesn't look at her while he's climbing back up. She'll follow him, but he can't look back."

"Does he look back?"

"Most often, he does."

"But sometimes he doesn't. Will he tonight?"

"Listen!" My father put his fingers to his lips and nodded. "Joy," he whispered. "Gluck. His name means joy in German."

. . .

"She called me a dirty Jew!" My mother, shaking, stood in the marble lobby of the opera house. She held my sleepy brother by the hand. "I can't believe it!" Her voice grew louder; people were staring at her.

"Shh!" My father put his hand on her shoulder, but she pulled away. "What really happened?" he asked.

Mommy's eyes flashed; she hated that he didn't trust her. "Jonny fell asleep. He's so little, his legs stuck out straight from his chair. As soon as the curtain came down, a woman beside me got up to leave, and Jonny's shoes scraped against her dress. She turned around and looked at me and said, '*Juden!*'"

"And?"

"And?" my mother repeated, outraged. "I kicked her. I kicked her in the shin! I kicked her hard! I'm not going to let anybody get away with that!"

"Jesus Christ!" said Daddy, his face tightening in fear and dis-approval. "Are you sure that's what she said?"

"Of course I'm sure!"

"Are you sure she didn't say *Jungend*? Youth?"

My mother was white with anger. "I'm not going back there!" she shouted. "I want to leave. If you want to stay, please, stay! I don't know why you even brought us here to this godforsaken anti-Semitic city. The war may be over, but nothing has changed."

"No!" I begged. "I want to stay! Please! I want to hear the rest of the opera!"

Jonny started to cry.

"Now look at what you've done," growled my father. He fished our tickets from his pocket. "You go sit here. Nobody will bother you. Deborah and I will take your seats. Give me your tickets. Hurry. It's about to start."

At the beginning of the next act, I sat on the edge of my seat, alert to this anti-Semite; I scanned the row of middle-aged women with their disciplined gray curls and precise loden suits as if I could identify a surviving Jew-hater from her features, from the cruel, thin cast of her witch-like mouth. I was curious to see what hate looked like, but I could not spot her and soon forgot about it. I was in no danger; I was sitting next to my father; with him I could survive any trip to hell.

. . .

We drove west from Vienna across a plain. Our turquoise car brilliant as a neon sign invaded desolate villages strung along the road. Brick barns, stucco facades, dusty and crumbling: they seemed to be empty in the raw, bare, early spring. We hardly ever saw people. If we did, they stared at us suspiciously. These villages were like the one where my father grew up, I imagined, and I pitied him his bleak childhood. These were the dark places from which he had escaped to the clean brightness of Baltimore.

As if I were talking instead of thinking, Daddy answered: "Ivančice isn't very far from here."

In Europe I was getting used to the feeling of dreams and reality colliding. "Have you ever been back?" I asked.

"I went back after the war. Just after the war, in 1945." He paused. We slowed down as we entered a village. Through an open door, a shaft of light caught the square, dung-encrusted hindquarters of a cow. "I went back to look for my family, to see if anybody was left." My father swallowed. I wished he wouldn't go on. "Nobody was. Of course. The Nazis had used the shul for a stable. They had emptied it out, all the seats, the ark, all the silver, the Torahs. It was filthy; it stank; the floor was strewn with straw. And nobody knew what had happened. Nobody. Nobody would tell me what had happened to the Jews. Nobody even admitted that they remembered who they were. I asked for people by name, and it was as if they had not existed."

We were past the village. My mother sped up. "Then a few months later," Daddy continued, turning around to look at me in the back seat, "I was sitting at my desk in Prague, and a man came to see me. He had been in a concentration camp. He was skin and bones. His head had been shaved. He had no teeth. 'Who am I?' he asked me, but I didn't know. I didn't recognize him. 'I am Goldmann,' he said. David Goldmann had been my best friend when I was a little boy, when I was just a bit younger than you are, Deborah." My father took a breath and faced front again. "He told me that he had shoveled the bodies of my cousins into the ovens at Terezin." He shook his head, fighting back tears.

We drove and nobody said anything. I felt my father's horror; I saw his best friend stoking an oven as fantastic as the oven of the evil witch in "Hansel and Gretel." I was becoming aware that my very existence, our parade south through Europe in our blue chariot was in itself the happy ending. The fields were tilled into black furrows, ready for planting.

Ahead of us I saw a white sign with an arrow pointing left. "Prag," the sign said. My mother saw it at the same time. She slowed down. "Look!" she pointed, her voice suddenly lilting, singing with delight. "Prague."

"Prague!" I shouted. "Let's go! Come on! Turn!" The road to Prague was in disrepair, pocked with potholes; the white center line had faded to a shadow. The road leading to the magic city was not traveled. I stared at the black letters in the sign: evidence. Prag. Prague was real, a place, not a memory. Mommy stopped the car just before the signpost. She and my father looked at each other with longing and with tenderness. "We can't," she said sadly. "We can't get in. They won't let us in. Prague is in a communist country; it is behind the Iron Curtain. It's worse than Hungary. They would take one look at our passports and turn us away."

"Or arrest us," Daddy added.

"Why?"

"The Communists did not like your father. He kept the borders open; he helped refugees escape from the East, from the Russians. He got into plenty of trouble. Oh, I wish we could go! Oh, Deborah, I wish you could see that city, the castle."

Rusted gates, the Iron Curtain: walls of sheet iron, perversions of Oz, locked us out. My mother put the car in gear and we went on; I kneeled on the seat and watched the sign through the rear window until it disappeared.

Seven

La Primavera

From the Piazzale Michelangelo, Florence spread before us in its shallow valley: the red hemisphere of the Duomo, the black and white stripes of Santa Croce and the Campanile of the Baptistery against the blue May sky.

"*Qu'è bella!*" breathed my father, as if he were about to launch into an aria. My brother pointed to the honey brick tower of the Palazzo Vecchio. "That's just like the Bromo Seltzer tower in Baltimore! But there's no clock." My father laughed. "Because this tower is real. It's the original, the one they copied."

Florence was how a city ought to be; this was the perfect place. Neither of my parents had ever seen it. They had dreamed of it and feared the discrepancy between their imagination and the reality. My mother wanted a dance of color, a painting come to life. My father, descendent of Goethe and the German romantics, sought the lightness and the redeeming ecstasy of the south. I'm not sure if his entrance into Florence—in our blue Plymouth laden with luggage and trailing bread crumbs and globs of strawberry jam—met the requirements of his imagination. He would have preferred to arrive on elephants.

My mother, who was driving, exclaimed at everything and pointed everywhere. "Nath! Nath! Watch where you're going!" My father pretended to be calm, but he was as excited as she.

"I feel like I'm home," my mother said.

Daddy laughed, but he did not disagree. This was going to be our home. I marveled at coincidence. Our first full day in Florence would be May the sixth, my ninth birthday. Florence would be all mine.

We crept up the hill along the via San Leonardo. High peeling stucco walls with flowering vines spilling over their tops hid the houses from the road. We were searching for number 72. At the same time Mommy was consulting a map. She did not trust my father to navigate. "Galileo's Tower is on this road, just a bit farther up the hill," she exclaimed. "Let's go look."

"I'm tired," Jonny wailed.

"There it is! Our house!" I called out. Enameled numbers, 72, were affixed to the wall beside a large, rusted, wrought-iron gate. Beside it was a smaller gate, for people. We nosed the car into the shallow apron, and my father pulled the bell. An allée of cypress trees stretched back downhill from the entrance. A tall, stoop-shouldered man appeared and flung open the gates. Our American tires crunched onto the white stone driveway, and the man directed us to the left, to our villa. I skipped behind the car, in the heat of its exhaust, into the sudden smell of cypress and earth.

A square, white-haired woman came out to greet us from the yellow house. She was the cook, her husband the caretaker. We called them the signora and the signore. Their daughter, Esterina, a young woman with a sweet and open face, lived with them. A gray striped cat emerged from under a thick laurel hedge. "What is his name?" I asked. But the signore and signora looked at me quizzically. They spoke no English. My father tried out his Italian, which he had not spoken for eighteen years, except in operas. In 1938, after leaving Budapest, he had spent the summer in the Val d'Aosta, hiking and studying composition. He translated my question. The words came slowly, and the signore and signora understood; nonetheless, the question stumped them. Finally, the signora shrugged and said, "Leonardo." It seemed careless, made up on the spur of the moment to satisfy a sentimental American child.

The signore led us upstairs; he and his wife insisted on lugging our suitcases. My mother followed them, clutching her pocketbook.

As we entered the house, the signore gestured toward a gloomy kitchen; that was where he and his family lived, in shuttered rooms on the ground floor. Our apartment, it turned out, had no kitchen; the signora prepared every meal for us. A refectory table stood on the wide landing at the top of the stairs; this is where we ate.

The furniture was dark and heavy, the rooms were cool, the tiled floors shone, and thick wooden shutters kept out the afternoon sun. My mother and I opened all the shutters. The windows looked out over the garden, where the signore grew our vegetables, and to the hills beyond: fields, vineyards, smells of oleander and basil. Beside the grand piano in the *salotto,* the big living room, doors opened onto a little balcony with a rusted iron railing. Jonny and I rushed out. "Be careful!" Mommy called. My father stood at the piano. He played a chord, and another; he sat down. The signore and signora trudged up the stairs with our luggage. My father began to sing. "*Di provenza il mar, il suol chi dal cuor ti cancellò? Al natio fulgente sol, qual destino ti furò?*" His big voice resonated against the tile floors and the bare walls; he was singing and playing as loud as he could, loving his sound. The signore and signora stopped to listen. When he finished, they smiled and applauded. Daddy stood and bowed. "*Traviata,*" said the signora, nodding passionately. "*Mi piace molto.*"

"What does that mean?" I asked.

"It means she liked it." He smiled. "My father loves that aria."

"The words to the music, I mean," I interrupted.

"He's singing about his home; he asks his son: 'What fate took you from the shining sun of your birthplace?'" Daddy looked at Mommy. "It sounds so right here. So right." He was laughing with tears in his eyes. For him, joy and sorrow were only a note apart.

. . .

I awoke the next morning to the sound of feet crunching on the gravel driveway and a shouted conversation in guttural Italian between the signore and the signora. Jonny and I shared a room; he was already up and out. Today I was nine years old. I was happy, absolutely happy, setting out on an adventure in a foreign land. I knew just what I was going to wear: my new dirndl. I lay in bed getting used to the room's ochre walls, the black spires of the cypresses, the exotic buzz of cicadas, the new smells of leaves; it was like resting at the edge of a fairy tale.

I heard heavy footsteps coming up the stairs and the clinking of china. I got out of bed. The signora lumbered onto the wide landing and set a big tray on the table. "*Buon giorno,*" she panted.

"Hi," I said shyly.

She wore an apron tied around her ample square body. She smiled at me, and I saw that she was missing an eye tooth and a couple of molars.

"*È molto magra, lei,*" she said.

I looked at her quizzically. She pointed to a big basket of rolls and brought her hand to her mouth. "*Signorina, lei deve mangiare,*" she said and pointed at me and brought her palms together. "*Magra.*" She repeated. "*Magra.*" Still, I did not understand. She lunged toward me and grasped my arm above the elbow. Her big callused fingers encircled me; I pulled back, startled. Just then, my father came into the room. He put his arm around my shoulder. "Darling, the signora is saying that you should eat," he explained. "She says you're thin. Next she'll tell me that I'm fat!"

The signora was right. I had recently noticed that I was thin; I had never thought of myself as anything but perfect, and I did not like it. I had no curve to my calves and only a small ball of muscle in my upper arms. And my father was, indeed, fat. He had a round face and a round belly, which comforted me; his stomach loomed staunch and secure, a boulder of substance. "I like you the way you are!" I declared.

My father hugged me and let me go as my mother emerged sleepy from the bedroom. Jonny charged up the stairs, his knees already grass green. We sat down to breakfast; my parents mixed hot milk and coffee in the huge cups, and broke apart the rolls and smeared them with butter. They exclaimed with delight at the taste of everything: the bread, the coffee, the fresh, white butter.

"I want Corn Flakes," my brother proclaimed.

"Jonny!" Mommy laughed. "How can you want Corn Flakes when you can eat bread like this?"

But Jonny began to cry, and he did not stop until my mother promised to search for cereal. I felt adult and smug as Mommy flavored my milk with a touch of coffee. The milk was different, richer, slightly sour and tasting of grass; it foamed in its pitcher, and seemed somehow more connected to the cow than what we poured from our American cartons. The little breakfast rolls, the *panini,* were softball-sized globes almost hollow inside, with a six-sided pattern baked into the crust.

"These look like Stars of David," I said. I had a habit of searching out Stars of David, searching the world for Jewish evidence. "Do you think that's on purpose?"

"No, I don't," Daddy answered. "It's just a hexagon, it's not a Star of David."

"I think it is," I insisted. My father shrugged.

After breakfast, Jonny and I explored the allée. The grass between the cypresses was uncut and lush and still held dew. It tickled my ankles. I took off my socks and sneakers and felt the cold on my feet. There was a swing at the bottom of the walk, a heavy rope and a wooden plank seat. I thrust my feet high in the air against the black points of the trees. In ancient Israel, my father told me, Jews planted a cypress tree to mark the birth of a daughter. For the Romans and therefore the early Christians, however, cypresses signified mourning, and they were planted in cemeteries.

After lunch I changed clothes. We had followed Mozart's trail east through Austria, to Salzburg and Linz, where Mommy had bought me this dirndl. It had a white puffed-sleeved blouse, which fit under a blue bodice above a red gathered skirt. A white eyelet apron tied around the waist. It reminded me of the costumes the characters wore in Smetana's opera *The Bartered Bride,* which my father had conducted at his opera company. My mother plaited my hair into two braids and tied ribbon bows over the rubber bands.

I was ready for the fairy tale to begin. But when I came into the living room where he sat at the piano, my father said: "Deborah, are you sure you should wear that?"

"Why not?"

He shrugged. "I don't know. People might think we're German."

"Don't be ridiculous," Mommy said. "It's her birthday present. If she wants to wear it, she can."

My father wore a sport coat and tie, my mother her silk sundress. We planned to walk down the via San Leonardo to the bottom of the hill, where it joined the viale Michelangelo. There at the corner was a gelateria, a little kiosk that sold ice cream.

Like a family of ducks, we walked in single file hugging the walls, my father first, my mother bringing up the rear. Vespas and little Fiat Cinquecentos roared past us, their engines chugging like lawn mowers. The driver of one of the Vespas whistled at my mother, who blushed; my father smiled possessively. The gelateria was crowded. Lithe, small men, ladies in black skirts and sturdy black shoes, a few children in skirts and short pants. When we entered, people looked at us. We were clearly alien. I wondered if they thought we looked German, if they were preparing to retaliate. I hoped not.

But my father took control of the situation. He addressed the gelateria's proprietor. He spoke loudly in his operatic Italian and explained that we were an American family living up the hill. The proprietor smiled effusively. There was a line behind us, but we were theater. The spectators grinned. I wondered if they understood opera, if, therefore, they believed my father.

"Well, have you decided what you want?" Daddy asked, aware of the line.

"Yes," I said.

The proprietor had begun to scoop out flavors for us on tiny shovel-shaped wooden spoons. Vanilla, chocolate, pistachio, hazelnut, strawberry. "*Ecco*," he urged. "*Voi devete provare!*"

Jonny, lover of the simplest foods, refused to taste. Customers laughed as he shut his eyes and sealed his lips. But I tried. Rich, smooth flavors, like the milk, utterly non-American, less sweet, more vanilla, more chocolate, more strawberry. "A triple. Vanilla, chocolate, and strawberry," I told Daddy in English.

My father ordered for us, and we moved outside. In the sun my ice cream melted and ran in sticky streams over my hand.

"Watch out for your dress, Deborah!" Mommy warned. Worried about her figure, she never ate ice cream. My gelato dripped onto the hard, trampled earth under the plane trees outside the kiosk. My father finished his dish of hazelnut. "Gelateria," he said, rolling the "r" thick as cream on his tongue, and I was beguiled, as always, by his pleasure in sounds and in the sound of his own voice. But did the passersby think we were Germans, hated and cruel? I wanted to be admired, like my mother, a bright stranger in this wonderful place. My father had warned me. Enemy, victim: they were too close; one flowered into the other.

"I think we should go home!" I announced. I started up the hill, running away from appearances. Thin. German.

I pushed open the little side gate at via San Leonardo, 72, and ran upstairs into my room and pulled off my costume. I did not love it less; I treasured it even more for its innocence, for what it could be forced to signify. I kept that dirndl until I had grown so tall that the waistband came halfway up my ribcage, but I wore it only in secret, never outside of my room.

. . .

Mommy, Jonny, and I parked our car along the Arno and walked along the colonnade of the Uffizi. We climbed the shallow marble steps to the second-floor painting galleries. My mother wore espadrilles and a sundress, and she carried a straw satchel with her book. She had started Young's *The Medici,* and she studied it all summer long. My brother and I ran ahead of her; we knew where she was going. We did this every day, the way we went to the lake in Maine.

My father had to work on his opera; we had to clear out. In the afternoons we went to a swimming pool filled with very cold water; my brother and I swam while Mommy worked on her tan. In the mornings, we went to the Pitti Palace, the Bargello, or the Uffizi. Mostly the Uffizi. Of all the museums, it was the largest and the coolest. My mother read to us from time to time about the exploits of Lorenzo and Cosimo de Medici. She pointed out their faces to us in their various appearances throughout the museum.

We preferred the early Renaissance galleries. There were benches in the middle of the rooms where she could sit and read undisturbed. The galleries were empty. Jonny and I had the corridors to ourselves, and we played tag and a kind of hopscotch with the ornate patterns of inlaid marble. We contemplated the Roman statues, the *Dying Gladiator,* the great wild boar, and the Medici *Venus,* set in her own round room. We visited the Michelangelo tondo of the Holy Family.

Afterwards we sat beside my mother and gazed at Botticelli. *The Birth of Venus* and *La Primavera* hung at right angles to each other. The slow ripening dance of *La Primavera* enchanted me and disturbed me, the groups of figures under a tent of fruit bright as stars. I loved the Three Graces with their translucent sweetness; I stood close to the canvas and studied how Botticelli worked with white to give the illusion of gauze. When I think of this now, I hear my mother's voice in my ear, rapt, talking to herself as much as to me. "Look at that line, that stroke of white, so thin it almost isn't there. That's how he does it!"

She had studied painting, but I never saw her paint. She sat in the gallery, her beautiful legs crossed. Her full skirt was draped over her round thighs; her thick, dark hair was caught in two barrettes, one behind each ear; and bright lipstick defined her mouth. She bent her head over her book and read of assassinations and intrigue and lust and playful erudition, and all of it had happened here, in this city. She sat still as a marble figure herself, a beautiful painted statue, with her long nose, narrow lips, and pointed chin.

When I asked, she identified the figures in the paintings for me. *La Primavera* unfolded as a mysterious story. I watched the wind breathe flowers onto Flora's dress. That blossom-covered gown was my favorite, but Flora's seductive, impudent smile, the sassy way she lifted her skirt as she skipped not quite out of the painting, made me uneasy. She was musing on a secret that had to do with Mars in the opposite corner. He rested his weight on one leg, his hip was thrust lazily forward, and he raised an arm to pick an apple from the canopy of trees; his flesh was disturbing: dense and solid beside the ethereal Graces. Neither he nor Flora looked at one another; they didn't have to. My mother smiled.

. . .

Looking at art did not satisfy my father; he needed to possess it. One afternoon, when I came back with my mother and brother from the *piscine,* the swimming pool, my father got up from his piano. "Deborah," he asked, "would you like to go into town with me?"

I hardly ever went anywhere alone with him. "Yes!" I exclaimed.

"Well, hurry up and put on some clothes. You can't go in a bathing suit."

I sat beside him in the front seat as we drove down the hill past the Piazzale Michelangelo into the city. We parked on a street near the river, and my father led me to a shop on the Lung'Arno. A little bell jingled as we entered. "Maestro Weisgall!" the proprietor of the shop greeted him. "Signore Bruschi," Daddy replied in Italian, "this is my daughter, Deborah." Signore Bruschi, sleek and urbane in a fitted black suit and a necktie of thick, ribbed silk, took my hand and bowed. His shop was furnished like an elaborate living room, like our living room in Baltimore but multiplied; ornate furniture and cabinets holding figurines crowded the floor, leaving only narrow aisles for passage. I began to explore, examining the ranks of little bronzes and guessing at the civilization that had produced them; I was beginning to recognize the difference between realistic Roman statues and the more abstract Etruscan ones. Larger Renaissance bronzes stood on shelves. "This is a Venus," Daddy told me. "This is Hercules shouldering a boar; this is the rape of the Sabine women, like the big statue in the Piazza della Signoria, do you remember?" I nodded, remembering everything because I was with him.

The door bell tinkled, and a couple entered. The man was stout and flushed from the heat; his wife wore a flowered dress and thick-soled white shoes. They were Americans. Signore Bruschi greeted them in English and invited them to look around. The couple wandered for a few moments, listening to Daddy explain the statues. Then the man stopped in front of a display of figurines. He picked one up, a little man about three inches high. "Excuse me," he said to my father. He had a southern accent. "Can you tell me just what this is?"

Of course he could. "It's Etruscan," Daddy announced in his deepest, most authoritative tone. "A Zeus, I think; it must have held a thunderbolt. Do you see how its arm is raised? It was probably made about 500 B.C."

"Five hundred?" Gingerly, the man replaced the statue. "Milly," he called, his innocent drawl breaking the hush of the shop. "Milly! Come here and look at this thing! It was made five hundred years before Jesus!"

There it was; the America we had left, our country, where the Palazzo Vecchio stood for Bromo Seltzer. We waited until they left the shop to laugh, to revel in our own sophistication. Then my father said, "Deborah, I have something to show you."

Signore Bruschi slipped into a little office in the back of the shop and returned carrying a statue in each hand: a pair of bronze horses. They were rearing on their hind legs, one leaped straight ahead; the other turned his head back and to one side. Their tails streamed out behind them. I stared. I recognized them immediately; they were Black Beauty and Ginger.

"They're Venetian, sixteenth century," Daddy announced reverently.

"Can I touch them?" I asked.

"*Si*," Signore Bruschi answered.

I stroked their greenish black backs, the knotted curls of their tails.

"Do you like them?" my father asked.

"Do I like them? They're beautiful! Can we get them? Are we going to get them?"

"I don't know, Deb, they're very expensive. Do you want them? Do you think we should?"

"Oh, yes, please! They're the most beautiful things I've ever seen!" I burned with desire.

"I don't know what your mother would say. We'll have to see."

He nodded to Signore Bruschi, who carried them back into the office.

"So we're not getting them?" Tears of disappointment gathered in my eyes, and I was ashamed to want something so badly.

"He's packing them up in a box for us." Daddy smiled. "We'll take them home with us now. But you'll have to work on your mother."

I burst out laughing. "They're ours? We own them?"

"So far." Daddy laughed, too, and we headed home with our spoils in a cardboard carton.

. . .

My mother was not ready when the guests arrived. The clothes she had rejected lay in sloppy heaps across the bed. Nothing looked right. Her face was flushed as she scurried back and forth between her room and the bathroom, currents of anxiety shimmering around her in a dangerous electric field. The bell at the entrance clanged, and the signore went to open the gate. Jonny and I raced downstairs and waited as a car drove up.

My great uncle Meyer Weisgal was Abba's younger brother. He lived in Israel and New York; he had been secretary to Chaim Weitzmann during the thirties and forties, the years when Palestine was a Zionist dream; he stood beside Weitzmann when Israel was declared a state. After Weitzmann's death, Meyer founded the Weitzmann Institute of Science in Rehovot, Israel, in his honor; Israel's first president had been a scientist before he became a politician. Meyer called himself a *schnorrer,* which is Yiddish for beggar. All he did, he said, was raise money: millions and millions of dollars. He knew everybody, every rich Jew in the world—politicians, actors, actresses, musicians: conductors, pianists, opera singers. My father expected things of Meyer; he expected him to be an automatic door opener, and Meyer had made promises. But one of Meyer's favorite stories—and, like Freddie, he was a master storyteller—revolved around the line "The check is in the mail." The check that never arrives, the promise unfulfilled.

Meyer emerged from the big black car. It was easy to guess that he and Abba were brothers, just as it was clear that they were also very different. Both had thick white hair, but where Abba's was silky and wavy, Meyer's was frizzy and unruly. Abba's blue eyes were round and dreaming, Meyer's narrow and clever. Abba, for all his lust for life, was also refined; Meyer traded on his appetites. He considered himself a peasant, a son of the people. Abba was a man of God; Meyer was a man of the world. Each was jealous of the other.

Meyer smiled at Jonny and me and looked past us. "Where's your father?" he asked in his gruff, thickly accented bass voice. Behind him, his entourage emerged. A lady with bangs and enormous jeweled rings, a gray-haired man in a fine gray suit, and a younger woman with a fur stole draped around her shoulders, even though it was June. I had never seen such opulence.

My father came outside and led them upstairs. Meyer put his hand on the waist of the younger woman to guide her through the dark stairwell. It was a Friday evening; we had already lit the Shabbos candles. Meyer and his friends crossed the living room and crowded onto the balcony to admire the evening sky over the steep Tuscan hills. "Where is the beautiful Nathalie?" Meyer boomed when he turned back inside. He did not wait for an answer and crossed the room to my father's piano. His manuscript was spread across the music stand. "So, *vie gets?*" Meyer asked carelessly.

My father nodded nervously. "Slowly."

"What is it again?"

"*Six Characters in Search of an Author,*" my father answered.

"Of course. I'd forgotten." Meyer smiled. He had a big man's way of making somebody else feel small. "And you have a performance?"

"City Center commissioned it. I assume I have performances." He emphasized the plural. He was already testy.

"When are they scheduled?"

"When I finish."

Meyer looked past my father, searching for the next thing. Now it was my mother. She stood at the entrance to the salotto. She stood still, waiting, uncertain. She wore her silk sundress, exposing her tanned neck and shoulders. Her glossy hair was smoothed back from her face, which was powdered and perfect. Her brown eyes took in the guests, their riches, their assessment of her. I have an image of her at that moment: eager and wishing not to be, expectant: of delight and disappointment equally. She stood there, shimmering with contradictions, so that I thought her wonderfully beautiful.

She crossed the room and Meyer embraced her. "Nathalie, you are magnificent! Didn't I tell you?" He grinned at the man in the beautiful suit; Meyer also had a big man's way of making somebody seem extremely important. Meyer held my mother until she pulled away, but she had left a bright trace of lipstick on his cheek. He took her by the hand and introduced her, and she laughed and smiled and offered drinks. "Do we have time?" my father asked. "When is our reservation? I don't think we have time."

"What do you mean, time? Of course we have time. We always have time. Our table will wait for us." Meyer helped my mother pour the drinks from a little table against the wall. I watched him fill glasses with Scotch, and I watched my mother watch him; I had heard her tell my father how terribly expensive liquor was in Italy. But she complained, laughing, to Meyer how difficult it was to make the signora understand that Americans liked ice in their drinks.

Conversation began. I remember only the sounds: the ice in the glasses, my mother's high voice and sharp laughter, the elegant man's English accent, the way the woman with bangs said one word and paused and waited for silence before she continued. My father took issue with everything she said, and my mother laughed loudly, as if she could conceal his disagreeableness. The woman in the fur stole said hardly anything. She sat beside Meyer on the sofa, very straight, clutching her wrap to her chest, listening to the words with a blank little smile, as if none of it mattered much, as if she were beyond such social effort. Daddy addressed several questions to her, but she answered with only a word or two. She spoke with an accent, but I could not tell what she was; maybe Hungarian, or a sabra, an Israeli born in Palestine. She had olive skin and black hair and wore diamond earrings but no wedding ring. I wondered what she was; she was surely something.

"Hugo!" Meyer exclaimed. "Hugo! I have a tremendous favor to ask of you."

My father looked doubtful.

"Listen to Margrit sing. Maybe you can help her."

"Help? What kind of help does she need?" my father asked. "I'm not a singing teacher."

"You know people . . ." Meyer began.

"Meyer. So do you. She doesn't need *my* help, I'm sure," my father answered with a gallant smile in the young woman's direction. She returned his compliment with a small smile, as if she agreed with him. "Where have you sung?" he asked.

"Oh, Hamburg, Munich—"

"Margrit," Meyer interrupted. "Sing for us, please. Hugo will accompany you."

The other conversations had stopped. My mother laughed in the silence. "Hugo doesn't accompany people," she said. Daddy shot her an angry look; I prayed that she would not answer back. Margrit stood and dropped her stole on the sofa. She wore a crimson, low-cut, satin dress that fit her figure. The spheres of her breasts rose from the bodice. She was short, but she seemed immense as she sauntered across the room toward the piano. Her perfume wafted behind her. My father followed her. "I'm afraid I don't have very much music with me," he apologized.

"Do you have *Traviata*?"

"Why, yes, I happen to have that. And I have *Otello*."

She nodded. Daddy handed her the scores. She leafed through *Traviata* and put it on the piano and leaned over him to smooth open the pages. My father played, and she began to sing "Sempre libera." Her voice was dark and rich. It ricocheted against the tile floor and the stucco walls; I could feel it in the tips of my fingers. Her breasts swelled as she breathed. She sang softly, and then her voice grew louder until it hurt my ears. My father crashed chords, matching her volume. Meyer listened with a small, proud smile of satisfaction. I wished she would stop. The beautiful sound crowded me out of the room.

When she finished, Daddy nodded. "Should we try something else?" His voice was tense with excitement. He began another aria. Margrit laughed, she threw back her head and her throat gleamed like the Venus's in the Uffizi. She rested her hand on my father's shoulder. She behaved as if she were on a stage, acting. "Now you are getting serious," she said. "Strauss. How did you know that I love to sing Strauss?"

My father shrugged, dislodging her hand. "With your voice that's what you should be singing."

I hated how beautiful she looked; how her dress shimmered across her hips, how her enameled nails gleamed triumphantly through the open toes of her high heels. My mother was standing behind the sofa now, in the shadows. She swirled her drink.

"It's getting late," she said, but nobody answered her.

Margrit sang. Mommy walked away from the sofa, but she had no place to go. She stood beside a bookcase in the corner of the room and listened, head bent, her long, fine mouth drawn in a pout. I went to stand beside her, but she ignored me. She fiddled with the necklace she wore, her long intricate chain with a clasp in the shape of a hand. She had no diamonds, no real jewels like the other women wore. The pair of bronze horses stood on the top of the bookcase. She and Daddy had fought over them. "Don't tell me Deborah wants them!" she'd screamed. "Why don't you just admit that you want them?" But they had stayed.

She traced with her fingernail the pattern of flowers on her sundress. It looked shabby compared to what the others were wearing, but I loved that dress; she had been so beautiful wearing it in the photographs from Prague. She was beautiful still, more beautiful than the other women here, but I was afraid to tell her; she wouldn't believe me. I reached out and stroked the soft, dead tail of Margrit's wrap. "Don't touch that!" Mommy whispered vehemently. She did not even look at me. I fled back to the piano.

Margrit's speaking voice was as silky as her soprano. "And do you write beautiful arias?" she asked my father.

"It depends on what you mean by beautiful."

"Let me see."

He rummaged on the piano for a copy of the first act of *Six Characters*. When he finished each act, he orchestrated it on long sheets of thick, translucent white paper. My mother drew the measure lines for him in black India ink, and along the margins she wrote the names of the instruments and the characters in her even, graceful, italic lettering. Then Daddy filled in the vocal lines and the orchestra parts with indelible India ink. This part of his composition was silent; he orchestrated quickly; he had already imagined the textures as he composed, but the process was painstaking. He kept the finished score in a large black portfolio. "Daddy, here it is!" I pulled at the folder, but he snatched it from me. He didn't want me, either. I hung, miserable, suspended in the awful space between them.

He propped the folder on the piano. "There." He pointed. Margrit furrowed her brow. She bent over, and I could see the gap between her breasts. She straightened and shook her head and laughed, a little descending arpeggio. "But it's so high!" she said. "And so difficult. The tempo changes so often." She turned away. My father played the first notes of his aria. "A quiet room," I knew it so well. It had worn ruts in my brain. But Margrit didn't care. She went back to the sofa and swaddled herself in her fur and stood, smiling, waiting for the others to understand what she wanted next. I saw Esterina waiting on the landing; she was to babysit.

"I'm starving," Meyer declared, rising. He guided Margrit toward the stairs with his possessive hand at the small of her back. "Shall we go? *Andiamo!*" he commanded with great gusto in his central European Italian.

My father wearily closed his score and laid it on the piano. My mother, instead of picking up her pocketbook, began to gather the glasses from the coffee table.

"Nathalie," Meyer admonished, "leave that. You are not the servant!"

She knocked over a glass. It shattered on the floor, splattering ice and Scotch. Her face was red. Dismayed and furious, eyes red with brimming tears, she glared at my father. They were alone in the room now, except for me and Jonny and Esterina.

"Nath! Are you all right?" he asked. "Did you cut yourself?"

"What do you care?" she hissed. "I don't know what possessed you to think that she would even look at your music!"

. . .

The next morning, my parents slept late. They emerged from the bedroom bleary and wary of each other, but they were talking. The storm had passed; they all did, leaving behind small damages, erosion. I never learned how to weather them. I took every angry exchange as if it had been aimed at me, too. I sought to fill the dead space between my mother and father, the vacuum of love.

On Saturday morning, when in Baltimore he would have been conducting the choir in shul, my father sat at the piano and played through what he had written during the week. The opera was due in a few months, but my father worried every note; it would never be ready on time. This morning he interrupted himself to play Beethoven. He had been learning Opus 111 since the war. He was fine on the slow movement, but the passages of triplet arpeggios eluded him. When he practiced them, he substituted his own notes, giving the sonata a twentieth-century edge that made him laugh. He stopped in the middle of a measure. "Let's go to Fiesole this afternoon," he said.

Our favorite excursion was to that ancient town in the hills above Florence on the north side of the Arno. The road wound through vineyards, past I Tatti, the villa where Bernard Berenson pronounced on the authenticity of Italian Renaissance paintings. Archaeologists were excavating an Etruscan temple and a Roman amphitheater. It cost five hundred lire to spend an afternoon among the ruins. Jonny and I had learned all the passageways in the amphitheater, the rooms behind the stage, brick underground chambers. We raced up and down the stone seats. We cavorted on the paving stones of the stage, certain that the Roman spectacles were not so different from Gilbert and Sullivan. The brick proscenium rose behind us; its marble had all been vandalized. Today we were especially noisy, celebrating our parents' most recent truce. Beside the entrance to the sites, two or three little carts shaded by umbrellas sold straw trinkets and gelati; for the most part, the ruins were empty on those hot white summer afternoons. White dust from the excavations covered the wildflowers and grasses that grew up between the chinks of the ancient brick and marble.

Mommy wore sunglasses against the hazy, glaring sun. She had on a white shirt and a full skirt and espadrilles. Her hair glinted with dark red highlights. She moved slowly in the heat and soon sat down in an arc of shade in one corner of the amphitheater with her book. On our excursions into antiquity, she brought *Memoirs of Hadrian;* she read slowly and thoroughly, and Hadrian and the Medici lasted her all summer. To satisfy my literary appetite, every week my father bought me novels from the English bookstore, lots of Dickens, and then Louisa May Alcott. In Florence, I read *Little Women* for the first of many times; for years, I inhabited that book. Jo wanted to be a writer. To do so, she would sacrifice anything. She cut her hair, she married an older man who did not demand domesticity and permitted her a vocation. I wished she didn't have to marry him. If

I were Jo, my whole being would have rebelled against that choice. Nothing Louisa May Alcott wrote, not even sequels, could persuade me of her character's wisdom.

While Mommy read, Daddy tied his handkerchief around his neck and explored the ruins with Jonny and me. Although we knew our way around, each week we hoped to find something different, some revelation, some new secret exposed. The archaeologists had roped off the area where they were working. They had excavated a pit just behind the amphitheater along the path to the Etruscan temple. We peered inside, at the white limestone dust and the exposed rock wall.

"What could it be?" I asked.

"An altar of some kind," Daddy answered. All ancient sites were places of worship, altars for the performance of arcane rituals and sacrifices; their excavation would yield keys to ancient mysteries. "I don't really know. But look over there!" His voice sharpened with excitement.

On a ledge opposite us lay some fragments of pottery: a tiny jug and the bottom of a vase. Nobody else was around. The three of us stared at the shards. "The archaeologists must have found them," my father said. "They can't be very valuable." He looked at my brother.

"I want them," Jonny said.

Daddy looked both ways. Only a string separated us from the treasure. "They shouldn't have left them there," my father said. "They're probably Etruscan pots."

Jonny looked at my father.

"Well," my father said, "go on! Hurry up!" He lifted the string, and my brother scuttled under and snared the shards.

"Wrap it up in your T-shirt!" Daddy said, and Jonny made an apron from the hem of his shirt. We raced back to my mother. Jonny dumped the pieces of Etruscan pottery into her lap. She laughed and smiled up at my father. "Hugo! I see what you're teaching your children!"

"What do you want? Do you want us to put them back?" I hoped she would say yes; not because I felt it was wrong, but because I hadn't been brave enough to loot the excavation.

But she shook her head, no. We left our booty with her and went off again to the temple. My father held our hands and steadied us while my brother and I climbed over the stumps of columns. He gave Jonny hints on how to scale the marble walls. Jonny's knees and hands grew white with stone dust. Daddy untied his handkerchief and wiped his forehead. Yellow daisies grew in a corner of the ruins, and I picked a bunch. "Give those to your mother," he told me.

"I will," I said. "That's what I was going to do." They were my offering. After a while, we headed back to her. The shadows were longer, the air slightly cooler. My mother was not where we had left her. Out of the corner of my eye, I saw her standing on the topmost row of seats. She stood straight, looking down into the steep green valley behind the amphitheater. Her legs tapered to slender ankles, her round arms to tiny wrists; her jaw in profile was delicate, and there was something about her posture that made her look utterly precarious.

"I'll never be that beautiful," I said.

My father studied me sadly. "Oh, yes, you will," he said. "Just wait and see."

Eight

A Love Song

By 1958, Baltimore had more traffic lights than any city in the United States. Like Christmas lights, dandelion yellow fixtures festooned each intersection. The city had hired a traffic engineer. He had cut new white cement highways through the old, gracious downtown grid. "They're obliterating architecture," my father mourned as we waited at six redundant red lights.

Along the new routes to shul, blocks and blocks of row houses with scrubbed white marble stoops had been demolished. Mounds of rubble, plaster, torn sheets of wallpaper, lay beside the sidewalks and sprouted weeds. The city looked bombed and desolate, like Europe.

"They're ruining Baltimore," my mother said.

"Americans have no sense of the past," Daddy added. In the distance, the gray American Palazzo Vecchio mocked Florence. The letters "BROMO SELTZER" replaced numbers on the clock faces adorning each of the tower's four sides.

Although I knew I shouldn't, I liked those traffic lights, how they dangled from their spider web wires in blinking celebration. I liked the clean white roads. Although my father had taught me to love the past, I also shared America's delight in the new. Not, however, the congregation's new sanctuary, an enormous prow of brick and glass and panels of turquoise enameled steel. It rose on a flat parcel of land surrounded by pristine asphalt parking lots and sapling trees. Soaring into the bland, suburban sky, it was a place without sorrow.

I went to Hebrew school there. Just the week before, already bored on the first day of class, I was looking out of the window at the emerald green sod and saw Abba get out of a taxi; he was coming to teach twelve-year-old boys their bar mitzvah portions. After school, I nearly collided with him in the hall. He wore his double-breasted suit and his boulevardier's hat; as a gesture to the suburbs, perhaps, he carried his rustic walking stick with the horn handle carved with his initials. He was a nineteenth-century man trapped in this cinder-block hall; he was not happy to see me, and I stared at him, feeling suddenly alien, suddenly a party to his betrayal.

In the end, the congregation had had no choice but to keep the Eutaw Place synagogue for Abba. My father and the choir stayed with him, forcing the hiring of a second choir in the suburbs. They hoped that their music would be enough to lure people downtown, at least for the High Holidays. This Rosh Hashanah, Abba had stood alone on the bimah, without the rabbi, without the president of the congregation. He stood straight in his white cambric robe and tall white velvet hat, his hands spread out across his carved lectern. He sang the melodies of the Musaf service, and the choir responded. Their voices reverberated against the synagogue's limestone walls. I perched on the ledge of the choir loft in my usual place, tall enough now that I could see over the brass curtain rod. I had grown taller than my mother. To brush my hair back into a ponytail, she had to stand on the stairs, two steps above me.

I watched Abba with sadness and anger. The shul was barely half full. I recognized most of the worshippers: Surosky the butcher, Mrs. Werner: old people without cars; Lillian Forman, who loved music. The walnut pews no longer had prayer books waiting in the racks on their backs. The watery stained-glass windows looked cloudy, stagnant, unclean, and dense shafts of dust motes caught the light within the open dome. Several hooks on the velvet curtain that screened the choir loft ledge had come loose, and the brass curtain rod was greasy and unpolished. There were no flowers on the bimah.

Abba sang as if the house were sold out, and the choir responded with a passionate edge to their voices. The music was no

longer safe, not even here. Who could tell how long the congregation would keep this building? Who could tell when Abba's voice
would be silenced? Then the music would die: not in concentration
camps but in the oblivious affluence of America. I tried to sing and
tried to hold on to the notes in my head. Who could tell? This might
be the last time I would ever hear it.

After services, only a few people waited to greet Abba. They
shook their heads and swallowed; they embraced Abba and my father
and Uncle Freddie as if this were a funeral, not a holiday. Mrs. Forman
reached her short round arms up to my neck and hugged me.
"Deborah, you are growing so tall, and so beautiful. I hardly recognized you up in the choir loft. You're going to be as tall as Aranka, as
tall as your grandmother. Your grandfather must be so proud of you."

I blushed. But this was the purpose of the synagogue: to mark
changes. "Blessed art Thou O Lord our God who has kept us alive
and brought us to this season." That was the prayer one said at the
start of each holiday. I was growing to hate changes. I wanted my
body not to grow; I wanted to stay always where I was. Even preparing to leave for Maine had been hard, and packing the house in
Maine and returning to Baltimore was worst of all.

My father had finished *Six Characters in Search of an Author*,
finally, two years late, and performances were being scheduled in New
York, at the City Center. City Center: those words hovered over our
house, glamorous and fateful. He was going to spend more time than
ever in New York this winter. Everything was going to change.

Abba went to his study to take off his robe. Surosky hung
around, waiting to lock up. There were no longer funds for a shamas,
so Surosky volunteered. Abba emerged onto the bimah, dapper in
his double-breasted suit and cane and Borsalino.

"At least we didn't have to listen to a sermon," Uncle Freddie
said as we walked home down Chauncey Avenue. It was a clear, cool
Saturday in late September. The linden trees were turning; the yellow leaves looked like fragments of sunset. Negro families sat on
their stoops. Over the door posts of the house where my father's
cousin Klari used to live, a sheet of paint curled like a loose strip of

wallpaper. Radios blared top-forty songs into our holy afternoon. The people watched us pass. "Good afternoon, Reverend," they called. "How are you today? Happy New Year!" And Abba doffed his hat and smiled.

"Safe?" he scoffed. "I *am* safe. What do they know from safe? Those *mishigoyim* on the board don't know what they are talking about."

· · ·

That fall, I was in sixth grade. There were forty-three children in my class, and our neighborhood was growing fast. Blocks away from us, where there used to be woods, bulldozers toppled trees and gouged into the red Maryland clay. Rows of cellar holes waited like bread pans for concrete batter. My friend Barbara and I passed this construction as we walked home from school. I was tall, but Barbara was taller. She already wore a bra, and she needed a real one, not just the elasticized bandeaus that many girls wore. We watched the houses rise fast as quickbread, almost identical loaves of neat brick and white clapboard with picture windows that offered views of other picture windows.

One day in early October, a plush lawn appeared in front of one of those houses. Two days later, a signpost went up beside the white concrete path. "Model House," the sign read, "Open for Inspection." We walked by the sign every day for a week and a half. Finally, on Friday afternoon, we stopped in front of it.

"Let's go inside," Barbara said. She had thick, dirty-blond hair that fell in waves to her shoulders; she had told me that she stuck rollers into her hair at night before she went to sleep.

"Do you think we should?" I asked.

"That's what it's for. For people to go in and look around. Who cares if we go in?" The new concrete of the walk seemed as pristine as a ribbon of white icing. The tips of the blades of brilliant fresh grass fringed the edges of the concrete. We approached the front door, with its three little rectangles of glass arranged like stairs. We rang the bell, and electric chimes sounded in a honey-I'm-home arpeggio. Nobody came to the door. Barbara turned the handle, and the door swung open.

We went in. Flagstones paved the little vestibule. The house was completely furnished. A guest book lay open on a little table. I wrote my name and address: Deborah Weisgall, 2707 Whitney Avenue, Baltimore 15, Maryland, USA, The World, The Solar System, The Universe.

"That's silly," said Barbara. "The universe. Who cares?"

"I do," I answered. Who cares? was Barbara's rallying cry. Who cares? she answered to everything. I surveyed the house. Where the flagstones stopped, three steps covered in beige wall-to-wall carpeting in a pattern of swirls led down to the living room. Two layers of drapes, sheer fiberglass under a heavier layer printed with beige ferns, adorned the windows. I stepped on the carpet. My sneakers sank into its thick pile, and I left footprints. A huge sofa took up most of the room, along with a pair of armchairs. Plastic plants decorated the end tables. There was not a bookshelf in sight, but there was a huge console television. Its blank screen reflected the room upside down like a convex mirror. There was no piano.

In the kitchen the avocado enamel sink matched the stove and refrigerator, and the counters were avocado Formica. In a little breakfast nook, ruffled café curtains with a folksy print of recipes hung at the windows. I imagined the mother of this kitchen. She wore a shirt-waist dress and stockings and high heels, and an apron that matched the curtains protected her dress. She whipped up angel food cake mixes; with her pert brown curls, she even looked like Betty Crocker. She always smiled. She never lost her temper. She had everything she wanted.

The wonderful thing about this house was that nothing terrible was going to happen in it. Life here was peaceful. The children would come home from school and lie on the rug in front of the television, and their feet in their white socks would wave like flags of contentment. Their father would park his car in the garage every evening at five-thirty, and dinner would be ready, and they would have mashed potatoes every night. I yearned to live here. It was easy and sublimely safe, like a television show. It was a home for families who did not ask existential questions. Here, everybody would play for laughs, not tragedy.

Barbara had disappeared. I went looking for her. The bedrooms were up three stairs, the upper part of the split level. She was not in either of the children's rooms. The boy's was done in a manly brown plaid, and the girl's had pink organza curtains and pink polka dot bedspreads on the twin beds. I stood in the doorway getting my fill of that room. This is what girls were made of, and I wished I were of that stuff, too. It would be so much simpler. I knew what my mother would say about that room: it was sentimental and in bad taste. But my mother had no idea. I stepped inside—even the wall-to-wall carpet was pink—and stroked the shiny bedspread. It felt thrilling and wicked; in this pink and ruffled room it would be easy to be a girl. This was a place to think about lipstick and Barbie dolls. I pulled my hand away from the seductive fabric, afraid to get caught, afraid that Barbara would spy on me.

But I found Barbara in the master bedroom at the end of the hall. She had taken possession of the big bed. She'd kicked off her sneakers and lay on her back; the blue quilted bedspread rumpled around her in plush waves. I saw her reflected in the wall of mirrored closets, and I wanted to climb onto that bed with her and feel the slippery nylon under my own bare legs. Barbara's big, protruding gray-blue eyes watched me from under her dirty-blond bangs. She pouted; she wore frosted-pink lipstick. Dark crescents of sweat stained the armpits of her white blouse, and I could see through its straining cotton the circular stitching on her bra. She rolled sideways; her straight skirt hiked high above her pink knees; she pointed her toes, and her feet in their bobby socks arched in lush, beauty-queen curves.

"Debby," she smiled; I couldn't get her to stop calling me Debby. "Do you know what *fuck* means?"

In the mirror I could see that I had become bright red. "Yes," I lied. But I had no idea. My parents never used words like that. I cringed at its filthy, grunting sound; it meant something ugly.

Barbara nodded, knowingly; so I was in on her secret. "When I'm in junior high, my mother is going to let me go out on dates. I'm going to go out with Marc; we're going to go steady. He's so cute. Don't you think he's cute?"

"Yeah, he's okay." He had freckles and a blond crew cut.

"So what don't you like about him?"

"He's short."

She shrugged. "My mother says he'll grow."

I was shocked. In a million years I could never talk to my mother about boys and dating. I had never tried, but I knew. It was too dangerous; my father would find out. Barbara ran her hand down her side to her waist and up the rise of her hips and smiled at me. "I'll let him get to second base. Next year, in seventh grade." She rolled over on her stomach and giggled.

Miserably, I giggled, too. I had no idea what she meant by second base—not a double, I was pretty sure. Baseball was something I knew; I played almost every afternoon, spring and fall, with the boys in the neighborhood in the big yard that belonged to the house next to ours; I was one of the few girls good enough to play. I should know second base. Marc played with us sometimes. I stood frozen with disgust and admiration. I needed to know what she already knew, but I couldn't ask.

Lazily, she sat up. "Wanna dance?" she asked.

"There's no music."

"Who cares? I can hum. Come on!" She swung her legs over the side of the bed and held out her hand. I walked around the bed. "Take off your sneakers," she commanded. I did.

"Okay. Let's go." She grabbed my hand and began rocking slowly back and forth as she sang "Apple Blossom Time," by Tab Hunter. Barbara loved Tab Hunter. Head down, shoulders hunched, elbows bent and tucked close to her body—she was cool and wicked. "Turn!" she breathed, twisting my wrist. She stopped and shook her head. "Don't you get it?"

No. I didn't. I could run faster than even the boys; I could bat and I could field, but I couldn't dance. I wasn't sure that I should dance. I pulled my hand away and watched as she took little steps by herself and spun, humming, with her eyes closed and a dreamy smile on her wide pouting mouth, imagining me Marc.

"I've got to go," I said, bending down and putting on my sneakers.

"Why?"

"It's Friday. It's Shabbos."

"So? Who cares?"

"I do. I've got to get home. My mom will be worried." I was lying again. My mother never worried. And we ate late; what I hoped was that there was a game going on. I left the bedroom and stepped silently down the carpeted hall. It would be terrible to live in such silence, I thought now. The only music would come from the record player: canned strings as thick as Campbell's tomato soup. This house would deaden voices. It frightened me; there was no room here even for a prayer.

Barbara followed me outside. Her shirt was untucked and the back of her hair was mussed. I walked on ahead of her. "Deb!" she called. "Deb, wait up." Reluctantly, I did. Barbara smiled. "I'll teach you to dance, if you want."

I nodded. I did want, but hated to admit it. I was not used to having to learn things from my friends. It was I who taught them. We walked without talking until we came to her corner. When Barbara walked, she swung her hips like Marilyn Monroe, whom she admired; she trawled along the sidewalk, its squares of concrete perforated like saltines. She was invulnerable. On that sunny afternoon she was practicing love, but it had nothing to do with love as I recognized it. It was free of pain. This was love as wipe-clean as Formica, as comfortable as a sofa, crisp and clean and well defined. I was crazy with jealousy: not of Barbara herself, but of her ability to measure love in bases. Love did not scare her the way it scared me.

She stopped and squinted at me. "What about now? *American Bandstand*'s on."

"My father's home working."

"I don't mean your house. There's no place to dance at your house. And anyway, I'm scared I'll break something at your house and your father will yell at me. My mother's not home."

I shook my head. "I can't."

"What about tomorrow?"

"I don't know."

"Why not?" she persisted.

"I don't know. Okay. Sure."

"You know, Debby," Barbara said as she started down the sidewalk to her house. She half-turned toward me. The sun caught the fine white hairs on her arms and glanced off the roundness of her breasts under her cotton shirt. I wanted to look away, but she had caught me, too, caught me by her secrets. "I don't think you should play baseball anymore. You're too much of a tomboy. Boys aren't going to like you."

"So what?" I retorted. "Who cares?"

I started to run. My feet pounded on the sidewalk. My legs wheeled under me. My thighs burned. My breath hurt. My skirt caught between my legs until I stopped and bunched it around my waist; I always wore shorts beneath it so that at recess I could hang upside down on the jungle gym without exposing my underpants. I could do whatever I wanted. I could play baseball, all my life. It did not matter if I couldn't dance. I could run. I could hit. What did it matter if boys liked me or not?

I ran the three blocks home; I ran through our ragged hedge and up the front walk. Panting and hot, angry and frightened, I flung myself down on the bottom step. Mittens emerged from under the porch and rubbed against me. I patted him, and he arched back and forth under my hand. In the yard next door, two boys who lived down the street, Michael and Stuart, were tossing a ball back and forth under the heavy canopy of beech and sycamore. My father's music hammered from his study. "Hey, Deb!" Stuart called. "Wanna play? Peter's coming!"

It was just another afternoon, sunny, dusty. I still had all the time in the world. The days were getting shorter, that was all that was changing. I could play baseball.

I called back. "Sure. Just a sec. I'll be right out." My voice sounded separate from me, calm and easy. Who was that? Still who I wanted to be, strong and fast, tall, still possibly a boy, I ran inside, tossed my skirt on the floor, and grabbed my glove and bat.

. . .

That winter, my father sometimes spent half the week in New York; he continued to teach at Juilliard and the Jewish Theological Seminary, but he had opera business, as well. Performances of *Six Characters* were scheduled for April 1959. He attended auditions; he met with the stage director and with the conductor. He came home with stories about the director and about a pregnant soprano named Beverly Sills with a marvelous voice who was taking the part of the Coloratura. This singer was wonderful and that one terrible, she understood the music, all he wanted to sing was Puccini; my father was extravagant with judgment.

In school, I was busy with a play, too. It was called *A Cowboy's Life*. I had written it and I was the cowboy. I had made up a story and dialogue to fit around the western songs that our class, which was the cowboy chorus, had been learning.

The morning of the play I tucked my hair inside my cowboy hat and pulled the brim down straight across my forehead. Manly and fierce, I frowned at myself in the bathroom mirror. My disguise was perfect. In my jeans and a plaid shirt, I could have been my twin brother. I strapped my two-gun holster belt low around my hips and tied the thongs at the bottom of the holsters to my thighs.

We had rehearsed for weeks in the school auditorium; the other leads—Michael and Peter, two of the boys I played baseball with—had permission to practice while everybody else was solving pages of multiplication problems and answering questions in reading workbooks. It was the auditorium's darkness that lured me, its seductive daytime darkness. Light shone around the edges of the auditorium doors: silver rectangles shimmering like aurora borealis in our artificial night.

. . .

Light slithered through the barn siding at the Hilltop Opera Company. I was four years old and played in the aisles while my parents rehearsed my father's opera *The Stronger*. I tried to interpret the white beams of sunlight winking in celestial code while the soprano sang and sang and my mother sat on stage at a little round table. She sat with her back to the empty rows of folding chairs; her elbow rested on the table as she smoked a cigarette. The director, John Scrymgeour, a slender young man with lanky brown hair and huge blue eyes, stopped the singer to fix a gesture; my father interrupted to correct the singer's intonation.

The singer sighed. "This part is awfully high," she complained.

"You're supposed to be a soprano," my father replied. My mother crossed her legs and uncrossed them. I ran to the stage and called her, and my father shooed me away. "Your mother's busy now, Deborah." But she wasn't doing anything at all, just sitting. Finally, after many hours, the soprano stormed off stage and returned and stormed off again, and again and again, until she got it right.

"Okay, Nath," John Scrymgeour said to my mother. "Now. Turn. Slowly, slowly. Remember, you'll be wearing a hat. They won't be able to see your face until you've turned all the way around. There . . . a bit more. Perfect! Now, smile. Not too much, not too much! Okay, okay! Look mysterious, look sly. You're the mistress, remember. Remember, this is *The Stronger*. This is your moment. He's married to her, but he always comes back to you. You have to do it all now; you haven't made a sound for half an hour while the wife has gone on and on and on. The whole thing hinges on your smile."

Mommy smiled. Her smile was not mysterious, and it was not sly. She could be sly, but not on demand. Her smile was sweet and open, bright as sunlight. Who could resist? I wanted her across the barrier of the stage. I ached for her and mourned her silence, disappointed that she had no voice and my father could give her nothing to sing.

. . .

Rehearsing for my own play, I swaggered across the stage in shorts, my skirt abandoned in a heap in the wings. I spoke my lines in a western drawl, and Michael and Peter answered me, my words in other mouths. We mimed sitting tall in our saddles; we pretended to lean against cardboard fence posts. Michael was shorter than me; Peter was taller. The day before during the dress rehearsal, Peter had slung his arm around my shoulder as we all sang "Git Along Little Dogie." His arm was brown, and I could see the blue veins starting up from his wrist; in the hot stage lights the fine hairs glistened gold. I stood still, riveted; touch shimmered through my spine like lightning.

The morning of the play, my mother kissed me as I dismounted from the car and straightened my hat. "Break a leg," she smiled. "And, Deb, remember—speak slowly. Slowly!"

"Mom! I know." I half closed the car door, slamming it on her doubt. "Why aren't you coming in with me?" I asked.

"I just have a quick errand to do. The play doesn't start for half an hour. I'll be there." The familiar anxiety roiled in my stomach. She would not be there; she would be late. I ran away, straight to the auditorium and backstage and hesitated behind a concrete-block wall, reluctant to give myself away, even to my own class. But I shivered with eagerness to be seen—and not recognized.

"Deb! Is that you? Is that really you?"

Mrs. Rhodes, my teacher, stood in front of me, laughing. She was tall and angular and kept her hair in a halo of tight, sandy curls.

"Yes, it's me. You couldn't tell? Really?"

She hugged me, dislodging my hat. I grabbed for it.

"Really!" she exclaimed. "You'll take the whole school by surprise. Now, come on, we better let the rest of the class see you, or they'll think their star hasn't shown up!"

Star. The word laced through space and lit me with its brilliance. Mrs. Rhodes thought I was a star. I strode behind her, and my holsters thumped boldly against my thighs. The class sat in a semicircle around the perimeter of the stage, leaving the center free for action. When I swaggered in, everybody stared. I stood for a second and said nothing, letting them wonder, letting them guess, and then I sat down in my place beside Peter. He stared too, and then he smiled. "I had no idea who you were," he whispered.

"Good," I said, laughing from happiness.

We took our positions under the bright stage lights and listened to the auditorium fill, the thudding of feet, the flipping of seats, the treble chattering of children. My brother was there with his fourth-grade class. I hoped my mother was back from her errand. Errands, always something, always late. My father was in New York, of course. His opera was the most important thing in his life, I understood that. He would watch me when he came home; I could put on a special performance just for him, he said.

"Shhh! Shhh!" Hushes hissed. The audience settled down. The principal strode onto the stage and praised our efforts. The curtains parted, and we began. I rode, I loped around the stage, I twirled my lariat. I spoke my lines. We all sang. Michael and Peter piled the cardboard logs for our campfire in the middle of the stage. The three of us stretched out on our stomachs; the grit on the stage floor prickled my forearms. The stage darkened. I gazed up at the ranks of gels like blue-white stars in the black ceiling, remote as real stars in the prairie sky. Peter's right arm lay parallel to mine, close, close.

Behind us in blue twilight, the forty other boys and girls in Mrs. Rhodes's sixth-grade class hummed like the wind across the prairie. I lifted my head slightly. We were supposed to be sleeping during this song, cowboys on the vast grassland; silver tassels of prairie grass met the horizon, and we lay alone against the curve of the earth beside our campfire. Peter lay with his head on his left arm, his face turned toward me. I gazed at him until he opened his eyes. I could see one eye, blue dark as the stage lights, startled blue seeing me, my eyes black in the shadows, and I saw him sensing something not quite me, something in the charged space between our arms, sensing it with alarm and sweet curiosity. The lights came up, and the play finished with "Home on the Range."

I took my bows, and during the second bow my cowboy hat fell off and my ponytail tumbled down my back. The applause faltered for a moment, and then it renewed, louder; I was unmasked, and I loved it. And whatever Peter and I had sensed hovered, translucent, like the moon in daylight.

. . .

I unpacked my suitcase and laid my new dress across the double bed in our hotel room. The Wellington Hotel on Fifty-sixth Street stood just around the corner from City Center. The whole family was here. We had taken the train from Baltimore; Nanny, my mother's mother, had come with us, and Abba and Uncle Freddie and Aunt Jeanne were due at any moment. My father had come up days earlier for the dress rehearsals. He was already at the theater; we hadn't even seen him yet. Tonight was the premiere of *Six Characters in Search of an Author*.

The hotel room was mauve. The ventilation system panted stale air. The window looked out on a grid of sooty walls and windows and gray daylight. The floor was jammed with luggage and cots for Jonny and me. The bed was already strewn with Mommy's clothes; she had brought too many for two days. She stood at the window. If the sun was shining, we could not tell. "This was my view when I was a little girl," she said in a small voice. "When I lived in New York, this is what I saw out of my bedroom. The living room, though, the living room had a lovely view. You could just see the George Washington Bridge."

"I didn't know you lived in New York," I said.

"I did. When I was five years old. I lived in an apartment house in Washington Heights. The George Washington Bridge was new."

"I hate New York. How could you live here? There's no grass and no trees. There are too many people."

"We didn't live here for long. We moved to Hartford and back to New York to a different apartment, and then to Baltimore. There was a park," my mother said. "And steps that went from one street to another, connected them because the hills were so steep. And an elevator in our apartment house. I loved the elevator. And my best friend lived in the building." She stood in a cotton bathrobe with her arms crossed in front of her chest; her face shone with cold cream. "I wonder if your father is coming back to the room."

Jonny bounced on the bed and landed on my dress. "Get away!" I yelled and pushed him off onto the floor. He gazed at me, hurt and furious. I pumped myself full of righteous rage, ready to defend myself, but all Mommy said was, "Jebra," her hybrid word when she couldn't decide whom to name first. She looked at her watch and bit her lower lip. I felt mystified and vaguely dishonest, as if I had caught and hurled at my brother some emotion not mine. I had never connected my mother with New York; I could not imagine her here; I could not picture her growing up anywhere but in Baltimore. In my history of the world, when she was a child, she lived in one place. It was only my father who had been uprooted.

I patted my dress smooth. I had bought it by myself, alone, without my mother. On a Saturday morning, I took the bus with Barbara downtown to Hutzler's department store. I pushed through all the size seven dresses and chose a pale blue cotton with a boat neck, a full skirt, and a sash and charged it to my mother's account. The bodice was shaped by darts. I needed darts now; I had begun wearing a bra and hated its tightness around my rib cage, its white cotton jib-like cups, and what it signified. My body was diverging from my mind. I was no longer whole.

Except for a tiny woven pattern of darker blue squares, the dress was unadorned; my mother couldn't object to it, I hoped. Taste for her was a moral issue, and she got angry at me if I even looked at a dress she considered too gaudy or too frou-frou. But she said she thought this dress was rather nice. To go with it, she bought me a pair of patent leather pumps with little curved heels. They were my first high heels. And suddenly this spring I was eager for them, I was eager for beauty and its discomforts. I found I could breathe despite the bra. I arranged my shoes on the floor beneath the dress and put my new stockings and garter belt beside it. I was going to look beautiful and grown up for my father's opera. I did not think of my father at all or of my mother; I thought only of my entrance into the theater, my debut in a woman's costume. "Can I get dressed?" I asked. "Can I put on my dress?"

My mother nodded. She closed the blinds.

I hooked the garter belt around my waist. It dug into my hips and in combination with the stockings held me in traction. But it had to be endured; there was no other way. My mother brushed my hair carefully into a ponytail and tied it with a blue ribbon. She appraised me. "You look gorgeous." I twirled. The skirt of my dress brushed against the bed, and I stumbled on my skinny heels and nearly twisted my ankle. It didn't matter. In my new dress, I was beautiful, ready to go.

The family gathered in the lobby of the Wellington Hotel. It was a gray evening, threatening to drizzle. The adults talked to each other in quick, anxious sentences—raincoats? umbrellas? Where's Hugo? Gone already? Nath, you look fabulous! Are you nervous? Jonny and I walked along the sidewalk, not stepping on the cracks. We felt the need for good luck. I was skipping over the cracks between childhood and something else. My mother's shrill laughter caught up with us; it knotted my stomach. What if nobody liked the opera? her voice made me think. What if nobody came? In her voice I heard all potential disaster. During rehearsals a few of the singers and orchestra had complained about the dense atonal music, and some had trouble learning their parts. My father was hurt and disappointed by their indifference and their occasional animosity to his music. Jonny started to run, and I started after him. I wobbled but kept running, rebelling against the shoes I had coveted, determined to beat him.

"I won!" I shouted and stopped, breathless, blocked by the crowd in front of the City Center, people all going to see my father's opera. "Jonathan! Deborah!" my mother called. It was beginning. My father had told me the story: The family of Characters looking for their author interrupts a rehearsal in a provincial opera house. Their story, their opera, has been left unfinished by its composer. It is a melodrama—a story they are condemned to repeat until it is finally completed.

Mommy handed us each our ticket, and we gave them to the usher; I wanted to tell her who we were. The curtain was up on the stage, and so was the back scrim. You could see the scaffolding of lights, the stagehand's ladders, all the theater's mundane apparatus. For a moment, I was disappointed. I had envisioned my entrance against a crimson velvet backdrop. But excitement shimmered through the theater from the exposed stage. My father was behind all this, I suddenly realized, and the surprise and pride of it shivered through me. All these people had come here for the opera that my father had sat composing for years and years in Baltimore, in Florence, in Maine. Here he had suddenly expanded; his name filled the theater, and I was a part of him. Craning my neck like a young heron, I walked down the aisle to our seats, looking, wanting to be looked at.

The orchestra began to tune, the long, anticipatory A. I saw my father like an apparition at the back of the theater. I waved, but he didn't see me, and he didn't sit down with us. The house lights dimmed; the stage darkened. My father—my father, Hugo Weisgall—hovered in back under the balcony, but the current of his anxiety shot through me as if he had been holding my hand. My mother sat stiff, almost paralyzed.

A man walked onto the gloomy stage and switched on a lamp. The opening chords shot through the theater, jagged and electric as lightning. Another man came in and shouted "Lights! Lights!" My stomach lurched. The stage lights went up. The opera spilled from the stage. The rows of notes I had heard endlessly repeated on the piano, sung in his baritone and falsetto, worried, broken apart and reassembled, erased and rewritten, now poured one after the other in torrents of instruments and voices, flutes and trombones, sopranos and tenors, now harsh, now lyrical. I recognized every note, and at the same time I did not know the music at all. "Anthony's Pig" became a long, virtuosic sextet, and the audience laughed at the silly words. They laughed as the singers parodied members of an opera company. The Coloratura simpered. The director fumed; he didn't think much of this modern stuff they were rehearsing, this *Temptation of St. Anthony* by Weisgall.

In a trick of light, the Characters materialized. Dressed in deep Sicilian mourning, they invaded the stage. Their surrealistic blackness galvanized the bare space into theater. They imposed their story on the bored singers; they insisted on playing it out. I watched, sitting forward on my seat from excitement and anxiety and so that I would not crush the sash of my nice dress, aware that I could not separate the music from the drama, that I could not tell which engendered which. Theirs was a terrible story; they could not endure its repetition, but they had no choice.

They were a family: the Mother, the Father, the Stepdaughter, the Son, the Boy, the Child. The Child was a girl, and the Boy was supposed to be older than she was. They were silent roles. When he started the opera, my father said that my brother and I could play those parts, but it had taken him too long to finish. I was now taller than the woman who sang the Stepdaughter. My father had dedicated the opera to us, though. He was very pleased with the dedication, and I knew it by heart: "To my own two special characters, Jonathan and Deborah, who outgrew their parts while waiting for this opera to be finished." I, a character, who, at eleven years old, had already outgrown my silent role but could not sing.

The opera company laughed at the Characters at first, but they became swept up in the story. Something was going to happen between the Father and the Stepdaughter, something awful. I watched. It took place in Madame Pace's shop. Pace: it meant peace, *shalom*. In front it was a hat shop; in back behind a red curtain, it was something else. Eleven, almost twelve: what did I know? Not the things men and women did, but neither was I innocent. The Stepdaughter in her black mourning dress waited in the back room, coerced by Madame Pace. The Father pushed aside the red curtain. He offered to buy his Stepdaughter a crimson hat. She refused. Because people would ask questions about where the hat came from? the Father wondered. Can't you see? I couldn't wear it, the Stepdaughter sang. The Father replied: "How silly of me not to notice. You are in mourning. I know what we will do. We will take this nice little dress off." The music slithered and struck like a dangerous snake.

The Stepdaughter began to lift the hem of her dress. Up over her thighs: from the wings, the Director tried to stop her. I was terrified. Her dress seemed suddenly malevolent, her nice little dress, her beauty. She wanted this to happen. She embraced her Mother's husband. The sin, the shame, originated with her. I cringed. "Curtain! Curtain!" called the Director, and the curtain fell on the second act.

I have been told that there was a buzz in the theater that night, the realization that something marvelous was unfolding, that here was an American opera with a brilliant, largely atonal score that was dramatically compelling: an American opera that worked. Never mind that it was based on an Italian play, that the librettist, Denis Johnston, was Irish, and that the composer had been born in Czechoslovakia; that made it all the more American. I remember only the terror of the last act, when the Child drowns and the Boy shoots himself.

I was shaking after the gunshot, and still reeling with shame that the Stepdaughter would take the dress off and reveal her awful desire. Reality and illusion, my father told me; *Six Characters* was about reality and illusion.

Anxiety shimmered through the cast party afterward during the wait for the reviews. There were many, the *Herald Tribune*, the *Post*, the *Daily News*, but the only paper that counted was the *Times*, and its music critic Harold Schoenberg. Schoenberg despised modernism and atonal music; he was deaf to the opera's lyricism; its miraculous coherence as theater did not interest him, and so he called *Six Characters* derivative and difficult. My father was crushed. He had imagined fame and popular success flowering from this one review, vindication. He had expected to return to Baltimore a hero; he hoped that this opera would lift him free from that provincial city. He had expected everything to change.

We took the train home together. My father's despair penetrated him like a chronic pain returned. But nothing would change. Our life would stay the same. We would continue to live in our house in Baltimore, three miles from my mother's mother, four miles from my father's father. Nothing would change.

. . .

That spring of sixth grade we played baseball every night until the
ball turned blue in the twilight. We hit and lost the ball in the dark
leaves of the sycamore and the big beech. We played by ear, by
whooshes and thuds. We batted and threw lethargically, the distance
between us diminishing with the light. The evening smelled of cut
grass and charcoal fires. Fireflies winked. Windows flared into yellow rectangles. Mothers called, and the boys wheeled their bicycles
through gaps in the hedges and then rode home, standing up and
pedaling furiously. All I had to do was walk next door.

I always stayed until last. Last, I thought. This was the last
spring. We were leaving Baltimore and going to Pennsylvania, to a
town called State College, which was, my mother announced with
great enthusiasm, ten miles from the geographical center of the state.
She presented this fact as if it would make the move all right, an
adventure. My father had been appointed a distinguished visiting
professor at Pennsylvania State University; the appointment would
last a year. Not one of us, though, believed we would ever come back.
Everything had changed.

Everything would have changed anyway. I thought of the
huge junior high school on Park Heights Avenue with apprehen-
sion. When she entered that school, Barbara would let Marc get to
second base. I played first base; sometimes I pitched. Peter was always on my team. My brother was always on the other team. He had
to be. We had only one baseball glove between us, and it was for a
southpaw. I was left handed; Jonny was not, but he learned to throw
with his left hand. He never complained. I never knew if he dreaded
leaving Baltimore as much as I did. We kept our feelings from each
other, and Jonny kept his from our parents as well.

On this June night Jonny had gone in early to watch a television show. One by one, the other boys got on their bikes and rode
home. Only Peter and I were left. We stood in the middle of the yard
where the most light remained, and we tossed the ball back and forth.
I played lazily, judging the ball's slow trajectory and stepping to it;
at the last moment I stretched my arm so the softball thudded into
the glove's pocket; and then, in the same motion, my hands met in

front of my chest, and I grasped the ball and threw it back. Peter's movements, assured and languid, echoed mine. The ball spun a web between us. I reached to catch a wide throw, and I kept the ball, charged with connection now. I started for home. The hedge between my house and the field was less than a foot high. I jumped over it, and Peter followed.

Moths flickered their wings against the milky globe of the porch light and beat like snare drums against the screen door. We slid inside, eluding them. I braced the door with the heel of my sneaker to keep it from slamming. It was a Wednesday night; my father was in New York, and my mother had closed the door to her room. She would be lying on her chaise longue, reading. Jonny was in the guest room.

Peter and I went into my room. I closed the door. We sat on the floor, on my oriental rug. The putti over my bed looked down at us; from this angle they appeared disapproving. I had a little portable record player that closed up into a suitcase. I opened it and shuffled through my small stack of forty-fives, records I had bought with trepidation, half expecting my father to order me to return them. I put the Everly Brothers on the record player. I studied the dark hairs of Peter's sideburns, the smooth browned skin of his cheek, and the tendon in his neck that disappeared into the collar of his plaid shirt. His Adam's apple pushed against the tender skin of his throat.

We sat close to each other, like two Scotty dog magnets, attracting and resisting. "*I can make you mine, taste your lips of wine, anytime, night or day,*" the Everly Brothers sang in their close harmony. "*Only trouble is, gee whiz, I'm dreamin' my life away.*" Peter's brown fingers rested on the rug beside my hand, not touching. I watched his hand as if it were a wild thing, easily frightened.

It had grown dark outside. We sat there saying nothing and listening to the Everly Brothers. The phone rang in my mother's room. Peter started. "What time is it?" I shook my head; I had no idea. "I have to go," he said. "My mom will be worried."

I followed him downstairs, past the drawings my father had hung there: three large charcoal sketches of a naked woman. She was middle aged; she had wide hips, sagging breasts and belly, and red strokes burned amidst the black thatch of her crotch. Her bleak, explicit ugliness mortified me, but when I asked my father to take them down, he said that he had known the artist during the war, his name was Nympsh, and these were drawings of his Jewish wife. I did not see how any artist could have loved her, and then I thought, guiltily, that she was probably dead. Peter walked past her and averted his eyes.

I followed him through the hall and out the screen door through the veil of moths, across the porch, down the steps into the summer night, along the path to the hedge, and onto the sidewalk. We walked under a sycamore tree whose leaves blocked the streetlight. Abashed, I stopped.

Peter took a step away from me and then swiveled neatly as a pitcher checking a base runner. He lifted his arm in a smooth arc, and he embraced me. I bent back my head, and there, perfectly, was his mouth. I was not surprised. What surprised me was that I knew exactly what to do: how to tilt my head so our noses didn't collide, how to fit my arms above and beneath his. I was astonished at what I knew. I kept my eyes open. I kept it all: his mouth pressing against mine, that ecstasy of surfaces, the smooth heat of his skin, the imprint of his hands on my waist and shoulder. I felt his heart beating against my chest to its own rhythm that had nothing to do with my own heart. The humid breeze brushed the back of my neck. I was shivering. We let each other go. Peter ran home down the sidewalk, silent in his black Keds.

I closed the door to my room and lay on my bed and wrote a poem. It began: "A wonderful thing, so old and new." I wrote it in a kind of *terza rima*, each verse contained three rhyming lines. I copied it over in blue ink with my fountain pen onto a clean loose-leaf page. I folded the page into quarters and tucked it into my notebook. I went to bed with my kiss, playing it over and over again.

The next morning I ran off the school bus and found Peter on the playground playing dodge ball. "Here," I said, and handed my poem to him, and as I did, I brushed my hand against his. He did not look at me; he did not even say hi. When the bell rang, I followed him into school. Our desks were arranged in clusters; Peter sat diagonally across from me. All morning I stared at him, willing him to turn and look at me, but he did not.

At recess, I avoided him, afraid that I would not be able to stop myself from talking to him. That would be too dangerous, I knew. I had done something terribly wrong. But despite myself, I tracked his movements; he had to notice me. I would make him speak. I walked by Michael; he was reading something that he tried to hide when he saw me coming, but I recognized the piece of paper, narrow lines, from my notebook, blue ink, my handwriting. It was my poem. Peter had given it to him. I had been betrayed.

"Give that back to me!" I yelled. My voice blasted wild and shrill; I howled like a coyote. The bell rang. My face burned red; I trembled with rage and shame. The playground fell silent as students began lining up to go inside. I snatched the sheet of paper from Michael. The corner ripped, and he held on to the tiny white triangle.

"Deborah!" Mrs. Rhodes stood in the middle of the playground. "What is going on?"

"Nothing," I said.

She approached me. My neck was damp with sweat.

"What is that?" She pointed to the paper in my hand.

"Nothing."

"May I have it, please?" She held out her hand.

I put my hands behind my back. "No," I said. I had never defied her. I was her star. I waited for her to force me to hand it over. I pressed my lips together and closed my eyes to keep the tears in. I crumpled the poem in my fist. Everybody watched me. I stood in the bright June sun, cornered.

Mrs. Rhodes approached me. I shook my head, helplessly. She raised her hand and I thought she was going to grab my arm and make me give up the poem, but she touched my shoulder, instead. "Go inside, now," she ordered the class. "You go to the girls' room," she told me softly. "Go and wash your face. Take your time. When you feel better, then you can come back to the classroom."

I stayed in the pink-tiled bathroom gazing at my red face and red eyes. I blotted my cheeks with wet paper towel and waited for the pressure in my chest to subside. When I returned to class, the shades were half drawn against the sun, and heads were bent over math problems. Mine waited at my desk. Peter didn't look up as I crossed the room and took out my pencil.

After school, as I headed for the bus, Michael ran after me. "Debby!" he shouted. "Debby! Wait up!" He blocked my way. "You didn't write that," he said gently, offering consolation.

I wanted to punch him. How could he imagine that I would use somebody else's words to reveal my heart? "I did so. I did so write it! Move!"

"You couldn't have. You copied it from somewhere."

"I did not."

"Come on. It's too good. I know you couldn't have."

"Well, I did! I did write it. It's mine." I pushed past him and climbed into the bus. In the way of boys—in the way of the world—I should not have written that poem. I should have denied susceptibility: to the kiss, to pleasure, even to the rhyme. I should have kept it all secret. That was love, which required feints and strategies, distance and calculation. I could not do that. Peter did not take the bus home that afternoon, so I did not even have the heartbroken pleasure of having him pass close by me on the way to his seat. Craven, I longed for him. After that day, he avoided me. He ducked out from under love, as any sensible twelve-year-old boy would do. He did not show up for baseball for more than a week.

On the last day of school, we were dismissed before lunch. Everybody gathered at the field. It was cloudy and still, muggy with no rain. The leaves of the sycamores drooped. While we were choosing up teams, Peter appeared. I did not pick him. Fizzing with nervousness, I tried not to look at him, although I couldn't look at anything else.

I batted third. Peter played right field, about twenty feet in front of the side wall of the neighbor's house. Michael pitched. I swung smooth and level; my body and legs and arms twisted in an effortless coil. I connected with a solid, resonant crack and watched the ball go. It soared over Peter's head. He leaped for it and missed. With a soprano crash, the ball shattered the neighbor's kitchen window. Home run. My team cheered; my brother, on the other team, cheered. Everybody was yelling, even Peter, in an impersonal way; breaking a window was cause for celebration. I loped around the bases and crossed home, elated and miserable, wishing I could stop forever right there, at that house-shaped diagram we'd scratched in the red Maryland clay.

Nine

Photographs

"*I chose Jesus for my Savior; you take Him, too! I chose Jesus for my Savior; you take Him, too!*" My eighth-grade music class belted out the words. I stood silent in the front row; I felt my face red with anger and embarrassment. I could not sing that, no matter how snappy the tune, no matter if it was only a song; I could not sing those words. "You take Him, too!" The nerve, the assurance, the cruelty: "Take Him!" That was no suggestion, but a command. That was at the root of it all. "You take Him, too!" Or else. No. Mr. Brocklebank, the music teacher, conducted from the upright piano with vigor.

Mr. Brocklebank was also my eighth-grade homeroom teacher at the junior high school in the town of State College, Pennsylvania. When we moved, I skipped seventh grade. I sat in the last row in my eighth-grade homeroom, a "W" in a roomful of "L's" and "M's," enrolled at the last minute, stuck in wherever there was space. The school was a big old brick rectangle with dark varnished woodwork and yellowed linoleum floors that rose perpendicular to the sidewalk on Fairmount Avenue about eight blocks east of our rented house. State College, that school, these were utterly alien places. There were six other Jews in the entire eighth grade.

I had already determined that Mr. Brocklebank did not know very much about music. He had called a piece of music a fugue when clearly it was not; I verified his mistake with my father and corrected him. Mr. Brocklebank looked at me now, and I stared back, defiantly, I hoped, but I was near tears. The song had eight verses, and each was riddled with Jesus. My classmates sang out wholeheartedly, their consciences free and clear, having chosen Jesus for their Savior, confident that everyone else had also done so. And at the same time that I hated those words and hated Mr. Brocklebank for choosing that song, I longed to join them. I yearned to open my mouth and announce that I chose Jesus and was just like them. I remained silent and stared.

Mr. Brocklebank frowned and lowered his eyes. He banged a final chord, and the period was over. We scattered to our next classes. It was a Friday in October; the school had a loose Friday air. As we walked down the hall and up the stairs to math, my new friend Cheryl chattered about the weekend. There was a football game tonight, and she was meeting Rob there; on Saturday she had a date with him, too. A movie. His friend John had asked me out with them for a double date, but I had to tell him that I couldn't go. This weekend was the last two days of Succoth, the fall harvest festival, and we were driving back to Baltimore as soon as Jonny and I got home from school. We had been in State College for a month, and we had returned to Baltimore every weekend for Jewish holidays and once during the week for Yom Kippur, driving nearly five hours each way so that my father could conduct the choir.

I cradled my books in my arms; I used to admire my high school babysitters doing that, and now I was old enough to carry a stack of books home every afternoon. I talked to other kids as we walked west along Fairmount Avenue. I smiled. I laughed. I felt outside of myself, both amused and unbalanced by the discrepancy between the sound of my laughter and the tense ear with which I listened to the conversation, imitating its cadences, searching for footholds.

I walked the last three blocks alone. I would have no trouble, my mother had assured me, I was grown up and very smart and seventh grade would be a waste of time for me, and any school in a university town would be populated by the children of nomadic academics; there would be lots of new kids. But most of them, it turned out, had known each other since elementary school, and all had had a year to get used to junior high. Just finding my way from class to class through the maze of halls was complicated. Phys ed was twice-a-week torture: locker rooms in the basement that smelled of mold and alien sweat; reluctant games: inept, half-hearted maneuvers around the gym or playing field. I did not want to play, not here, not with these fleshy, lumbering girls who hated to run and preferred to watch. They were female and passive; I feared their maturity was contagious. Afterward we had to take showers; the teachers stood at the entrance to the shower room to be sure our bodies had gotten wet. Naked, cold, and humiliated, we filed past so they could check us off. The only way we could avoid taking a shower was by claiming to be having our periods; we could even skip gym altogether if we wanted by saying we had cramps. "Time of the month," we announced, encoding the truth.

After school, boys played pickup games on the high school fields near our house. As I passed by them this afternoon, I recognized Cheryl's boyfriend, Rob, and his friend John, carefree, the whole empty weekend before them. I wished to dump my books on the sidewalk and join them, but I knew better than to try. What Barbara said was true; girls did not play sports with boys. I watched John run, squat to field grounders, stretch to snag fly balls, and lope off the diamond at the close of an inning. He was distant, lanky and graceful; his voice, just changed, had a fresh, confident timbre. He shaved; I had seen the delicate stubble below his sideburns. I watched him at bat and the corkscrew of his swing twisted yearning through my body. I kept walking. I had lost courage.

If we didn't have to go to Baltimore all the time, I could have gone out with him. Maybe he'd never ask me again. Our car stood in the driveway, the trunk open and three suitcases and some paper bags beside it. Through the screen door, I heard the piano. A descending figure, high treble, again and again, and over it my father's voice. He was working on another opera, one act, set to the text of *Purgatory*, a play by William Butler Yeats. He sang: *"But there are some/ That do not care what's gone, and what's left:/ The souls in Purgatory that come back/ To habitations and familiar spots."*

I slammed the door. My father looked up, annoyed. "Deborah, what took you so long?" he demanded.

"Nothing," I answered sullenly. "I came straight home."

"Jonathan's been home for half an hour."

"We go to different schools, remember? He's still in elementary school."

He opened his mouth to rebuke me, but he said, "Well, hurry up and pack; I want to get going."

"Why do we always have to go back? What's so important about the last two days of Succoth, anyway?"

He looked at me, his blue eyes round and disgusted behind his glasses. "What do you mean, what's so important? Simchas Torah isn't important? Rejoicing in the Torah? The law, our history?" Then his tone changed; his expression softened from anger to bleakness, but his eyes held me. "Deborah," he said. "they're all important. All the holidays. It's not enough to celebrate Yom Kippur and Rosh Hashanah. You have to keep them all, observe them all. Judaism is a way of life."

"We don't keep kosher. You don't go to services here."

He lowered his eyes. "And I have to conduct the choir. I can't leave my father."

"But we're so far away!"

He looked up. "What can I do? I couldn't stay in Baltimore."

"Why not? What's better about here? You have to go to New York every week anyway! Why couldn't we just stay in Baltimore?" My eyes filled; he had confided in me; he shared my loneliness, my dislocation, but I knew he would not share my wish to belong to this town in the geographical center of Pennsylvania and to live among the gentiles.

"I need this job. The seminary and Juilliard aren't enough; composing isn't enough. I have to support you and Jonny and your mother. How else are you going to live? Not to mention go to college? Christ, I don't know when I'm going to get a chance to work." He played that anxious treble figure again. "Don't let your mother see that you're upset," he said quietly. "This is hard for her, too. Now, hurry and get your things together. I'm going to pack the car." He got up from the piano.

I stood there. "What's that opera about?"

"A man who kills his father and then kills his son. It's a great play. You should read it."

"Not too cheerful."

"Life isn't cheerful. Now go on!"

I ran upstairs. The furnished house we rented had a persistent smell, damp and rotten, like dead mice in the walls. It had a green shag rug in the living room and horizontal knotty pine paneling. My room was painted pink, which, only a year earlier I had thought was the perfect color, but rosy reality cured me of desire. My mother rented the house because of its piano and its large size. She craved space, and part of her loved complaining about how ugly the house was, how filthy, how hard she had worked to clean it.

I folded my best clothes into my suitcase and added it to the row of luggage. Even for a few days we loaded the car as if we were afraid to leave anything behind. My mother drove relentlessly to beat the sunset. The road crossed the gray folds of the Allegheny Mountains. At Lewistown we followed the Juniata River to Harrisburg, where it joined the Susquehanna, then down to York through Pennsylvania Dutch country, with its wide fields and big barns looming in the late afternoon light. We crossed into Maryland past Hagerstown, then into the glare of lights marking the depressing suburban sprawl surrounding Baltimore.

We pulled up in front of Abba's house. Brown leaves banked the curbs; chipped brown paint littered the front yard of the house next door. We greeted the neighbors as we hauled our luggage into the house, humid and redolent with steaming chicken soup. Abba's *lulav,* his palm branch bound with myrtle and willow, lay in a white florist's box on the dining room table; his *esrog,* a fragrant Israeli citron, nestled in lambswool in its silver container. Jews carried these symbols of the harvest to synagogue during the holiday. "Where have you been?" Abba greeted us as we entered. "Hurry, we're late. We're late for shul."

"Jesus, Papa," my father protested. "We can't take the kids out of school every week."

My parents slept in the bedroom Abba had abandoned after Lady died; Jonny and I slept across the hall, in a room that had belonged to my father and his brother. The room was dark; its windows looked into the windows of the house across a narrow passageway. The glass was grimy, almost opaque. The bathroom was at the end of a long hall, next to a study, a room lined with bookshelves with a grand piano in the middle. That upstairs study seemed haunted, as if my father and Freddie had left pieces of their lives there, bright pieces once, dulled with dust.

Dusty anxiety settled on me. There was barely a minyan at shul. Services were quick, and my brother and I and our cousins raced home in the tired October twilight and crowded into the *succoh* on the back porch. During the eight days of Succoth, Jews were commanded to live in little booths, *succoth*, to commemorate the forty years the Hebrews wandered in the wilderness after the redemption from Egypt. We did not live in the succoh, but we ate there every night. Abba's succoh was set up just outside the kitchen door: a bright tent, yellow canvas printed with a frieze of grapevines barely big enough for a folding aluminum table and picnic benches. He used to have a wooden succoh, a dark, collapsible room like a stage set or a playhouse. I didn't like this canvas one as much; it seemed too modern and convenient. A lattice of evergreen branches formed the roof; the lattice had to be loose enough so that you could see the stars through it. Fruits and flowers hung from the roof, and vines twisted around the aluminum tent poles. Children were supposed to help decorate succoth, but Lil Forman, from the congregation, prepared Abba's. Perfection counted for more than participation.

Freddie poured Scotch and bourbon for the adults, Pepsi for the children. He sloshed soup on the tablecloth as he helped Ozelia hand around the wide bowls filled with broth and noodles. The holiday candles lit the canvas walls a deep ochre, and we made shadow puppets with our hands. I looked up through the drying green boughs for faint stars twinkling through the city smog. A damp autumn chill rose through the floor. Abba and Freddie and Daddy sang; my mother and Aunt Jeanne chattered shrilly, competing with the men's voices. Crowded around the table, we were happy. I forgot to regret the football game I was missing; how could I miss this? Succoth was easy. There was nothing we couldn't eat, nothing to repent, no arduous restrictions. My father's birthday fell around Succoth. We celebrated the harvest, we celebrated finishing the annual reading of the Torah in the synagogue and starting over again. I loved seeing the lopsided scrolls: Deuteronomy rolled to the end, Genesis unrolled at the beginning, holy circles.

There was a soft *thunk*. The succoh shivered. Something heavy thudded onto the wooden porch just outside. We sat still, silent. The candle flames swayed. In the alley there was a faint scrabbling: feet kicking up loose pebbles. "What was that?" Jeanne demanded. "Shh!" hissed my father.

Abba stood up and pushed aside the flap of the succoh. Daddy and Freddie followed him outside. We waited, not exactly afraid, but alert. I finished my soup. My father came back and stood at the entrance. "It was a rock," he said. "Somebody threw a rock. It's out there, on the porch. Freddie's calling the police." Behind him I saw Ozelia leaning against the back door, blocking the cheerful kitchen light, her arms crossed in front of her chest, her anxious eyes scanning the darkness.

"Who was it? Did you see anybody?" We rushed questions at him; he answered them with a no. "It was probably just a kid," he said, but his face was white and worried. I believed him. It was probably just a kid, and the police were on their way. Ozelia collected our bowls, and Mommy got up to organize the turkey. I slid out behind her. In a few minutes two policemen tramped through the back door: white, round, fleshy faces, hats in hands, leaning deferentially toward Abba. They picked up the rock, a hefty cube, gray and squared-off, a cobblestone from the alley. I could see the gouge of raw wood in the chipping porch paint. There was a white chalk-like mark on the yellow canvas of the succoh. The policemen clattered down the porch stairs to the high wooden fence behind the overgrown garden and peered out into the alley from the back gate. Nothing. Carefully, they latched the gate. "We'll take a look down the alley, Reverend," one of them said to Abba. "Don't worry. It was probably just a kid. Some——" He opened his mouth to say something more, and he glanced at Ozelia.

"A kid," my father repeated quickly. "Just a kid. I'm sure that's all it was."

The policeman shrugged. "Go ahead with your holiday. Me and my partner, we won't be far away if you need us."

I was afraid that Daddy would decide to correct his grammar.

"You sure you don't want a drink, Officer?" Freddie asked.

The policeman shook his head and laughed. "No, sir. Good night, now."

Freddie showed them out; their laughter grew fainter through the house. Abba sat down again at his place. When Freddie came back, he poured himself another drink. My mother, flushed with the heat of carving the turkey, shoved her emptied glass across the table toward him, and he filled it. My father's pale eyes flickered over their little transaction.

"Ach——" Abba sighed. He took off his glasses and rubbed his eyes. He shook his head and ran his hand through his thick white hair.

"It's over, Papa," Freddie said. "Forget about it."

Abba put his glasses back on. "Forget about it?"

It was always there. The war: there was no word then——no Holocaust——to name the destruction.

Mommy glared at Freddie. "How can you forget? How? How? How many times are we supposed to forget? Do you have any idea what you're saying? Do you know how stupid it is? Do you? Tell me!" Defending Abba gave her courage, but from her mouth the words sounded wrong. My stomach turned. My heart closed against her.

"Nath!" my father admonished. "Nath! Please!"

"Please what?"

Her voice struck shrill chimes against the aluminum poles of the succoh, anger as sudden and unpredictable as a thrown rock.

"Please what?" she growled again.

"Please don't!" I screamed.

"Don't what?" My mother narrowed her eyes at me. "How dare you talk to me like that! How dare you tell me what to do?"

"I wasn't—" I began.

"Everybody! Everybody!" Abba slammed his hand on the table. Plates and silverware clanged through the cloth against the metal tabletop. "Everybody! This is yom tov. Do not spoil it with arguing." His voice was thick with curdled consonants. "We are here, we are together. What more do you want?" He had intervened for me, and my mother did not challenge him.

. . .

Each time we came back to the shul something else had broken: the arm of the old school chair in the anteroom fell off; a pane cracked in one of the blue and green windows across the balcony. The old men with their lulavs and esrogs, the palm fronds brown and brittle and the fruits' yellow skin withered after the holiday week, marched in procession behind the scrolls of the Torah, and Abba leading the procession sang psalms as he passed around the perimeter of the nearly empty shul. His voice echoed as if it came from far away, some past place. It was as loud as ever, but I could hardly bear to hear it. What was the use of singing if there was nobody to listen?

Afterward while we waited for Abba, Mrs. Forman, faithful as always to my grandfather and his music, sought me out. She reached up and wrapped her short, plump, white arms around my neck. I bent down so she could kiss me. "Deborah," she said, "Deborah, you lovely young lady. Are you preparing for your bat mitzvah? When will it be? Richard's will be in April. I wish he were here; I know he'd love to see you, but he has to go to shul in Stevenson; they made that a rule." She shook her head disapprovingly.

I broke out in a guilty sweat. In seven months I would turn thirteen. If I were a boy like Mrs. Forman's son, Dickie, I would be memorizing a portion of the Torah, a paragraph from the Five Books of Moses and a longer section from the Haftorah, the writings of the

prophets and the books of judges and kings. I would learn the blessings and the chants and prepare to sing them in the synagogue as
proof that I was becoming an adult, a member of the community with
full responsibilities to uphold the ancient covenant between God and
His chosen people. *Bar mitzvah:* son of the commandment. *Bat
mitzvah:* daughter of the commandment. Since the war, girls were
beginning to do this, too. Certainly, I, Abba's oldest granddaughter
and Hugo's daughter, would become bat mitzvah. But we had not
talked about it. My father had not brought it up.

And I was afraid. I could not sing all those words. I would forget
the tune; I would wander out of tune. The thought of it made me sick
to my stomach. I would get lost. Abba would have to correct me; I could
already hear his gruff voice breaking into my hesitating silence. Dickie
Forman, sturdy, black-haired, his mother's pride, could do it; any boy
could do it, and probably almost any girl, but I could not.

Mrs. Forman smiled. She meant well. She assumed, always, that
I could do what I could not. I could not sing.

"I don't know," I said. "We're not here this year. I don't know
what we're going to do."

"Maybe your grandfather can record a tape for you."

I nodded. "But we don't have a tape recorder."

Mrs. Forman frowned. She started to speak but pressed her lips
closed—disapproving of me, I thought. "Give my love to your
mother, dear. Tell her we miss her."

I nodded, but I would not convey the message. My mother did
not miss them.

Abba was just coming back from his study. He wore his
Borsalino and carried his cane; he stood confident as a general.
Surosky the butcher closed the front doors to the synagogue and
walked up to the bimah; he stood beside Abba like a devoted aide-
de-camp. He was small and bent, his lips purple as raw meat. He
walked to the side door with us. When we were all outside, he locked
the door and tried the handle. Dry brown sycamore leaves littered
the cement sidewalk and crackled under our feet. It was much
warmer here than in the gray mountains of Pennsylvania.

I walked beside my father. Bat mitzvah: the words beat against my teeth. I was afraid to ask, afraid that he would say yes and afraid that he would say no. He was talking to Freddie; he would not want me to interrupt. I did not ask until we were driving to State College, on the winding last leg of the trip. It was dark, and I could barely see the shape of my brother in the other corner of the back seat. I thought he was asleep.

"Am I going to be bat mitzvahed?" I asked. My voice squeaked.

"Bat mitzvah," Daddy answered. "It is a noun, not a verb."

"Bat mitzvah. Am I?"

"We're not in Baltimore."

"We go back all the time."

He did not answer me immediately. Finally, he said, "How will you learn it? There's nobody in State College who can teach you."

"I don't know. Mrs. Forman said that Abba could make a tape. But we don't have a tape recorder." Now I hesitated. "But you could teach me." I wished I hadn't said that. He was not patient with musical matters. He would become frustrated and yell. I could already feel my breath tangling in my vocal cords, squeaking and croaking.

Mommy drove fast; as we sped around the curves, our head-lights swept over the rocks along the sides of the road. My father stared straight ahead. I leaned forward and put my chin on the back of the front seat.

Daddy had a beautiful speaking voice, deep and resonant, sweet at the edges. "Do you really think it's necessary?"

I did not answer.

He went on. "For boys it is, of course. There has to be a cer-emony to mark their coming of age. But for girls, it's not the same thing. You know when a girl has grown up."

"Girls get their periods," my mother said.

"What's that?" my brother asked. Nobody answered him.

Period: a sentence, a punishment. My father turned around in the seat. It was not so dark in the car that I couldn't see his expres-sion: aggrieved and betrayed.

I did not want that blood. "Don't tell Daddy!" I'd begged my mother when it happened the first time. "Please, don't tell him." But she did. I heard them whispering in his piano room, and as I left for school, he stood by his door and gazed at me. He said nothing, but his injured, unhappy look was unbearable. I had lost him. That curse, that leaking mess, that monthly excuse for incapacity: I hated what it did to me. I would give anything for it not to define me, to be my ceremony.

But I did not protest. My father did not think I could sing, and he was right. That settled it. His glorious noise was not for me. He did not think there was any reason for me even to try. He would not help me anymore; I had grown up.

. . .

Matzo crumbs from last night's Seder littered the cloth on the long table in Abba's dining room. The chairs were pushed away, as if we had just gotten up. I stood in the living room beside the stairs looking into the dining room. It seemed like a stage set, not real without actors, without us. I stood there suspended, looking, waiting for something to happen.

In the corner of the living room, the television set whispered. My brother sat on the floor in front of it. The television was an experimental one: closed, it looked like a blond wood box. The screen was in the lid. You lifted the lid, turned the set on; the cathode ray tube sat in the box and projected its picture onto the screen. A member of the congregation had given Abba the set. We weren't supposed to watch on yom tov; technically you weren't supposed to turn on lights or even the burner on a stove, but nobody had told Jonny to turn it off. He was watching bowling. One camera was fixed on the duckpins, another aimed at the players. The commentator whispered the players' names and the score; the sounds of the wooden ball rumbling down the alley and the tumbling pins were louder. The clapping from the spectators sounded meager, like the applause at a poorly attended concert of modern music.

My parents had gone out. "Come on, Hugo," Freddie urged. "You've got to see this painting. It's gorgeous, an American primitive."

"Primitive isn't my taste," my father said. "I won't like it."

"You'll love it, Hugo, I promise you. And it's a steal."

"It's probably a fake."

"Hugo! Don't you think I know anything about art?"

My father narrowed his eyes.

Freddie laughed. "Okay. That's why I want you to take a look at it."

"Where is it?"

"In this antique shop on Charles Street."

So they went, my father and my uncle and their wives, grown children uncomfortable about commerce on a holy day. They asked me if I wanted to go, but there was nothing worse than waiting around for my parents in an antique shop. They examined everything until their fingertips were gray and dry with dust; they desired a few things, discussed them, disagreed about them. Sometimes they bought, and then they argued afterward about whether they should have spent the money. The whole process was urgent and combative and fraught with mistrust.

As they left, a warm breeze slithered in through the open doors. It was spring in Baltimore; in State College the trees were still bare. I missed this soft Baltimore spring, but I was trapped inside. "Why don't you call one of your friends?" my mother had suggested. But most of them were in school; they did not skip school for Passover. I did not really want to see anybody. I had nothing to say, nothing to connect me with them anymore. We were not coming back here, and we were not staying in State College, either. I had made friends there; Cheryl had horses, and she and I galloped bareback through the Nittany mountains; I had sung Christmas carols and felt the thrill of surrendering to the majority. And Mr. Brocklebank never again had us sing "I Chose Jesus for My Savior." After the summer, we were moving to New York. While we were at shul this morning, my mother had met with a real estate agent to sell our house in Baltimore.

In the kitchen, Abba clattered a dish, probably inspecting the gefilte fish. There would be twenty-three people for the Seder tonight. He had cooked everything himself, for both nights. He was tired. He came out of the kitchen and started into the bathroom when he saw me. "Where's your brother?"

"Here," I said. "In the living room, with me."

Abba nodded and grunted. When he came out of the bathroom, his shirt was unbuttoned and the tails hung out of his trousers. I could see his *kittel*, the fine linen pinny he wore under his shirt. It had fringes like a tallit at each of its four corners. He crossed the dining room to where his daybed was squeezed behind the opened dining room table. He peered into the living room at the television set. "What is he doing?"

I shrugged. The questions Abba asked me were always about logistics. He never asked my opinion, or what I was doing with my life, or how I felt. If he had, I would not have known what to answer in order to keep his attention. "What is that?" he asked.

"Bowling," I said.

Abba shook his head, disapproving, but he looked too weary to enforce God's commandments. "I'm going to lie down. A little nap," he said and motioned for me to close the sliding French doors separating the living room from the dining room. I sat on the stairs for a few minutes. A woman in a shirtwaist dress and neatly folded socks and bowling shoes straight-armed the ball down the alley and got a strike. "Isn't there anything else on?" I asked Jonny.

"I'm waiting for the Orioles' game," he answered.

I went upstairs to the bedroom he and I shared. I stretched out on the unmade bed to read my book. I still wore my dressy clothes, a woolen jumper and a blouse. I unhooked my stockings from my garter belt, pulled them off, and let the straps dangle against my bare thighs. All the windows were closed. The air was stale. No sunlight reached this room. I tried to read, but I could not concentrate. I thought of my father in here, a boy who spoke no English fresh from grim Europe. He had never described Ivančice to me. All I knew was that his house had a courtyard with a coop where they kept geese. I imagined its gray and dusty buildings, their walls strung along a road. It was like the villages we'd driven through on the plain southeast of Vienna, hopeless places with no trees, no hills, no elevation at all; no wonder my father had jumped off the roof of the garage with garbage can lids.

This room, this whole floor, held their foreignness; it smelled of their unknowable life before America. This house contained homelessness, theirs and my own. Theirs had been much worse than mine. A strange language; a country to which he could not return. I was moving only two hundred miles away. We came home all the time. I got up from the bed and crossed the hall to the room where my parents slept, the room that used to be Abba and Lady's bedroom. Shouts from the street cut through the silence. The blinds were still drawn. I opened them, lifted them aside—slats filmed with grime— and peered out through the veil of translucent leaves. Boys were playing kickball in between the ranks of parked cars, boys my age home from school, or maybe they hadn't even bothered to go. I let the blind clatter against the windowsill. My mother hadn't made the beds, and the sheets, their underwear, pajamas, hangers, and shoe bags were tangled together. The lavender spreads spilled onto the floor. On the ebony dresser, Lady's silver-backed mirror and hair- brush lay on a linen mat amid the clutter of my mother's cosmetics.

Lady died in this room. The thought of death caught me by the throat. I inhaled deeply, taking in living air, to shake it loose. Death attached to her things, her lavender spreads with their designs of round cotton tufts, her brush and comb. I gazed at myself in the big mirror that stretched the length of the dresser. With my broad forehead, I looked like my grandmother, my father said; I was tall, like her. Would I die like her? Keep your hair back, my father said, so I can see your forehead. I shook my hair into my face. I stood on the bed to see all of myself. Lady was not beautiful; she was too sad, too severe. Was I beautiful? Even if I didn't have straight hair or a straight nose? I jumped off the bed and took Lady's mirror and climbed back and balanced on the footboard. Who would ever love me? What was there to love? I looked. My skin was smooth. My hair shone. I smoothed my skirt along my waist and legs. I was slender. I smiled and studied that smile for flaws; to seduce myself was hardest of all.

This was vain. I was afraid I'd be caught. "What are you doing?" Abba or Jonny would ask, and I would have no answer. I put the mirror back on the dresser and I mussed the linen runner around it so my mother would not guess that it had been disturbed. I stood still in the hot room, listening. The shouts outside continued, and the television voice had changed pitch, higher and more urgent and backed by a chorus of shouts and cheers. The ball game. I tiptoed out to the landing. I felt isolated, removed from those ordinary sounds, held in a suspended state of being. I would not go back into the sad room where I slept. I started down the windowless hallway that led to the back room.

Light poured in from the French doors that led to a tiny balcony above the back porch. I tried opening them, but they were stuck. Motes of dust floated in the still air. Nobody ever came in there now. The grand piano with a standing lamp beside its bench occupied the middle of the bare floor, and bookshelves covered the walls. On the upper shelves, books were neatly arranged, but paperbacks were piled haphazardly on the lower shelves. The air smelled dry and papery; I breathed dust. I had no idea who had used this room, whether prayers or ballets had been composed on the closed piano. But the room held emotion in its bright austerity: hope, ambition, disillusion, a mixture of all three.

I opened the piano lid and left black finger marks in white dust. I pressed a yellowed key, the B below middle C, slowly, softly, and it made no sound. I pressed it harder and still it was silent. I struck the C; it twanged like an untuned violin. I shivered, afraid that it had been heard.

I closed the piano and prowled the room and pulled down one of the books on the upper shelves. Its black leather spine had faded a greenish gray. Its pages were onionskin; their gilding had tarnished. I opened it to the frayed ribbon bookmark. It was in German, printed in tiny, dense Gothic letters, paragraphs long as a page. I could not even decipher its alphabet, more exotic to me than Hebrew. It had been my father's, I guessed. He had written his dissertation at Johns Hopkins on seventeenth-century German literature, I knew that

much. "If you become a composer, you will live in poverty," Lady
had warned him. She had wanted him to become a doctor, and so he
earned a Ph.D. and became Dr. Hugo Weisgall upon completing a
dissertation that had something to do with the cult of the Virgin
Mary: a strange subject for the son of cantors, or not so strange for
a young man hungry for history and defying his pious mother.

I did not speak a word of my father's native tongue, the language
he hated to speak but loved to sing. I put the book back. My fingertips
were flecked black with fragments of leather. I picked up the paper-
back book on top of one of the piles. It was a mystery, Mickey Spillane.
Spillane and Tolstoy: those were Abba's favorite authors. The book's
cover, its celluloid cracked and peeling away from the cardboard, fea-
tured the silhouette of a man in a fedora. A smoking cigarette hung
on his lip and the barrel of a smoking gun made a threatening black
diagonal across the cover's left-hand corner. Between the cigarette and
the gun appeared a redhead with green cat's eyes. Her breasts and
thighs burst from her tattered bodice and skirt.

I opened the book, and a clump of pages popped from their
binding. I scanned the pages of dialogue. Babe, moll, tough words,
police procedure, curves, figure: euphemisms for sex. I searched for
more sex. I felt dirty. I put the book back. The room depressed me,
with its discarded books, its abandoned inspirations, its alien traces
of familiar men. Standing in that room, I felt estranged from them;
I knew so little of my father and grandfather; they would tell me so
little. I ached to know, but perhaps my soft life had kept them silent
and persuaded them that I would never understand. Perhaps my
father assumed that a daughter, especially an American daughter,
could never burn with his passion to connect with the past.

Slowly, I walked along the last wall of books toward the door,
hoping to find a title in English. Over my head, in the corner of the
last row of shelves beside the door, I saw a shoebox. It had no lid,
and the thick white paper of photographs curled over its edge.
Curious, I stood on tiptoe and tilted it off the shelf. A pack of pictures slid onto the floor. I kneeled beside them and put the box down.
When I turned the photographs over, I saw that they were all prints

of the same image: a snapshot of my father in uniform. It was a wonderful picture. On his collar were pinned his brass crossed rifles. He looked young and jaunty, bolder than in his wedding picture. He stood outside; I recognized the tiny square of lawn in front of Abba's house. It looked tended; a rose bush grew inside the clipped hedge. My father squinted at the camera and smiled in noon light. His boat-shaped hat rode bravely on his curly hair. Perhaps he had just enlisted. I knew that expression: eager, energetic, fired by just the air he breathed; he thought he was going to make a difference. It was how he looked when he told us we were moving to New York.

I turned over another photograph: Uncle Freddie and Aunt Jeanne. They were young, smooth and gleaming. Jeanne's hair was arranged in a pompadour over her forehead. She wore a pale suit, and a corsage was pinned to her lapel. Her lips had photographed black as her hair. Freddie wore a boutonniere; it must have been their wedding day. Just beneath that, I found a picture of my father with Lady. He was wearing his uniform and hat and his smile; she looked somber, dismayed by his military bravado. I knew that look, too; I had often seen it on my father's face when he had been disappointed. Just under that, I found a snapshot of the dog, Lady, a blond, silky-haired terrier mix that my father had when he was growing up. I did not think it odd that we had called my grandmother by a name she had used for a pet.

I dug deeper into the box, wondering what else I'd find, what other clues. Pictures of him as a little boy, at my age, at my brother's age. Perhaps a record of his flight from the roof of the garage. "What happened? What happened?" My brother and I would demand. "Nothing," my father always answered. "I jumped off the roof of the garage with a garbage can lid in each hand. I flapped the lids, but I didn't fly." "Did you hurt yourself?" "No." "How old were you?" "About your age." "Whose age?" Which age: thirteen, eleven, twelve, ten? He never told us.

From the bottom of the box, I pulled a thick sheaf of photographs, thirty or forty of them curled and nested together, their white backs uppermost. I spread them apart as if I were extending a tele-

scope. The backs were all stamped: "Secret. Property of U.S. Army."
I had no idea what they could be; maybe my father had been a spy. I
turned them over.

Bodies. Naked, emaciated, and hairless, whiter than chalk in
sunlight. Bodies heaped into a truck bed like peeled forked logs, spilling out the back.

Shaven skulls shadowed black with stubble. Huge joints: elbows,
knees, wrists, ankles. Nipples, penises: remnants attached to corpses.
Dead eyes stared, black mouths gaped.

Two men in striped rags supported a naked third, his skin spun
like a cobweb over ribs and hollow pelvis. They displayed him. I
stared at his sex.

Survivors with Stars of David on their striped rags and identical, empty faces starved past identity, past youth or age or gender
into grotesque similarity. They were all Jews, like me; many could
have been girls like me. Girls born to soft lives.

I could hardly breathe. I picked up picture after picture; I could
not shut my eyes to their sharp, glossy detail. Random bodies tossed
like the Egyptians by the closing waters of the Red Sea in the
Haggadah's triumphant illustration. Each picture was shot in brilliant light; the noon shadows were short and strong. This was evidence. It must have been a beautiful day when the U.S. Army entered
this camp.

My father had been there. He had been here at this concentration camp. This was what he had seen. He had gone in with the liberating U.S. Army. He spoke the language. He had seen the real color
of the bodies; he had smelled them. He could have spoken his mother
tongue with the survivors. He did, and they had answered him; they
had no other language. This was his war. This was what Mrs. Werner
remembered. Mrs. Werner had sat at the Seder table the night before
with her tight gray curls and clown rouge, packed into her navy serge
dress, her ankles swollen above the laces of her black old-lady shoes.
This was where her family had gone. There was a terrible prayer in
the Haggadah. "Pour out Thy wrath on the nations that do not know
You," it began. "For they have eaten Jacob and destroyed his places."

We said it when we opened the door for the prophet Elijah. "I hate that prayer," Uncle Freddie said. My father insisted on chanting it. "The Warsaw ghetto uprising began on Pesach," he retorted, silencing his brother.

There was a photograph of a sign: a black skull and crossbones above the words: "Achtung Danger Typhus." I memorized the picture: a shovel leaning against a wheelbarrow, the round toe of a shiny American army boot intruding on the still life. I was hungry for those pictures. I could not stop looking at their obscene details, at naked, commonplace death. I looked at them until I was stuffed and sickened.

I hid the photographs under their camouflage of snapshots and replaced the shoe box on the high shelf. I nudged it until it looked to be exactly where I had found it. Nobody would know what I had seen. I would never tell.

I felt light-headed. I stepped silently down the hall like a thief back into the spring afternoon. A roar came from the television. Home run. Below me, I heard Abba's bed creak. The door between the dining room and living room slid open. I hurried to the upstairs landing. Abba said something to Jonny. "Where is your sister?" I thought I heard. I rushed halfway down the steps; my garters tangled between my thighs.

Abba in his undershirt and kittel, his white hair spiky from sleep, peered around the twisting staircase. I stopped just beside the window where my grandmother's dusty plants languished. I was almost directly above him. He looked up at my bare legs. I slapped my skirt down. He regarded me with a slow, wicked smile, as if he saw me for the first time.

Ten

Innocence

In September of 1960 we moved to Great Neck, Long Island. My father had become a professor of music at Queens College in Flushing, while continuing to teach at the Jewish Theological Seminary and at Juilliard. We drove from Maine in one day and crossed the Throg's Neck Bridge onto Long Island. My mother navigated the eight-lane highways and mysterious road signs: Van Wyck Expressway, Northern Boulevard, Grand Central Parkway. As we drove east on the Long Island Expressway, we passed a tall smokestack. "That's Queens College," my father announced. "Distinguished school. You can recognize it by its crematorium chimney."

For my father, every achievement was in some way a disappointment. It could always have been something better. The sight of that ugly smokestack pulled me out of the pleasant suspension of travel. I was sorry that the long drive from Maine was ending; in New Hampshire I sank into the white noise of wind and engine. I held on to Maine, the simple blue sky and water, evergreens, crisp white afternoon clouds, and the maples' early red. Maine was out of time, always summer; only the maples gave away the truth. In Maine I was all ages; I picked up traces of my younger self every June and wove them into who I had become over the winter. I held on to Maine, already memory, as we drove past apartment houses, row houses, acre after concrete acre where a tree was an afterthought, until we reached Great Neck and the landscape changed.

A suburb of New York City, it seemed more rural than our old neighborhood in Baltimore. My mother had bought the house of her dreams, a beige stucco Tudor on a corner lot on Maple Drive. We drove down our new street for the first time. It looped and curved, and there were no sidewalks. Huge oaks shaded the street, and, while it was hot, it was not oppressive like Baltimore. "It's so kempt," said my father, with admiration. He valued bourgeois punctiliousness. Our house, empty over the summer, was the one with the brown scruffy lawn. A boring hedge of azaleas banked the facade. In the spring when they bloomed, my mother assured me, they would be beautiful, but our lawn, I guessed, would never achieve neighborhood standards.

Inside, the house was white and clean. My mother had had it painted; she had left us for a week in Maine to supervise the move. It had large rooms with casement windows and two maid's rooms behind the kitchen. A plumbing-fixture distributor had built it and installed bathrooms everywhere. I had my own bathroom. This house would hold all our possessions, all the furniture that had languished in storage for more than ten years, all the crated paintings, all the Meissen dishes that had remained packed in barrels since my parents' return from Prague, and all my father's books. Shelves had been built into almost every room for the thousands of books he already owned; there was ample space for those he continued to buy. Everything would be fine. We would be happy. My father would become famous.

Over the mantelpiece between the turquoise ducks hung St. Anthony in his familiar agony, his twisted limbs welcoming us. My pair of bronze horses pranced on shelves protected with panes of glass, as if they were on display in a museum.

A cream-colored rug with a pattern of golden tree branches lay on the living room floor. It was so beautiful that I hesitated to step on it. "Where did this come from? Why haven't we used it before?" I demanded. My parents laughed. "We had it in Prague. We never had a house big enough before," my father said. "In 1938 the Munich Pact was signed on this rug."

"What was that?" I asked.

"That was the treaty the Nazis used as an excuse for invading Czechoslovakia. My mother went downstairs and sat by the radio in the basement of Chauncey Avenue, and she wept."

"Why do we have this?"

"It's beautiful, isn't it?" my mother asked. "And isn't it ironic that it ended up in a Jewish family?"

I went from room to room searching for what I had never seen: an inlaid table, a large painting of a witch trial, a tapestry depicting Brutus stabbing Caesar. Even St. Margaret had come home; she stood beside the front door on a specially constructed little shelf. She fit right in. Mittens followed me, sniffing, batting at threads, skittering away from every invisible-to-the-human-eye creature he encountered.

A glorious Waterford chandelier hung in the dining room. Chains of crystal ropes draped from a canopy, and crystal branches arched from a central crystal trunk. The prisms shot rainbows onto the walls. I stared, enchanted; so this was Prague. "Now we need a dining room table," my mother said. "I wish we still had the table we had in Prague. It could seat eighteen. Hugo, do you remember?"

My father nodded. "I told you not to sell it."

"When were we ever going to have seated dinners for eighteen? Not in Baltimore! And we couldn't take everything we had with us."

They had taken almost everything, though. I had never seen the ranks of Bohemian crystal delicately and elaborately engraved with some pope's coat of arms. It filled one entire cabinet in the pantry: claret glasses, Burgundy glasses, hock glasses tinted palest yellow green, champagne saucers, tumblers, port glasses, sherry glasses. My mother washed them all, and I dried them. They gleamed, faceted and etched, each one flamboyant and excessive.

"I want to go to Prague," I announced, and my parents smiled.

"I do!" I protested.

"We're not laughing at you," my mother said. "I wish I were in Prague right this minute."

And in the midst of our rush to unpack and organize and find clothes for the first day of school, my father went into his piano room and sat down to play. "*Andulko, mé dítě*," he sang, the lilting Czech folksong that he loved most of all. "Deborah," he commanded. "Go find that book. It's in the carton from Maine."

"It's still in the car," my mother said. "Under everything. She'll never find it. We don't have time for this. There's so much to do I don't know where to start."

My father shrugged and began the song again, improvising the accompaniment. His new piano room had windows that reached to the floor. The piano resonated against the glass and the empty bookshelves, and his big voice filled the room and spilled out into the rest of the house, through its open windows and onto Maple Drive. He sang it once and then again, and he sang the sad folksong that he loved almost as much. Then, as always, he switched to Schubert, to the slow chords of "Wanderers Nachtlied." He sang to his own piano part, harmonies originating with Schubert but his own, the feeling identical: major and minor alternating, mixing delight and despair.

I loved the sound of his piano, clean and brilliant on top, warm in the bass. I stroked its gleaming ebony case. I recognized the permanent sprinkling of red eraser dust between the pins and the frayed red felt lining the slots where the music stand fitted into the lid. I had not heard it for a year. My father sang his songs of wandering, and I felt at home.

"Hugo!" Mommy laughed, "the neighbors are going to think that a crazy family has moved in."

"And they'll be right," he answered and kept on playing. His pale eyes were bright and hot with happy expectation.

A song came into my head, an unworthy tune, one of Freddie's popular songs, but Jewish Great Neck reminded me of it, and, despite myself, I began to hum.

"What are you singing?" Daddy asked, hearing me for once.

"Nothing," I said. "It's just a song that came into my head."

"Louder. Let me hear it."

I was afraid I'd go out of tune. I wasn't really sure of the tune, so I said the words instead. They were Freddie's:

When you're in love, the whole world is Jewish,
When you're in love, nobody is a goy,
The moon is a yarmulke high in the sky,
And each day is Yom Kippur.

"The song of Great Neck!" My father laughed and banged a crashing, ponderous waltz. "Now, how does it go? *When you're in love . . .*"

My mother interrupted. "*When you're in love, you don't do the dishes.*" She sang in her tuneless way, but she grinned with a broad, wicked smile. "*When you're in love, you don't unpack the car. The house is a pigpen, there's nothing to eat. And it's not even Yom Kippur!*"

My father stopped playing and gazed at her with stunned admiration. "Nathalie! That's fantastic! You just made that up? I'm telling you, you could do anything in the world if you just made up your mind to do it! Come here!" He stretched out his arms and she walked into them and he embraced her.

. . .

Miriam Buxbaum's mother met us at the front door. "So this is Debby," she said in a nasal New York voice. "Miri's told me so much about you." I smiled and did not tell Mrs. Buxbaum that I hated being called Debby. She wore a suit and stockings and pumps, and her hair rose from her forehead in an artificial blond puffed arc. A precise swath of blue tinted each eyelid; pale pink perfectly defined her lips. Miriam wore makeup, too, green eye shadow and a thin stripe of eyeliner. No lipstick: girls in Great Neck did not wear lipstick. Miriam was as well kept as her mother. Her dark hair shone. Everything about her seemed buffed and polished; even her calves gleamed between her plaid pleated skirt and her neat white socks.

It was a rainy day in early November. Wet leaves matted the roads and our lawn, but the Buxbaums' had been raked green and clear. I wiped the rain off my shoes. The house was a split level, red brick and white clapboard, sleeker and grander than the models I used to visit in Baltimore. *Oklahoma* played in the background.

"Miri says you like music," said Mrs. Buxbaum. "We all love Rogers and Hammerstein."

"I like operas better than musicals," I said. "Musicals are pretty boring."

"I see," said Mrs. Buxbaum. "Well, aren't you hungry? Miri, come see what I got for you." She led the way into the kitchen.

"Why is your mother all dressed up?" I whispered to Miriam.

Miriam looked mystified. "That's how she always looks. Maybe she had her hair done."

The white carpet showed streaks from the vacuum cleaner. So this was what a model home, lived in, looked like. I glanced into the living room, done in earth tones, and I knew exactly what my parents would say. There was nothing in it worth looking at. Overstuffed sofas, a glass coffee table, everything so new they might as well have left the price tags on. New and clean, blissfully without history. A contemporary brass Chanukah menorah swirled on a sideboard, and a Chagall print swirled over the fireplace: Chagall the Jewish artist. The print was blue, but its frame was the same color as the beige sofa. As far as I could tell, every family in Great Neck owned a Chagall.

In the kitchen, I could faintly hear the Buxbaums' maid's radio playing rock and roll. Mrs. Buxbaum put a prettily arranged plate of pastries on the kitchen counter for us and asked us how school had gone that day and if we wanted milk.

"No, thank you," I said. "Do you have Pepsi?"

"Miriam doesn't drink Pepsi. Her teeth."

Miriam rolled her eyes. She and I were in the same English class. "The work is so hard," Miriam moaned.

"No, it isn't," I said. "What's hard about it?"

"That report we have to write. Five pages. I'll never be able to write that much about a book."

"Just choose a book you like."

Miriam groaned. "You're such a brain. You don't understand."

"You wouldn't be in this class if you weren't smart." But Miriam did not care so much about being smart; she was popular. I was interested in popularity, and I was interested in brains; I was trying everything out.

Mrs. Buxbaum said: "Debby, try an éclair. They're absolutely delicious. Have you ever had one? Do you know what they are?"

I nodded. "I had them in France for the first time when I was nine." I loved éclairs, at least I loved my memory of how they tasted.

"Lucky girl. Take one of these. They're fabulous." I took one and bit into it.

"Well, what do you think? I have to go all the way into the city to a special bakery to buy them. They're the real thing."

I tested the pastry cream against memory. This was heavier. The pastry itself was soggy, not crisp and melting and airy on my tongue. In the four years since we had been to Europe, I had been trying to match the taste of foods: little artichokes and the signora's *latte portoghese*. In America there was nothing comparable. Mrs. Buxbaum smiled at me. I knew she wanted me to tell her how good these were, but that would not have been the truth. They were nowhere close to the ones I ate in Orléans.

"They're good," I declared. "But they're not as good as real French ones. I don't know what it is. And I've tried lots of éclairs, too."

Mrs. Buxbaum looked annoyed. "Well, I see we have a real sophisticate on our hands," she said. "First opera, now éclairs."

"My father writes operas," I said, trying to explain. "And these éclairs aren't that bad."

"Thanks a lot," Miriam said.

"Maybe you girls want to do your homework together," said Mrs. Buxbaum and left the kitchen. I couldn't tell where she went; the carpeting muffled her footsteps.

I ate another pastry. I was starving.

"Want to see my room?" Miriam asked, standing up.

"Sure." I was eager to witness her abundance. I both envied it and mistrusted it.

"What about those éclairs. Shouldn't we put them away?" I asked. My manners improved away from home; at home my mother was always after me to do my chores, and I had lots of them: I washed the dishes, I vacuumed the house, I dusted. I hated the work.

Miriam shook her head. "No, the maid will do that. Just leave everything."

Ruffled spreads covered Miriam's twin beds. Shelves held games and dolls, fancy dress dolls that looked pristine and untouched. A closet stretched along one wall, and a full-length mirror hung beside it like a picture. "Want to see my clothes?" Miriam opened her closet, which was as neat as her room. A whole row of skirts hung side by side, each a different color, and beneath them were ranged pairs and pairs of sneakers. Dark blue, white, lavender, green, beige, gold: a rainbow of Keds. And beside them, another rainbow: an assortment of neat little Pappagallo leather flats like pairs of colored pencils, all stitched in a delicate loafer design, all lined with striped canvas. I gazed at her closet in awe and envy and some astonishment. "You have so much!" I exclaimed.

"Not really. Everybody has this many clothes."

"Not me. I don't." I had three pleated skirts: a gray one, a blue one, and a dark plaid threaded with red squares. I had a straight skirt, too. I rotated the skirts so I didn't wear the same one two days in a row. I had three blouses and three sweaters, and everything went with everything else. I had one pair of white sneakers and one pair of heavy made-in-Maine penny loafers.

"I know." Miriam paused and gazed at me seriously. "Debby," she said, "Debby, you've got to get more clothes. You wear the same things every day. I mean, you're a really nice person, and really smart, and you're really cute, and people really like you, but they make fun of you because of your clothes. You've got to do something about them."

I nodded agreement, too stunned to be angry. "I don't care about clothes. They aren't that important," I lied.

"I didn't mean to hurt your feelings. I'm just telling you for your own good. You're not mad, are you?"

I shook my head. "No." I wasn't mad; I was desolate. Until now, I had imagined that I was going to be all right in Great Neck. But I was nowhere near as sophisticated as these girls. I was not anything like them, nor could I be. For Miriam, clothes were innocent. You wanted them, you bought them. Nobody complained. Your father paid the bill. He wanted you beautiful. Your mother urged you to consider another skirt. It didn't matter. Nothing mattered, except for you and what you wanted. Miriam left the lights on when she walked out of rooms. She floated as lightly as that Chagall bride in her living room, and she never had to sink to inhabit the hovels along the bottom margin. I studied her for the rest of the afternoon, trying to divine her knack for the easy, wishing for the secret of her levitation.

I knew my mother would be late picking me up, and she was. Finally, out of Miriam's window, I saw her car pull up. She honked. I grabbed my jacket and my books and fled into our familiar disarray. Grocery bags filled the back seat. I would have to unload them and put everything away. "I want a pair of Pappagallos," I said.

"Pappagallos? What are they? Doesn't that mean 'parrot' in Italian?"

"Shoes. Everybody has them. I need a pair."

"Oh, you do?" My mother was wearing her espadrilles; the canvas was soaked from the rain.

I burst into tears.

"What's wrong with you?" she asked. "Are you crying like that over a pair of shoes?"

"No!" I yelled, hating myself, lying again. I believed that I really was crying over shoes, not for the hopelessness of my desire.

. . .

I marched down the center aisle of the synagogue in Great Neck with my father and my brother. It felt strange to be part of the audience, but my mother had refused to drive back to Baltimore for the last two days of Succoth. "This is ridiculous. I've just organized this entire move, and I can't possibly make another trip. Four times in a month! If we are living here, then live here and don't run back to Baltimore every time you want to go to shul. I don't understand why you can't stay away for once. This isn't even an important holiday!"

And we had a place to go. We had joined the synagogue so my brother and I could go to Hebrew school. Jonny had to start preparing for his bar mitzvah in a year and a half; I was enrolled in the high school, three times a week. I had never been to services anywhere but Chizuk Amuno, except once in Florence, when my father had taken us on a Friday evening to the Sephardic synagogue, where the miracle of hearing the same Hebrew words rendered all the other differences insignificant. I had felt immense and tiny, a fulfillment of God's blessing on Abraham that his children would multiply like grains of sand. I walked in now with the familiar sense of anticipation. What would happen here would be mysterious and beautiful, and the words and music would tie me to generations of Jews.

The carpet underfoot was thick, and the seats were upholstered. The pale blue plaster walls and white-painted windows resembled the dining room of a colonial restaurant. It was comfortable; everything about Great Neck was comfortable. The choir, draped in black robes, stood off to the side on the bimah. I felt sorry for them; they had no place to go to talk or to read the paper, or to escape the rabbi's sermon. But, I realized, neither did I. I was stuck in my seat. I picked up a prayer book; at least that was the same one we used in Baltimore.

The cantor was a tenor; he had dark hair under his velvet hat. And he whined. Oy, oy, oy, his voice rose in complaining cadence, sharp as a baby's wail. His voice broke in pain, and tumbled, defeated, and rose again. Would God listen to this? There weren't even any tunes to beguile Him. Incredulous, I waited for the cantor to shape up, but he didn't. My inner ears began to sting; my throat ached. I could not recognize anything except the words. The ancient words of praise and supplication twisted into fretful whinnies. God, please, answer these prayers just to get him to shut up. I wanted to stop up my ears to the miserable, repetitive notes and block out the choir's depressing, murky harmonies. I wanted to scream. In my head, I tried to remember our music, but this noise was blotting it out. At this same moment, in our dingy shul, Abba was singing and the choir without my father was doing its best to keep up with him. Didn't this audience know how ugly their music was? Didn't they know what they were missing? Some people hummed along with the choir. I wanted to run away.

Then I heard my father's voice. His baritone cut through the choir and the cantor. He was singing our tunes, our responses to the prayers. I looked up from my prayer book. My father's eyes were closed in pain, but he sang in triumph. I hung on to his song, its clarity and its joy; on to my father's voice I hung the choir's harmonies, filling myself with its sound, breathing to its rhythm. I reveled in our familial subversiveness; I wanted to cheer.

After services, my father took us up to the bimah to meet the rabbi and the cantor. He introduced himself, and the cantor laughed, a bit ruefully, I thought. "Dr. Weisgall," he said. "It's an honor to have you here. I was wondering who that was singing in the audience. What brings you here from Baltimore?"

My father explained. "And my son," he put his hand on Jonny's shoulder, "my son will be bar mitzvah next year." Jonny grinned.

"*Mazel tov*," said the cantor. "I'm sure that we can make some arrangements if your father will be here."

My father nodded and smiled. "Well, it's good to see you. It's been several years, a long time, hasn't it?" The cantor turned to the next person in line, and we stepped down from the bimah and headed outside, ordinary members of the congregation, audience, watching and listening, powerless to affect the service.

As we left, my father pointed to a short, square man ahead of us. "Do you know who that is?" I shook my head, no. "That's Richard Tucker. The opera singer. He lives in Great Neck, too; he trained as a cantor."

"Like Abba."

"But Abba never became an opera singer."

"Why not?" This was the first inkling I had that the connection between cantors and opera did not exist solely within our own family; that my father and grandfather were playing out a musical struggle between a parochial and a secular life that was not unique to them. "Why not?"

"Because your grandmother threatened to go back to Ivančice if he didn't find a steady job." He was growing impatient.

"How did you know the cantor?"

My father shrugged. "I taught him. He went to the Cantors Institute at the seminary."

"You teach all the cantors? Daddy! I didn't know that!"

"All the Conservative cantors. I helped found the Cantors Institute. Why?"

I had not until this moment understood the implications of his days at the seminary. "Why can't you teach them our music, then? Why don't they sing it?"

My father shook his head. "Because they don't want to sing it."

"But once they've heard it, how can they not want to? Don't you even try to convince them?" I thought he was giving up.

He shrugged again, dismissing me and them. "They have their own music that they like to sing. People do what they want to do."

"I'm never going back there," I said.

"Abba will be glad to hear that."

"Why doesn't he move here?"

"What makes you so sure they'd want him? No, I'm afraid we'll have to go to Baltimore." My father stroked my head and smiled sadly. "And what's worst is that they have no idea how ghastly their music is."

My father was no evangelist. If people didn't want his music, he was not interested in changing their minds. He often said that Judaism was not an evangelical religion. It was an exclusionary faith; converting to Judaism was not easy, and even if you were a Jew by birth, it was still difficult to fulfill your obligations.

My father never offered to teach me what he knew—about religion or music, although his books were there for me to read if I wanted. If singing in Abba's synagogue or at the Seder was prayer, then my father did pray, but was he making a connection with God or with his fathers—with history? Maybe he doubted his religious qualifications, since he did not go to shul every Shabbos now that we no longer lived in Baltimore, neither did he insist that my mother keep a kosher home. But despite that, I think he was vulnerable to prayer. There was a part of him, however small, that did believe. He could not explain it or justify it; it was a part of him that history could not dislodge. Faith survived in a stubborn, lyrical place close to his need to make music, and he questioned that, too, almost every day.

. . .

Half-door, hall door,
Hither and thither day and night,
Hill or hollow, shouldering this pack,
Hearing you talk.

Purgatory echoed through the house. My father sang the Boy's part in falsetto, the Old Man's in his own baritone.

Study that house . . .
Stand there and look,
Because there is somebody in that house.
(Falsetto) *There's nobody here.*
(Baritone) *There's somebody there.*

His eyes shone with excitement one night as he came into the dining room for dinner. "These words! Nath, I know what you're going to say—that the audience never hears the words. But, my God, they're marvelous!"

"If the audience never hears them, what does it matter?" asked my mother. She was fussing at the stove. I hated this argument.

"It matters to me," my father answered. "I set the words. After all, Schubert set Goethe."

"A lot of good it did him."

"Nath, sit down, please. What are you doing?"

"I'm just organizing so I won't have so much to do later."

"While you're organizing, everybody else is almost finished."

My mother said over her shoulder: "You should have chosen a comedy."

"It's a little late for that kind of suggestion," said my father, and added, sarcastically: "I'm going to eat, if you don't mind, so at least my dinner isn't cold." He took a bite of brisket. "It's fantastic poetry," he said, maybe to himself, maybe to me. "And who knows if this damned opera will ever get performed."

My mother heard. "Deborah, come here!" she called.

I looked at Daddy for help.

"Your mother's calling," he said. "Go see what she wants."

She wanted me to put a pot in the sink and soak it. I came back to the table, gobbled the rest of dinner, and began to clear the plates. Jonny had already disappeared. We didn't have a dishwasher; my mother thought you might as well wash the dishes if you had to rinse them before you stacked them in the machine. She finally came to the table; she chewed slowly and methodically cleared her plate. As soon as she finished, I grabbed her plate and swabbed it clean and went up to my room to do homework. I was tired; I was always tired. I stayed up too late reading and listening to music. Downstairs, I heard my parents talking, back and forth, voices cutting into one another, on the verge of argument. I closed my door and moved my radio to the center of the rug. The radio was plastic, turquoise and cream, and portable, with the antenna built into the swivel handle. In Maine, at night sometimes Jonny picked up the Baltimore station that carried the Orioles' games. Here in New York, I listened to classical music on WQXR.

When my father was not home, I sat under the piano, where we kept our record player, and played Mozart's symphonies, and Brahms and Beethoven. When he was in the house, I took the radio and turned it to a whisper, keeping the sounds to myself. Music laid me bare, and I dreaded being caught. My emotions incensed my parents. "Stop being such a Sarah Bernhardt!" my mother shouted if I seemed too happy, or too sad. Mittens, on the prowl, slithered into my room. He crouched just out of reach: with me, but on his own terms. I took out my books and drew the gold curtains across my window. My room could have been a chamber in a castle. The rug picked up the deep yellow of the curtains, and the curved woodwork of my French armchair echoed its arabesques.

I sat on the floor and opened to my algebra homework. I stared at the parentheses and x's and y's. I turned on the radio. Piano music. Eighth notes in the bass, low sounds lapping like waves, a rumble like far-off thunder, and then a long, slowly lilting melody. It played right through into my heart; it transfixed me; I could barely breathe. I listened for a few moments and then grabbed the radio by its handle and raced downstairs into my father's piano room. He sat frowning at a manuscript page with a pencil, eraser end up, poised over a measure. "Daddy! Daddy! What is this? Listen!" I set the radio down on the side of the music stand and turned up the volume. The theme repeated, higher. My father put down his pencil. He nodded. "So," he said, tenderly.

"This is the most beautiful thing I've ever heard." I regretted saying that; he hated when I used superlatives.

But he didn't contradict me. "It's Schubert, the B-flat Sonata." He turned the volume higher until the notes of the piano rang tinny against the small speakers. It didn't matter. "*Meine tochter,*" he said and covered my hand where it rested on the radio handle with his. We listened, and he gazed at me with a sad half-smile until I lowered my eyes; I couldn't bear to watch him any longer, to see such pain and pleasure merged. "Sometimes I think the slow movement is even more beautiful," my father said. "Schubert wrote this just two or three months before he died. He never heard it performed."

"How old was he?"

"Thirty-two." He shook his head.

The movement began. My father closed his eyes. After a moment, he said: "Deborah, take it away. I can't bear to hear this."

I tiptoed upstairs, carrying the precious sound back to my room. A few days later as I was rummaging in the pile of records beside the record player we kept under the piano, I found a recording of the Schubert sonata, played by Arthur Schnabel, along with another new record, of Schubert's C Major Quintet.

"Did you get these for me?" I asked my father that night.

But he had retreated. "I thought we needed them," he said.

. . .

Beat! Beat!
This night is the anniversary
Of my mother's wedding night,
Or of the night wherein I was begotten.
My father is riding from the public-house,
A whiskey-bottle under his arm.

My father sang and banged hoofbeats on the piano. I stood at the doorway to the living room. In my outstretched arm, I held one of our silver candlesticks. "There. That's your cue, Deborah," John Scrymgeour said, "those hoofbeats in the orchestra. That's where you come in."

Purgatory was finished. It was going to be performed, at the Library of Congress. And I was in it. My father had given me a part; I was the Old Man's mother, who died giving birth to him. Actually, I was her ghost, a soul in purgatory condemned to reenact her sin over and over. It was, of course, a silent role. I was fourteen; the apparition I was playing was supposed to be seventeen or eighteen. "Dressed up, you'll look that old," John, who had directed my father's operas at Hilltop, reassured me. He was directing *Purgatory,* and he had designed the opera's sets. He was building them, too, with my mother's help, in the garage.

"You'd think that after a certain point you wouldn't have to do everything yourself." Daddy shook his head over the stack of lumber when it was delivered. "I shouldn't have had a family. If I hadn't had a family, it would have been easier." Nine or ten slabs of plywood, about a foot wide and eight feet long, they were supposed to represent the lightning-struck tree and the burned-out house where the play takes place. After we rehearsed on this cold January afternoon, we were going to paint them black with gray streaks. John had figured out a system of slots and braces so they fit together. They also fit into the back of our station wagon, so that we could drive them down to Washington for the performance. This was bare-bones opera, which is why I was in it. I was free.

The play's stage directions listed only one ghost, but in the opera there were two: me, the mother; and the drunken groom from a racing stable, her husband. I hadn't met him yet. He was a Juilliard student. John Scrymgeour had told me that he was tall and handsome. My father came in from his piano room and sat down.

"Now, Deborah." John, slender and small, danced like a sprite across the rug. "You cross the stage, holding the candle. Walk like a dancer, you know how they walk." I didn't. "Here, like this, toe first, then heel." He took the candlestick from me and, holding it shoulder high, stepped through the living room.

I tried.

"Deborah, you're watching for your lover. You're wildly excited, but you know what your parents think of him. You feel dirty; it's as if you're wearing dirty underwear." He smiled wicked encouragement; his blue eyes, enormous behind thick glasses, glittered.

I turned bright red. I thought dirty underwear was disgusting, leaked blood, or worse. My eyes flicked over to my father, but his face showed nothing. I understood why he put me in this role; it was both reward and punishment for being pretty. Like Sleeping Beauty, I should have fallen into a coma the instant I grew up.

"Do you understand?" John asked.

I nodded, but I did not understand. I concentrated on my feet. Toe, heel, toe, heel. I held the candlestick high and looked straight ahead, imagining love. But it was not supposed to be love. Desire, then, but I could not imagine desire dirty. Fierce. Almost hopeless, yes, but still bright, like a childhood dream: while I slept, I rescued a wounded prince and laid his head in my lap. Desire flowered in darkness and lit the night with a dream of a happy ending.

"That's better. Lean forward a bit more. For the performance we'll get you a candelabra," John said. "And a wedding dress."

A week later we rehearsed in a practice room at Juilliard, at the corner of Broadway and 122nd Street, just a block away from the Jewish Theological Seminary. The room had a scuffed piano, gray walls, gray floor, a heavy, soundproof door. The singers, the Boy and the Old Man, stood in the center of the floor. John Scrymgeour and my father had folding metal chairs. I sat beside my father and watched the door for the arrival of the person who was going to be the other ghost. The singers went through their parts; John darted around them and pulled them into different postures; my father interrupted them on musical issues.

My father asked questions—"How would it sound if you sang more softly there? Or make the crescendo earlier?"—and he listened intently for the singer's experiment. "What do you think?" he asked them and the accompanist, and he considered their answers. Sometimes he took their suggestions; sometimes he didn't. It was not at all the process he described to my mother over dinner. At home, he castigated singers, he talked only of battles that remained unresolved. But this was nothing like that. He was completely engaged; he sat forward on his chair. The score lay opened across his knees; he conducted with his right hand, graceful, precise gestures, and the singers paid close attention. My father breathed with their phrasing; he shaped the words as they sang.

I had seen him like this; I had memories of this from Hilltop; it was a memory of sensation more than of sight or sound. I remembered the atmosphere, dry and still, purpose sparking like heat lightning. John Scrymgeour had been there, too; then, my mother had taken the silent role. Now I sat and watched this collaboration jealously. This was what I desired more than anything: this passionate engagement, this excited interest and charged courtesy.

The latch of the soundproof door clicked; the door opened, and a young man walked in. The singers stopped. "Hello, Malcolm," John said and smiled fondly. The young man was tall, sturdy, his longish brown hair arched back from his forehead, his dark blue eyes scanned all of us. He was going to be my husband, the groom in a training stable.

> *Looked at him and married him,*
> *And he squandered everything she had.*
> *She never knew the worst, because*
> *She died in giving birth to me,*
> *But now she knows it all, being dead.*

That's what I was supposed to have done. I looked at this person, and I wasn't sure what I thought of him. My father nodded perfunctorily. "This is my daughter," he said, in a deep, foreboding voice. The baritone playing the Old Man laughed. "And stay away!" he rumbled. My father glared.

John's quick, nervous eyes darted from the singers to my father. "Since we're here, why don't we go over these entrances.

Malcolm, Deborah enters stage right. You enter stage left when I cue you."

"*Beat! Beat!*" the singer sang. I began walking, holding an imaginary candelabra.

"Here." John thrust an umbrella into my hand.

"*Look at the window; she stands there listening,*" the Old Man sang.

"Stop," John said quietly. "Stop there, after thirteen paces. Turn your head. Listen. Listen."

"*There's nothing but an empty gap in the wall,*" the Boy sang. "*You have made it up. No, you are mad!*"

The Old Man:

> *This night she is no better than her man,*
> *And does not mind that he is half drunk,*
> *She is mad about him. They mount the stairs,*
> *She brings him into her own chamber.*
> *And that is the marriage chamber now.*
> *The window is dimly lit again.*

"Malcolm," said John. "You're onstage. Come here." Malcolm approached. "Now, look at her. You'll both be behind a scrim, but the audience will still be able to see your face. Face her. Look at her. You're not too steady on your feet. Now, slowly, raise your hand, slowly."

"*Do not let him touch you!*" The Old Man's voice tore through the room. A slow, agonized, descending line, five notes of equal duration. The Old Man sang, and my father sang with him. Six words, plain on the page: *Do not let him touch you!*

"Malcolm, reach for her now. Just after that line. That's right. Put your hand around her waist. Go ahead, don't be delicate. You're drunk and you want her."

Malcolm touched me, tentatively. I shivered and glanced at my father, but he was concentrating on the score.

> *Deaf! Both deaf! If I should throw*
> *A stick or a stone they would not hear;*
> *And that's a proof my wits are out.*
> *But there's a problem: she must live*
> *Through everything in exact detail,*
> *Driven to it by remorse, and yet*
> *Can she renew the sexual act*
> *And find no pleasure in it, and if not,*
> *If pleasure and remorse must both be there,*
> *Which is the greater?*

The Old Man ranged from anger to despair, to yearning, to that final detached, defensive musing. I had heard this aria a million times in fragments, splintered phrases, a line or two, sometimes only a phrase. I heard the words like music, not with particular significance but with emotional meaning. I did not, in a detached way, understand them. I did not understand not finding pleasure, but the Old Man's grief—and his musing threat—vibrated in every note.

"This is when you embrace her. Malcolm, you grab her waist and bend her backwards. Deborah, you hold on to the candelabra." I held the umbrella aloft.

"Is it going to be lit?" I asked.

John laughed. "It should be."

"Just don't burn the theater down," my father said.

"Okay, let's give it a try." John nodded to the accompanist. "*Deaf!*"

Malcolm caught my waist and arched over me. With my free hand I clutched at his shoulder.

"Yes! Yes!" whispered John.

"*If I should throw a stick or a stone . . .*"

With his left hand, Malcolm supported my shoulders.

"Now kiss her."

Malcolm bent his head over mine, his lips close. I quivered from their little current of electricity, and I felt my face redden with pleasure, and with shame. My father was watching, watching me arch backwards under this man, watching this man take the weight of my body in his arms

"Perfect." John purred his commentary under the music. "Now, hold it. Deborah, try to keep the candelabra steady. I know, it's just my umbrella. Practice, though. That's better. Find a comfortable place. Not too low. Good, good."

"*Those two lie upon the mattress begetting me.*" The Old Man spit out the words.

"That's when the lights start to fade."

Malcolm helped me straighten up. My father walked away and bent over the score with the Old Man and the accompanist. Malcolm stood beside me. "Your father wrote this?" he asked. He had a deep, silky voice.

"Yes," I answered proudly, leaning on the umbrella.

"It's interesting," he said.

"Have you read it?"

"Have you?"

"Of course. I think I know it by heart."

"How old are you?"

"Fourteen," I answered, wishing I could lie when it would do me some good.

"You looked older." His voice lost some of its silk.

"I know."

. . .

I pulled on my wedding dress in the ladies' room of the Elizabeth Sprague Coolidge Auditorium at the Library of Congress. It was heavy satin, with a wide skirt supported by stiff petticoats and a low bodice. It was not very clean; the hem was black where it had brushed the floor during countless performances. It came from a costume shop; John Scrymgeour was pleased that it had turned up, even though my mother had to sew a new series of hooks so that it would fit my narrow back. The performance was going to begin in an hour. I crossed the hall to the door leading backstage, to a corridor lit by gray fluorescent lights. I peered through the black curtain. John was fussing with the sets. Abstract and eerie, they stalked the length of the stage, a cross between telephone poles and Stonehenge.

Malcolm appeared beside me dressed in a loose white shirt and vest, breeches and riding boots. "I've been looking for you," he said. "We have to turn into ghosts. This is for you." He held out a stick of white makeup.

There was a mirror in a back corner. I stroked the greasy stick over my cheeks, as close around my eyes as I dared, on my nose, my chin, down under my jaw. "How's this?"

Malcolm considered me. Gingerly he reached out and rubbed my temples where the makeup hadn't reached, and he dabbed more on my eyelids. "You have great eyebrows," he said.

I loved standing close to him.

"Now." He hesitated. "You need more here." He took the white stick and quickly rolled it across my bare chest. It rose and fell over the swell of the top of my breasts. I flinched.

"I'm sorry," he said. He had blushed beneath his ghost white. "Here," he handed me the makeup. "Put this on your neck and under your chin." He stamped away in his heavy boots.

"Where are you going?" I called after him, but he had disappeared.

I prowled backstage. John hurried past and nodded. "I'll bring your candelabra in just a minute."

Through the curtain I could hear the audience arriving. At least some people would be there; I had been worried that we would be playing to an empty theater.

I turned around and saw my father. He stared at me for a moment, as if I were indeed a ghost. "Deborah!" he exclaimed. "Deborah! I didn't recognize you. You look so grown up! Like a bride." He kept his distance. He stared. I dared not say anything.

"Well." He cleared his throat. "I'm looking for John. Have you seen him?"

"He was onstage." My voice sounded pinched and high. A child's voice; didn't he hear that? My head buzzed, I breathed shallowly, I stepped over electrical wires, afraid of falling. I retreated to my spot in the wings. The orchestra sounded its A.

Malcolm appeared beside me and squeezed my shoulder. "So," he smiled. "Here goes. Break a leg. See you in your bedroom!"

Half-door, hall door. The music raced by, dark as night, relentless. *Beat! Beat!* I grasped my candelabra, unlit—flames were too dangerous—and counted steps. Slowly, toe first, into the cold draft of the stage, blue white behind my scrim. One, two, three. Thirteen steps. I waited. He appeared, large, breathing heavily, rocking on his heels. *Do not let him touch you!* He embraced me and bent over me. I reached up and met his mouth with my open mouth. I felt him shiver and start to recoil, but I had him. He was helpless to do anything but kiss me, kiss me for measures and measures, for an entire aria. I tasted his mouth with my tongue. It was sweet, and he smelled powdery and white. I understood: this is what women do. I kissed him and did not count, knowing by heart how long it would last.

. . .

After the opera, my father spent extra hours teaching, making up for the time he had missed in rehearsal. The reviews had been predictable and uncomprehending—bad. He cast around for the text of his next opera, but he found it hard to muster enthusiasm. My mother argued with his choices. She complained about the drips of paint from the sets we'd left on the concrete floor of the garage. *Purgatory* had happened, but, once again, nothing was different. My parents were disappointed and depressed. They existed on faith in miraculous change, in events that would lift them from drudgery into a state in which everything was new and gilded, in which even the light was always dramatic, golden, heightened.

Their voices rumbled late at night through their half-closed bedroom door, low growls against white, sibilant whispers. At night, their voices were interchangeable. I lay awake stiff and listening. They held each other responsible for their expectations and disappointments. Even in this big New York house, I heard them through the thick walls, misery resonating in rooms built for comfort. I played the radio and blocked out their noise. I spent hours on the telephone talking my way into my friends' lives.

During these weeks of late winter, the sky stayed gray and low. Icy mist crystallized in the damp air. It clung to limp rhododendron leaves, to withered azaleas; it coated the brown oak leaves rotting against the foundation of our house. It entered the house and rimed the inner panes of my bedroom windows with frosty crescents before I woke up on a Sunday morning. I lay in bed under the thick comforter, *persinka,* my mother called it, that she had brought back from Prague. It was covered in cotton printed in a paisley pattern. I contemplated the stylized leaves and listened. I mistrusted silence; it was like the stillness before a thunderstorm.

My father was already in his upstairs office; I heard him pacing, opening cabinets and pulling out boxes. I missed his noise of composition, his piano banging through the house, his voice singing all the parts, worrying the notes until they achieved the precise tension between lyricism and dissonance. Silent, he was not himself. I dressed and hurried downstairs, late for Hebrew school. My parents' bedroom was still dark, I could see through the half-open door. Jonny was downstairs in the basement watching television. I called him and called my mother. No answer. I called again, and heard the bedsprings creak. "We're late! You have to take us!" I called.

She came downstairs, bleary-eyed, her nose red, her hair pulled back messily into a barrette. She started the car. It spewed frosty white exhaust into the chill air. "I don't know why you can't walk," she said.

Neither of us answered. She was late picking us up, too. We waited at the curb. We didn't talk to each other, except to ask, "Why isn't she coming?" Jonny's bar mitzvah was approaching. Abba had made tapes for him so that he could learn the chant and the blessings. My father was teaching him. Cold seeped through the soles of my shoes. Finally, our mother showed up, speeding around the corner, looking distracted and frazzled. We complained about waiting and about the cold. "I had so much to do!" she retorted. "So much."

"Even on Sunday?"

"Picking you up just had to wait." When we got home, I saw that all the breakfast dishes still littered the table; she had been waiting for me to clean up.

That afternoon, silence swaddled the house, dense like inimical fog. I sat on my bedroom floor in the gray light, a blanket around my shoulders, doing homework; my room was always cold, and my parents would not turn up the heat. I stared at my geometry book; geometry was visual and elegant, and each proof unfolded like a mystery story, but this afternoon, I could not focus. I listened to the quiet. From the basement, I heard faint rumbles from the television. I did not know where my mother was, perhaps on the chaise longue in their bedroom, reading one of the books that she could make last for months. My father stayed in the back room.

I thought to go talk to him, even, I imagined, to comfort him. Jonny wouldn't come upstairs; my mother might be too absorbed in her book to interrupt us. I pushed open the door, which was slightly ajar. My mother hated closed doors. When I tried to close mine, she came along and opened it.

My father was at his desk reading. A fluorescent lamp aimed cold light on the lined page, light as bleak as the gray afternoon. "Hi," I said.

He looked up, startled, and laid his arm across the notebook he was reading. Notebooks were piled on his desk, lots of them, composition books with black and white mottled cardboard covers, older notebooks with green covers. Underneath his forearm, I recognized his crabbed, angular handwriting, lines and lines of writing.

"What are you reading?" I asked.

"A journal. A diary. I kept a diary all my life, until after the war, until your mother came to Prague."

"And I was born."

"And you were born." He said that with an edge of irony I did not understand.

"Did you keep them when you were my age?"

He nodded.

"Can I see them? Can I see your diaries?"

"No."

"Why not?"

"Because there are things I don't want you to see. I don't want anybody to see them. There are things that are too difficult."

The photographs, I thought, the awful photographs. That was what he wrote about. "What kinds of things?" I dared ask.

"Nothing. Nothing that I can tell you. I'm giving them away. I'm giving them to the Library of Congress, my papers and my manuscripts. Nobody will be able to look at them until after I'm dead. And I'll get a tax deduction." There was bitter satisfaction in his voice.

"That's not fair," I protested. He was slamming a door, locking me out.

He shrugged. "It's not a question of fair." He looked at me. He took off his glasses and rubbed his eyes. His blue eyes looked startled in the flat light.

"Has Mother read them?" I asked jealously.

"Your mother?" He shook his head. "No." He shook his head again. "No. She hasn't read them. She wouldn't have any interest in reading them." He looked up, and his eyes were wide and angry. "That's why I'm giving them away." His voice, though, was quiet; I thought he was shielding her. "Come here, Deborah," he said, in that odd, gentle, intense tone. I took a step closer. "Your mother," he went on, "your mother. Do you know what she is?"

Suddenly terrified, I backed away a step.

"Do you know? Do you want me to tell you?"

I waited for his answer.

"She is a whore. Your mother was unfaithful to me during the war, while I was away. She had an affair, an affair with some doctor. And she told me. She told me about it. I will never forgive her for that; I will never forgive her for telling." He kept his eyes on my face. They blazed with nurtured fury.

I hated her; I hated her for what she had done, and for what she had led my father to expect from me.

Then he looked away. He hid his face in his hands. I walked out of the room and carefully left the door open.

. . .

Dodi li va'ani lo. "My love is mine, and I am his, who grazes among the lilies." I knew a melody for those words from the Song of Songs, an Israeli melody, sensuous and undulating. I hummed it, and then I opened my mouth and sang it low, imagining myself dark, sunburned and black-haired, and my lover with his belly of ivory, his legs like marble pillars, his raven black curls. I read the Song of Songs in English; I read it in Hebrew, puzzling out the meaning of the words. I prayed that it really was about earthly love and not, as I had been told in Hebrew school, a metaphor for God's love for Israel. I read it in secret. I tasted its words like kisses. It celebrated what I desired and must not want. "O daughters of Jerusalem! If you meet my beloved, tell him this: That I am faint with love." Lust was betrayal, but this voice was not ashamed. "His left hand is under my head, and his right hand embraces me."

On Yom Kippur, before the memorial service, there is a section of the prayer book devoted to Jewish martyrs, recounting the stories of those who were killed for their faith. Children whose parents were living used to leave the synagogue during the memorial service; remaining brought bad luck and meant their parents might die. But my father, scoffing at superstition, always made us stay. We listened to the stories. The rabbi who recited the Shema while he was flayed, the rabbi who was wrapped in the parchment of the Torah and set on fire. "The letters," he cried to his weeping disciples as the flames consumed him, "the letters are flying free! The parchment is burning, but the letters are flying free!" Jewish virgins who refused to convert and were condemned to death by being dragged behind galloping horses. They fastened their skirts to their legs with iron pins rather than expose themselves. What was the greater virtue, I wondered, fearing the answer: that these girls kept their faith or that they preserved their modesty?

Eleven

Experience

I was sixteen. While most Great Neck adolescents were sent to socially responsible summer work camps or arts or language camps, I continued to go with my parents to Maine. My mother and father did not have (or did not want to have) money to spend for my summer excursions, but, much as I longed for freedom, I could not picture summer apart from Maine; it would be too painful to imagine what I might be missing.

In the summertime I burned with potential. Returning to Maine, to its perpetual summer, finding in the emptiness of the house the relics of myself I had left behind the previous September, I compared them to the person I had become. I found myself stronger, smarter, and the summer stretched empty and full of possibility. But as days passed, I began to hate how slothful I was. I read, I dreamed, I swam, I cleaned the house. I thought about trying to get a job in a gift shop, but my mother refused to promise to drive me the seven miles into Camden every day; it would have been unbearable for her if I managed to escape. "I have too much else to do," she told me.

"Why don't you start painting again?" Too much to do, she answered, but there was only room for one artist in our house. Her errands sustained her. While she shopped for vegetables or whatever it was she passed her hours choosing as she waited for the laundry at the laundromat, I prowled the shopping streets of Camden, all three of them. Jonny and I started at the Village Shop, where we studied shelves of colored pencils, watercolors, and pads of drawing paper.

Next we haunted The Smiling Cow, a gift shop built over the waterfall where the Megunticook River emptied into Camden harbor. We
sniffed muslin pillows stuffed with balsam pine needles, toyed with
key chains in the shape of maps of Maine, and coveted kits for making plastic models of airplanes. When we tired of desiring, we hung
over the balcony, suspended in the waterfall's foam and white noise.

These places still lured Jonny, but this summer I quickly grew
impatient; I was pulled outside. I wanted to see who was passing; I
wanted to be seen. I felt eyes on me, eyes bright as sunlight glinting
off my smooth surface. I longed to fly into admiring eyes and become unglued in their heat.

· · ·

Abba stepped off the Greyhound bus in Camden. He wore his city
clothes, his suit, hat, and shoes, but he carried his country cane, the
one with his intertwining initials carved into the crook of the horn
handle. The bus stopped in the middle of Main Street, halting north-
bound traffic on Route 1. Abba raised his cane, saluting us as my
mother, Jonny, and I waited on the sidewalk in front of the Village Shop. The driver opened the hold; he extricated Abba's scuffed
leather suitcase and placed it gently on the curb. "Thank you very
much, sir," Abba said as he shook the driver's hand.

"Thank you, sir," the driver replied. "It was a pleasure. Have a
great vacation. I hope I catch you on the way back." Abba had this
effect on people; he made everybody revere him.

He visited every summer for two weeks. He came in August;
every year he fasted on the Ninth of Ab, the anniversary of the destruction of the temple in Jerusalem in 70 A.D. He slept on a sofa bed
in my father's piano room; he hung his clothes on hangers hooked
over door knobs and piled books—his mysteries and his prayer
books—on my father's writing table. He awakened early and went
to sleep late. After breakfast he marched west along the road, toward
the land that he and Freddie and my father had bought together a
year or so earlier: a hundred and fifty acres of blueberry barren and

second-growth forest on the slopes of Levensellar Mountain, about a mile from our house. He picked blueberries in the hot sun. He walked in the woods behind our house, where we rarely went, using his cane to push aside the underbrush. He knew our land better than we did. One day he discovered an enormous, battered pine, a vestige of the ancient forest. We all, even my mother, who hated to walk and jumped at the rustle of branches and leaves against her calves, followed him back where we had never gone before. The five of us barely encircled its trunk with our outstretched arms.

The new land included half the shoreline of Levensellar Pond, just below the mountain, but the road skirted the water, and there wasn't much room to do anything besides park the car and go for a swim, which I didn't like to do there. "Why don't you want to go to Levensellar?" my mother asked me several times a summer.

"Because there are bloodsuckers," I answered. There were leeches in Lake Megunticook, too, but there were also other people. But we went to Levensellar with Abba, and we went to the ocean, too. Abba possessed a child's immunity to cold. He waded into the frigid bay at Lincolnville Beach without hesitating and, with water sleeking off his white hair, he paddled happily toward Islesboro. While my father worked, my mother took Abba where he wanted to go.

He had a nose for Jews. He found the Jewish hotel owner, the Jewish bookseller. Abba assumed that the whole world was Jewish. If he suspected, he asked. He was hardly naive; he was, instead, willfully optimistic. He embarrassed my mother and delighted Jonny and me. He bought a nineteenth-century fish chopper from a Jewish antique dealer. My mother cleaned it for him and took him to the fish market, and Abba produced gefilte fish, to my father's horror. My father could not abide the smell or taste of fish; even feeding the cat was torture. After the manufacture of gefilte fish, our kitchen reeked for a week.

Abba picked bushels of ripening, wormy apples from the trees remaining in the decaying orchard that surrounded the house and, with my mother, cut them up and boiled them down into applesauce.

He exhausted her. He taught Jonny gin rummy and sat outside with
him at our white metal table for entire afternoons playing cards.

· ·

In Maine my bedroom window faced east. Morning light threw a
shadow grid of parallelograms from the window panes against the
blue cotton curtains, and when I awoke I could tell by the light's in-
tensity whether the day was bright or cloudy. This morning it was
bright. I had slept as long as I could. It was a Saturday, not that it
made any difference. I parted the thin curtains. In the shade of the
old cedars beside the house, the dew had not yet dried, and little
canopies of gossamer glimmered over the grass. The eastern sky
above the whale-shaped ridge of Mt. Megunticook shone white with
reflected sunlight, and a light breeze from the east blew the smell of
hay into my bedroom. I let the rectangles of sun heat my body as I
stood at the window, paralyzed by love.

   If I stayed still, time would stay still, too, and I would not have
to wait for the phone to ring; I would not have to dread its silence. I
had known him only slightly more than a week. I knew some of the
musicians who summered here, studying and living in apartments
in Camden. I had met them on my own, in the mysterious way of
connecting that people have. Olivier—he had been born in France
to a Jewish father and a Protestant mother—was a pianist studying
at the Curtis Institute, where my father had also studied. He was in
Maine to visit friends and take a lesson or two from his teacher. Not
that he needed lessons; his was a rare talent, and everybody knew it,
as did he. Lessons served to connect him to ordinariness. His ability
frightened him. He regarded it as not belonging to him, but as some
quality that had become attached to him almost against his will, and
he carried himself like the arbitrary vessel containing that gift. He
was afraid of cracking. He was nineteen and he had lived alone for
three years, since he was my age.

   His skin stayed white from the hours he spent indoors practicing; it was not sickly but glowing and dense like alabaster. He was
tall and thin. His eyes were blue green, wide set, and their expres-

sion alternated between bemused and baffled; his hair was thick and dark blond. He spoke in a soft voice, as if he were always telling secrets, and he enunciated each vowel and consonant precisely in a slightly foreign way; listening to myself in duet with him, I found my speech sloppy and slurred, American.

I had heard—and watched—him play. It was in the assembly room of the Congregational church in Camden, as he rehearsed for a concert he was giving on Sunday afternoon; that would be tomorrow, I remembered, and after that he would go back to New York for a week to see his parents, who were arriving from Paris. Olivier sat at the piano and looked at his hands; he held them outstretched over the keyboard as if he were not sure what they would do when he set them loose. His expression lost self-consciousness. His mouth, his thin, curving lips, opened; his eyes softened and closed, then opened again; and he leaned toward the keys, preparing to embrace the music.

He played the first measures—it was a dance by Schubert. I caught my breath. He played the waltz rhythm in the bass and the singing melody in the right hand; touching the keys and listening to their response, then answering back with his fingers. I fell in love right there, quick as the waltz, watching him love the music.

He had to call. I prayed that he would call. Probably later, probably he got up late. But he was so busy; he had so little time to spare from practicing, and I had nothing at all to do. The screen door banged, and Abba walked down the fieldstone path from the back door, a path disappearing under lush crabgrass, to the row of cedars. He carried a prayer book, and a tallit was draped across his shoulders. He sat on a folding canvas chair under the trees. A shaft of light gleamed in his white hair. Mittens, belly low to the ground, stalked the fringes of Abba's tallit and pounced, trapping himself in the white silk threads. Abba untangled him. He sat with his back to the house, in full view of Route 173, and he prayed, as he did every morning. He never asked us to join him, not even my father. There was something about the way he was sitting, facing away from us, facing east toward Jerusalem, that made me feel I was intruding even by standing at my window and watching. I wondered what the people driving by in their pickup trucks thought of my grandfather under the tree.

The house was quiet; there were no voices coming from the dining room. It was safe to go down. I passed the phone on the chest by the stairs. It sat black and dumb; it would never ring again. The table, littered with breakfast dishes, crumbs, knives caked with jam, a softening stick of butter, a wedge of cheese oozing to the edges of its tinfoil, awaited me. I made toast and poured a glass of orange juice and pushed away a plate to make space for myself on the side of the table nearest the phone. A residue of anger had settled in the room like dust; I awoke to it every morning. It belonged to my parents, but I took the blame for it. Cleaning up was my job.

The door to my father's piano room was shut. I heard a ripple of notes; he began work as soon as Abba cleared out; even on Shabbos this summer. He had another commission, an opera based on Racine's play *Athalia,* about a biblical queen. My mother was probably in the shed, off the dining room, where the farmer from whom they'd bought the house had kept his cows. My parents had rebuilt it into a big summer living room. I had no idea where Jonny was. I hoped nobody would disturb me yet. It was just ten. Either Olivier would call now, or it would be too late.

The phone rang. Its electric trill coursed through my body. It rang again. I didn't dare get up. What if it wasn't Olivier? It rang a third time. I looked at it. "Who's going to get that?" my father yelled.

"I will!" I shouted back and lunged for the telephone. "Hello!" I panted as if I had been running.

"Deborah?" Yes. Olivier. He pronounced each vowel in my name, and lingered over the last "a" as if it had no "h" at the end.

"Yes," I said.

"What are you doing this evening?"

"I don't know."

"Can I see you? I can pick you up about 7:30."

"Let me check." I put the phone down and ran into the shed. My mother, still in her bathrobe, was sitting on a bench beside the window, reading yesterday's newspaper. "Can I go out tonight?" I asked breathlessly.

"Good morning," she answered. "Aren't you going to say good morning?"

"Good morning. Can I?"

She shrugged. "Ask your father."

I opened the door to the piano room. "Can I go out tonight?"

"Your grandfather's here." My father didn't turn around.

"He's been here for a week. He's staying for another week."

He crashed a discord and glared at me. "I don't give a damn what you do."

"It isn't 'til after supper," I protested. "Shabbos will be over."

He kept playing. I closed the door.

. . .

In the late afternoon, I took a shower and washed my hair. Usually in the summer, I just let it dry and pulled my curls back into a tight ponytail. This time, though, I set it on big rollers and sat on my bed under the plastic bonnet of my hair dryer. When I emerged from inside its hurricane to test for dryness, I heard my mother clattering pots in the kitchen, and I prayed she wouldn't be angry at me for not being there to help.

But she said nothing when I came downstairs, my hair still in rollers.

"What are you doing that for?" Jonny asked.

"I just feel like it," I answered, furious.

"Leave your sister alone," my mother said.

Without being asked, I helped her serve. This evening, she lingered over the stove even longer than usual. "Nathalie, sit down," Abba demanded.

"Yes, Nath, please," my father echoed.

"Why should I sit down when I'll just have to jump up again?"

I ate as fast as I could and began to clear the plates. "I'll do that," my mother said, astonishing me. As I hurried upstairs to get dressed, my father got up from the table and went into his piano room and started to play. I stood on the landing to listen. He began the "Wanderers Nachtlied," with its peaceful, heartbreaking, slow opening chords. He sang the repeated notes of the song's first line: "*Peace hangs over all the mountain tops.*" Through my bedroom window a thin white edge of light glowed over Megunticook's ridge. The day's wind had died; just a cool breath entered the window. A star came out. I wished on it, speaking the wishing formula silently.

"*The birds call in the woods,*" my father sang, and then my grandfather's voice joined his on the aching, arching last lines. "*Only wait, only wait, soon you, too, will have peace.*" They sang at the tops of their voices, and my father yielded and let my grandfather carry the melody while he sang an octave lower, echoing the contrary motion of the bass line.

In the silence after the song, a dish crashed.

"What happened?" my father called.

"Nothing, nothing." I heard the anger in my mother's voice.

"Do you need help?"

"No!" she shouted.

He began the song again, and Abba sang it through. I brushed my hair out, admiring for a moment the way it refracted light from the lamp on my dresser, and crept downstairs to turn on the outside light for Olivier. As I came back into the kitchen, my mother looked up. "Don't you look gorgeous!" she exclaimed. She smiled at me in a sly and crooked way, jealousy and admiration mixed.

I turned away and stood in the doorway to listen. A few minutes later, I heard her go upstairs. My father was playing from memory; only his loose-leaf notebook of manuscript paper occupied the rack. Abba stood at the piano beside him, straight and glorious, his shoulders back, his chest out. His tenor reverberated throughout the room; I felt it vibrate through the soles of my feet. "*Warte nur, warte nur . . .*" he sang. "Only wait." He held the high note. He was in his eighties, but his voice remained as strong as a young man's.

They turned on the standing lamp by the piano and got out the book of Schubert songs and turned to *Erlkönig*. "Opus 1," said my father. "What a debut." He began the triplets thundering like horse's hooves and the ominous ascending scale of the stalking Elf King. He made mistakes, but filled in with his own invention. They divided the song. Abba, the tenor, began, setting the scene, and he sang the child and the seducing Erlkönig, the voice of death; my father took the father's part, galloping with his terrified child in his arms, trying to outrun fate. They sang with all their hearts; they knew the words from memory; they had, both of them, grown up on this. Their voices, their heat, filled the room; their noise battered me. My father pounded the last, slow, hopeless chords.

Olivier stood beside me. I jumped. "I'm sorry," he said. "I knocked, but . . ."

At the sound of his soft, unfamiliar voice, my father swiveled on his piano chair. "Who are you?" he demanded.

"This is Olivier, Daddy. Olivier, this is my father and my grand-father." I heard my own voice, wavering and weak.

"Olivier who?" my father said.

"Olivier Franck."

"Are you Jewish?" Abba scowled.

Olivier smiled. "My father is. I don't know if I am or not."

"Let's go," I said, blushing, anxious and ashamed.

"I liked your singing very much," Olivier said quietly. "I would love to hear more."

"I don't perform on demand," announced my father and started to close the song book.

"What if I played?"

"You can?"

Olivier nodded. He crossed to the piano. "I'll play. Then you can sing. I like to sight read." He looked down at my father, and my father considered him, suspiciously at first, then his look became challenging. And doubt appeared, too: self-doubt. My father knew he was no pianist. He got up and at the same time protectively folded his notebook closed.

Olivier sat down. He played a scale, rippling from the bottom of the piano to the top. The notes shimmered like wind on the surface of water. "Ah," said my father. His tone had completely changed; he was eager and curious.

"What would you like to sing?" Olivier asked.

My father picked up the book and flipped through the pages. "Try this," he said. "I never could play it myself. Believe me, it's not easy. But it's absolutely gorgeous. Now I just hope I can sing it."

He put the book down on the music rack and spread the pages open. "Auf dem Wasser zu singen," the song was. I did not know it. Something about water and singing. Olivier sat at the piano. I stood behind him, afraid to get too close. The lamp lit the white down on his cheekbones and his long, straight eyelashes. He was wearing a shirt with the cuffs unbuttoned, and his hair was still wet and ridged with comb marks. He pushed up his sleeves, and he peered at the score and tried fitting two or three chords under his hands. I studied the tendons in his tapering forearms, I memorized the hollows behind his wrist bones. He smiled at my father. "Oh, yes. I remember this. Schubert's barcarole."

My father nodded. Olivier played: octave leaps upward like cresting waves, then descending, babbling chromatic troughs, easy, liquid, treble notes like water glinting in sunlight. My father sang; the vocal part skimmed the piano, a third higher, like a tern hovering over the water's surface. I leaned over to turn the page, but my father was there first, flipping it at the right instant so Olivier did not have to hesitate. When it was over, my father grinned. "That was very nice," he said, smiling at the understatement. But Olivier was not ready to stop. He looked at Abba.

"An die Musik,'" Abba said.

Olivier reached for the book.

"I'll find it," offered my father. "Have you done much accompanying?"

"A little bit," said Olivier. "Unofficially. I wish I did more."

My father nodded. "You should do more."

"You should hear him play other things, too," I said, but my father wasn't listening to me.

Olivier smiled and started "An die Musik." Abba sang. "To Music": an ode to the redemptive power of art. I watched my father. His eyes were half closed, he was smiling a half smile, but he was fighting back tears at the same time. I felt my own tears rising in the back of my throat. It was because of the interludes between the song's verses, four measures of piano alone—there it was, in its resolving suspensions, all the consolation of music and the better world it revealed, its heartbreaking rapture.

The three of them, Olivier, my father, Abba, stood at the piano within the ring of amber light cast by the standing lamp. Watching them, I felt a rush of hope. This pale, tall, sturdy young man might earn me inclusion into that charmed place. I took a step forward.

Olivier turned and looked at me. "I think we should go, don't you? I borrowed the car; they might want it back. The people I'm staying with." He got up and shook hands with my father and grandfather and inclined his head slightly to each of them, a suggestion of a bow. "It's been an honor," he said.

"How long will you be here?" my father asked.

"I leave on Monday. I wish I could stay longer."

I watched Olivier to see if his eyes flickered toward me as he spoke. I couldn't tell.

"That's too bad," said my father. Finally, he looked at me. "What a pretty dress," he said. "I don't remember it. Very pretty."

. . .

Just outside, I stopped on the fieldstone path and listened. My father was playing again. He and my grandfather began to sing.

"What is that?" Olivier asked. "I don't know it."

"No. You wouldn't. It's "Yigdal." It's a Sabbath song." I stood still, stricken, feeling as if I were abandoning them. "My grand-

father wrote it." Their two voices battled each other and yielded,
rose again and intertwined. It seemed as if they were singing a song
that had lasted as long as memory. Their voices were fragile as
memory. How could I leave them? Abba had been here more than a
week. Why did they choose tonight for singing? I reached for the
handle of the car door, but Olivier had reached for it, too, and my
hand grasped his. I pulled back, afraid to give myself away. I burned
for him. He looked at me in the blue evening light and smiled.

The lake water was still as we drove past, a violet just paler than
the sky, reflecting electric lights like wavering torches, reflecting the
pointed silhouettes of the fir trees lining the shore, the mass of the
eroded hill that rose above the other shore, reflecting peace.

"What do you want to do?" asked Olivier.

"I don't know," I answered. "Just be." I knew exactly what I
wanted to do.

We drove to the house where he was staying. It was on Bayview
Street in Camden; we turned onto a thickly graveled driveway that
tilted downhill to the bay. The grass was precisely mown. "They
might be home," he said as we crossed the wide porch that jutted
above ledges. "You'd like them." No. I wouldn't. The tide lapped
and sucked against smooth rock: gray water edged with cold frills
of foam.

"It doesn't look like anybody's here," I whispered a wish on no
evidence.

And the house was empty. I wandered through the wide rooms,
registering their careless comfort, jealous of this connection between
money and music—why would these people, whoever they were,
have Olivier stay with them? I found the piano, in the bay of the living room, opposite the fireplace. Window seats were built into the
bay and fitted with cushions; through the open window I heard the
small surf and saw lights reflected in the bay like fallen stars, and
green and red buoy lights.

"Play for me," I said. "Play for me. Please."

I sat on the window seat. He sat at the piano. "Play what?" he
asked.

"It doesn't matter. Yes, it does. Play what you love."

"Why?"

"Because I can't. I can't play. I can't sing."

He gazed at me for a moment, and then he stretched his hand, pale and elegant, toward me. I watched his hand. His fingers were trembling. He touched my cheek so lightly that I felt the air compress and pause against my skin more than I felt the pressure of his fingers. "Deborah," he murmured. I held myself absolutely still, to fix his touch in memory.

He played his Schubert dances, lilting and yearning. I watched his arms, his back, the tilt of his head. I felt his hands as if they were playing me, as if I were the music under him. The room was dusky and blue, lit by the porch light. He finished a waltz and sat with his hands in his lap.

"Don't stop," I said.

He laughed. "Everything has to end."

"I wish you weren't going away. There are so many things I want to do. With you."

"But I have to go." He began another piece: Bach, each note precise and distinct and sweet, spare, inevitable lines spinning, braiding.

I put my hands on his shoulders. In the middle of a phrase he stood and turned and kissed me. He put his arm around my waist, and we stepped together across the dark, polished floor to the stairs. Night, cool and damp, sifted in through the screen door. His room was on the side of the house facing east. He did not turn on the light; the moon had risen by now. It was almost full; it streaked the bay silver, and the islands and distant hills floated black on molten metal. I could not kiss him enough; I could not get close enough to his heat, his cinnamon smell, his pale resilient skin. I did not want to stop, ever.

I could not keep back the words; I could not swallow them; they filled my throat like an irresistible song. Knowing their danger, I set my teeth against them, but they pried my mouth open. "I love you," I said.

Olivier lifted his head. I froze. In the moonlight his pale eyes widened in alarm, and then in sadness. His lips were swollen from kissing. He placed his hands on my shoulders and straightened his arms. He shook his head. "You don't," he said. "It's the music. You love the music. Not me. You don't love me."

I shook my head no. No. There was no difference; music was love. Surely he knew that. I pulled him back toward me, but he resisted. "It's late," he said. "We have to go." He held my hand downstairs; he opened the car door and closed it after I had gotten in. I sat beside him but did not touch him.

"I'll get out by myself." I kissed him fast, before he could parry. The house was dark. Thank God everybody was asleep. I didn't have to worry what I looked like.

He touched my cheek. "Don't cry," he said.

"You keep telling me don't."

"You're beautiful . . ."

"What good does that do?"

He kissed my forehead. I opened the car door and stood and cried under the lamp while he drove off around the cedars. I pushed open the back door slowly so it wouldn't creak. The cat, wet from dew, returned from hunting, arched against my leg. I picked him up and tiptoed into the dining room. The moon was bright enough so I didn't need a light. I started carefully up the stairs. A light came on in my parents' room, a light on the far side of the bed: my father. My stomach tightened with fear. I wiped my cheeks and eyes and tried to straighten my hair. Mittens wrenched himself out of my grasp and skittered down the steps.

"Deborah!" my father whispered harshly. "Deborah." He came out of the bedroom, disheveled himself, wearing his pajamas. He looked down at me over the banister. "Do you have any idea what time it is?"

"No." I did not.

"It's after two. I had no idea where you were. I was about to call the police."

"I was all right," I said.

He considered me, and his eyes grew cold with disgust. "You were? If you're going to do that with every man you meet, you're going to stop enjoying it." He turned around and went back into his room and turned off the light.

Through my bedroom curtains the moon lit a cold grid on the wall. Songs caught in my throat and beat against my heart. I ached from songs and feelings I could not voice. I choked on silence and remorse.

Twelve

Return

My parents and I squeezed into my narrow, shabby dormitory room. The walls were yellow, the woodwork scuffed brown, the ceiling higher than the room was wide. My empty trunk—it was a trunk my parents had owned since Prague, and it was still decorated with faded shipping labels—and my boxes took up most of the floor space. In the half of the closet that belonged to me, I'd hung the new clothes: tweed skirts, two dresses, a camel-colored duffel coat. I wore a skirt and a sweater, as did my mother. My father wore a tie and a tweed jacket. Tweed: independently we had each decided that Radcliffe College demanded tweed. My roommate, whom I'd just met and who had gone off with her parents, had been wearing a tweed skirt, too. She'd insisted that she preferred the top bunk, we'd pushed our desks side by side to share the window, which overlooked the Radcliffe Quad, and we had made a plan to go together into Harvard Square the next afternoon to buy Indian cotton bedspreads and open bank accounts. My parents smiled, proud and nervous. There was nothing more for them to do; it was time to go.

The oblique light slanting across the grass, newly green in September, reminded me of Maine. Maine had been part of Massachusetts until 1820, when, with the Missouri Compromise, it became a free state and Missouri a slave state. Maine was one of the reasons I had wanted so badly to go to Radcliffe, along with history. When I had visited Cambridge the year before and walked its ancient, frost-heaved, brick sidewalks, I trod on continuity. I lusted after the grand, austere Tory houses on Brattle Street. I had climbed the white marble steps inside Widener Library, past Sargent's pale murals of American soldiers in World War I, and in the wide stairwell I heard somebody whistling the slow movement to Brahms's Fourth Symphony. Transfixed by yearning, I stopped still; this was a place that would understand my heart.

The woman who interviewed me at Radcliffe had been arrogant. "Why should we take you?" she asked from behind her desk.

"Because you should." I had answered without thinking. "Because I want to come here." I didn't regret what I said; I figured I had no chance anyway. Nobody got into Radcliffe who wasn't first in her class. I was twelfth; in Great Neck we measured by hundredths of a point. But here I was. I walked downstairs with my parents, outside to Walker Street. We had just driven back from Rosh Hashanah in Baltimore. Yom Kippur would fall in the middle of next week, during the first week of classes. My mother thought that was anti-Semitic; in my parents' drama, it was her role to voice the unmentionable.

"All these colleges have Jewish quotas. You were lucky to get in."

"Maybe you weren't so lucky." My father had wanted me to go to Smith. Too many men at Harvard, he said. Precisely. He said I'd be distracted by men. I wouldn't realize my potential. I chose Radcliffe: three hundred women to twelve hundred men. I had already worn out the Radcliffe sweatshirt that a friend had sent me the week I was accepted.

"Mother!" I protested. "This is not anti-Semitism. Most people don't travel hundreds of miles just to go to shul. There's nothing I can do about Yom Kippur. I'll stay in Cambridge. I'll find someplace to go." We agreed that would be for the best. It would be pointless and expensive to fly all the way to Baltimore for just one day.

We had parked the car, a black station wagon now, in the fall of 1964, halfway down the block. Even the air smelled of knowledge, cool and sharp. Here were the uneven bricks beneath my feet, where I would walk for the next four years and emerge utterly changed. Here were other girls and their families moving into the red brick buildings with their cherry red doors: friends, rivals. I knew none felt as unsure as I did, as free-floating, as ready to be new. I was on my own; I had never lived away from home before.

"Be good," my father said. "Be good," he repeated into my ear as he embraced me.

"We'll call you Friday," Mother said. "You know, if you want to reach us, just call, let it ring once and then hang up. We'll call right back. Call if you need anything. I'm always home." Her eyes filled with tears. She turned her head to hide them, then turned back, trying for a smile. "And who's going to wash the dishes?"

"Good question," I answered, and we all laughed, relieved to have survived weeping. We never did get a dishwasher, or a maid. It was my mother's protest against the worldly excesses of Great Neck; it was her protest against me. I was overjoyed to be leaving all of that behind, and I was not looking forward to Radcliffe's requirement that each student work in the dining room once a week.

They got into the car and took a long time settling themselves. Mother rummaged in her purse. Maybe she'd misplaced her keys and we'd have to go back up to the room to find them. I waited. No. She dangled the keys in the window. She started the engine with a roar, and they pulled away. I was on my own. I swallowed and armed myself with a cheerful smile, covering elation, anticipation, and abject fear. Everything was about to begin.

All summer I had studied the Harvard course catalogue. It read like deliverance, the key to mysteries. History of criticism; the archaeology of Palestine, Greece, and Rome; Italian painting, one course per century; Proust; Shakespeare. Half courses, full courses. Page after page, a catalogue of reinvention. By now I had narrowed it down somewhat. I would take that course in criticism; after all, it was an essay I had written on Keats that got me into Radcliffe in the first place. My father had suggested that I might become a critic. Not a poet; if I were a poet, he said, by my age—I had turned seventeen in May—my calling would already be evident. Look at Keats, he had reminded me, dead at twenty-five. So I had to learn what criticism was; I was not really sure. I would take German to understand

Schubert and to read learned texts, Greek because it was necessary
for a classical education. I resolved to be studious and virtuous, neither male nor female. My mind would fly free from my body.

I planned to escape—I was leaving behind my mother's anger and
my father's reticence, his dire predictions that I would never fulfill my
potential. I was beginning. I walked back into the dorm. Many of the
girls already knew each other; they had been together at boarding
school. They did not appear to feel either blessed or amazed to have
arrived at Radcliffe. I had never seen so much blond hair in one place.

· · ·

I had come with one friend. She had graduated first in our class,
and her ability to clarify for me the mechanics of calculus was what
enabled me to graduate from high school. Anne and I ate dinner together that first night. "I thought I was blond," I whispered to her at
the round table populated with girls with thick straight golden pony-
tails. "In Great Neck you are," she whispered back. Anne, whose hair
was glossy and dark, did not have to worry about appearances. I
imagined with adolescent small-mindedness that she was secure in
her status as valedictorian.

That first night at college, I lay in the bottom bunk; my roommate shifted, and our wooden edifice creaked. I tried to sleep. At
home I fell asleep to whatever played on my portable radio, but Jonny
had claimed the radio for his baseball games. So I had no music; I
desperately wanted a record player, and I couldn't afford one. Love
was there in music, in the arc of a melody, in a modulation, a shift to
a major key, in what could not be touched.

The next morning we registered, lining up, winding in and out
of the crowded Radcliffe administration buildings, filling out forms.
I signed up to take my swimming test, required of all incoming fresh-
men. I received my bursar's card, white with the Radcliffe shield in
red and my name and serial number embossed beneath; with it I could
enter the stacks, join the Coop, validate my intelligence. The card
glinted in the sun, shining and plastic, my most treasured possession.
I hadn't made a mistake; here was proof that they expected me.

As we finished the registration gauntlet, a person descended upon me. The first thing I noticed was his green blazer; its fabric folded at his elbow soft and luminous as velvet; I wanted to touch it. He was stocky and fair, with pale eyes and pale eyebrows and small teeth. He introduced himself, Kevin was his first name; I knew from his last that he was Jewish. He was a senior, and he invited me to lunch.

"Why?" I asked.

"I'd like to get to know you."

"I'm having lunch with my friend," I said, flattered, corrupt.

"She can come, too."

He took us both to lunch; then he took me to dinner. He had a car. His blazer was cashmere. He took me to dinner again the next night, and he laughed when I said I wanted two desserts. "Why not?" He indulged my greed, and I couldn't resist. He had money. He had time; he never seemed to go to class. He had nothing to do but me. "What would you like to do most?" he asked.

"Go to Maine. I've never seen it in the fall. I've never seen it changed." The next morning he showed up at my criticism class. Aristotle was the subject of the lecture, the *Poetics:* pity and terror. Pity and terror, yielding the deepest delight. "Come on," said Kevin after class. "We're going to Maine."

The sky was a deep, luminous blue. On Megunticook, the blueberry barrens had turned garnet against the gray ledges. Through the branches of bare trees, the landscape had become almost transparent. I could not speak from its beauty. "It would have been better in a week," Kevin said.

"Let's climb to Maiden's Cliff," I said. "It's a short hike; the view—the lake and the mountains—they would be so beautiful from up there."

"Hike?" Kevin laughed. "Why hike? Anyway, I don't have the right shoes. It's just as pretty driving." He leaned across the front seat and kissed me. I did not like his smell. I liked kissing, but I did not like kissing him.

"It's not pretty. It's beautiful!" I watched the landscape through the car window, soaking up the sight of it through the glass. The sun heated my face; when I rolled down the window, the wind chilled me; I loved the difference; I loved the smell; I yearned to be in it. Kevin drove. He was getting impatient. He turned on the radio, some kind of easy listening. I stared out the window. This is what it would be like: comfortable, safe, distant, insulated.

I had lost innocence, if innocence was faith in love. I had lost it the way women lose beauty, helplessly; I had watched it ebb. It was my fault. If I had been disappointed in love, I had also disappointed. I had rejected young men; I had undone them with scorn; I had frightened them with ardor. Because of what I looked like, I wielded power; I had learned the lesson of my mother's beauty. What I knew best about sex was its capacity to injure. But I would go through fire and water for whom I loved; I would endure, to Mozart's stately music, for a Tamino. I would deck myself out in feathers and hop around the stage if Pappageno, with his bells and gaudy baritone, wanted me. But Kevin had his dignity; he was no birdman, and he kept an umbrella in his car—probably a fire extinguisher in his trunk, too. Without him, however, I would be unable even to get to Maine.

When I got back to the dorm, my roommate said that my parents had been trying to reach me. She hadn't known where I'd gone, and she thought she'd worried them. I called home, let it ring once, and hung up. My mother called back immediately. "Where were you?" she demanded.

"I went to Maine." I sounded smug.

"Maine? How did you get there?"

I told her about Kevin. "Oh," she said, "well, that's fine. We were just worried." I heard the phone click: my father picking up the extension.

"Deborah," my mother said. "Deborah, we have something to tell you. Mittens . . ."

"What? What happened to him?"

"We don't know," began my father. "We let him out two days ago in the morning, and he hasn't come back."

"Have you looked for him? Have you called him?" My voice rose in panic.

"We've looked everywhere. Your mother has driven up and down every street in Great Neck Estates. We've called the police. Nothing."

"So he's gone?"

"He's disappeared."

I began to sob.

"He left home when you did," my mother said.

. . .

"*Das Volk*," said the German instructor. "*Das Volk*." Our first word in German. Neuter. The people. I knew about that *Volk* and the killing it accomplished. I was not of that people. I sat through the class, but I did not go back. Instead, I signed up for Hebrew. Spoken Hebrew: the living language, the grammar, the structure of everyday sentences. A mistake, Kevin thought; the course would be too much work, and the class was small, so I would have to show up.

He asked me to spend Yom Kippur with his family, and I agreed. It was so easy; his mother called to invite me herself. I told my parents.

"Where does he live?" asked my mother.

"In Newton," I answered. "It's kind of like the Great Neck of Boston."

"So the drivers are rude?"

"In Boston they're rude everywhere."

"That's wonderful, dear. He sounds like a nice boy."

"I know that family," my father said, sounding relieved, as if the problem of my future had just resolved itself. "I think you're doing the wise thing."

But—I wanted to protest—no. I was just beginning. Nothing was resolved, nothing determined; didn't they understand? But Kevin was listening to my end of the conversation. I called from his apartment, not collect, another extravagance he encouraged. "Anything about the cat?" I asked. I was sure he would turn up, sure of a happy ending.

"Nothing."

"Have you been looking?"

"Your mother has."

"How's Jonny?"

"Fine. What's new with you?"

"Nothing. I'm taking Hebrew instead of German."

"Oh, that's interesting. We'll talk to you from Baltimore. Erev Yom Kippur. Before shul."

I asked Kevin if he would take me back to the dorm for dinner. I had hardly eaten a single dinner there; I hardly knew the other girls. Some of them frightened me with their sunny high spirits, their smooth good manners, their web of connections. They made me feel rough and dark, and I did not trust their good will. The world was not an easy place. "Why are you in such a hurry to get to know them?" Kevin asked. "You have plenty of time to do that." He'd already made reservations at a restaurant. He took me back to the dorm to change.

· · ·

Always the afternoon before Yom Kippur began, the light seemed to turn a particularly rich gold; the wind stilled; the world stilled. Even in this Puritan city, on this day in late September, when I looked out my window at the students crisscrossing the Radcliffe Quad, on their way to the library, to a late class, in the midst of ordinary gentile things, I sensed a descending quietness, whether it came from my own soul or from God.

I was dressed and ready and waiting for Kevin to come and pick me up for dinner with his parents. I wore my best woolen dress; I'd washed and dried my hair, enduring a midday hour under the plastic hood of my hair dryer to straighten my curls. I was feeling vaguely uncomfortable, pampered, cared for, coddled by this family I did not yet know. It was just after four. I called Abba's number in Baltimore. "Hello!" my father shouted into the phone.

"It's me. I was calling to wish you a good yom tov. I'm being picked up in a few minutes."

"Oh, darling." His voice softened. "We just got in. Your mother isn't even in the door. We were just talking about how we missed you, but how happy we are that you're settled, that you're in good hands."

I wanted to be happy, too. "How was the trip down?"

"Traffic was terrible. I don't know why. Your mother drove; she's extraordinary."

In the background I heard Abba call, "Hugo! Hugo! What are you doing?"

"Papa, I'm coming. Deb's on the phone. We have plenty of time. All I have to do is change!" I heard in my father's voice all the anticipation, the nervousness, the holy anxiety that accompanied Yom Kippur. The Day of Antonement, of *Tishuvah*. Repentance, but not exactly repentance, more like return. A noun formed from the root verb; all Hebrew grammar—nouns, tenses—blossomed from two or three letter roots with the addition of prefixes and suffixes, with shifts in vowels. Return: I felt a lightness in my limbs; I imagined my father and Jonny—Abba, too keyed up, would have gone on ahead after eating almost nothing—the two of them, Jonny now taller than my father, walking the three blocks to the shul, past the boarded-up shoe repair, the boarded-up pharmacy, the decaying brick and brownstone houses. In the soft, dry afternoon, they would walk under the linden trees, which still had most of their leaves. It was warm in Cambridge; it would be warmer in Baltimore.

"How's the weather?" I asked.

"Warm. Warm but not hot, thank God," my father answered.

"It's warm here, too."

"Do you want to talk to your mother? Let me get her. Hold on."

No. I wanted him, but I said yes. "Nath!" he called. "Nath! It's Deborah!"

"Darling!" And in her voice I heard all the tension, all her fear of Abba's righteousness, and of my father's, all her anger at her own shortcomings. "Listen, have a wonderful time—if you can have a wonderful time on Yom Kippur. I've got to give your father and brother something to eat. You would think that Ozelia would be able to do this. There has to be something, something to tide you over for the fast. We should be able to sit down and have a proper meal. I just don't understand . . . this place is such a mess."

"It's not supposed to be a big deal before Yom Kippur, Mother. Just a snack, really."

"But it has to be something!" She caught herself. "Oh, darling. We miss you! Have a wonderful time, and thank the Roses for us!"

I swallowed hard. I would be all right. I checked myself out in the full-length mirror in the ironing room next door to our bedroom. My smooth hair, not blond, not brown, picked up a rainbow of colors in the golden light. The blue tweed was a good color for me; I wore black pumps. I was wearing a light cloak of numbness, too. I was only doing what Jews everywhere did, attending Yom Kippur services wherever they happened to find themselves on that day. I was independent, embarking upon my own bildungsroman. All I permitted myself to feel was a quick tingle of relief that I was four hundred miles north of that familiar anxiety and my parents' tense truce. I pretended that I didn't miss them, or the choir loft in the dingy synagogue, or Ozelia's slow progress through the confusion in Abba's kitchen. The phone in the hall rang. Kevin was downstairs, the girl at the bells desk announced.

The Roses lived on a winding street, in a low house hidden by evergreens and maples. They embraced me, though we had never met. Mr. Rose, stocky as his son, smiled as if he, too, understood that everything was settled. The table was set; dinner was ready. Mr. Rose started to light the candles on the table. "Shouldn't we say the b'racha?" I asked. He looked surprised and then pleased. "Go ahead, dear, you say it." I did. Kevin smiled with possession.

The Roses were quiet; they were calm. They asked me about my father, about my grandfather, about the congregation in Baltimore. Yes, they knew people in the congregation; it was a wonderful community. We had salad and roast chicken for dinner, and we had plenty of time; nobody was rushed. We could have been going to the movies afterward, and we already had our tickets. The synagogue was a vast modern building, about two miles from their house; it reminded me of the sanctuary in Stevenson, convex and swooping, organized for spiritual uplift. And it was not called a synagogue; it was a temple. We parked in the lot and walked through the big, carved front doors. Our seats, bought and paid for with a hefty contribution, were toward the front of the auditorium. The vertical pipes of an organ formed an element of the soaring decoration. The Roses greeted a few people; I felt queasy.

I pulled a prayer book from the slot in the back of the seat in front of me. It was Reform, so there were not the facing pages of Hebrew and English translation. There was much more English, with snatches of Hebrew interspersed like exotic black and white decorations in the text. I scanned the familiar prayers for reassurance that I belonged here. There was a choir, men and women in black robes. They would not sing our music. Kevin had said that they were pretty good. "When was the last time you heard them?" I asked.

"When do you think? Last year, last Yom Kippur." He pronounced "kippur" as if it were a smoked herring.

I would be all right; I had survived services in Great Neck. As the rabbi and cantor—wearing ordinary black robes, too, not holy white—approached their side-by-side pulpits, a blast sounded from the organ, a long, ominous, murky minor chord. If it had been a soundtrack, the villain would have stalked on screen.

The congregation stood; I stood with them and awaited the solemn beginning, waited anxiously for the cantor to trumpet the first words of the ancient Aramaic legal formula: Kol Nidre. That, at least, had to be the same tune everywhere. "All sins," the rabbi intoned in English, "all sins we have committed before God, according to the age-old prayer . . ."

Then the cantor, facing the audience, threw back his head and howled, high and keening, a cosmic complaint. The chorus echoed him. It was awful and ugly; it was a polyphonic kvetch, devoid of compassion, empty of awe. No! I wanted to shout. No! This was not a prayer, not an appeal; this was a contract with God, an erasing of transgression, a statement of intent marking the beginning of return. At this very moment, in Baltimore, Abba was standing facing the holy ark of the Torah, facing God, beginning the first repetition, low, at the bottom of his range, so each succeeding repetition could start a tone higher. Those Aramaic words, that archaic formula, threaded backwards over time: years, decades, centuries, millennia; every year since the days of the temple in Jerusalem they had been sung and repeated, repeated, repeated: a negotiation with God. Legal words setting forth a law of mercy, a mechanism of redemption, a melody that started as a chant, plain and sober, but that rose and flowered and finally subsided. I yearned for it; it was mine; I belonged to it.

What was I doing here? I was in an alien place. I was not this kind of Jew. This was not the sound of my faith. I bowed my head under an enormous, desperate wave of longing. I bit my lip. I tried to still my shaking shoulders. The organ bellowed. I burst into tears.

"Dear, what's wrong?" Mrs. Rose asked.

"I have to go home!" I sobbed.

She put her arm around me; I breathed the motherly comfort of her perfume and cried.

"It's all right," she murmured. "Of course you do. Of course."

The service thundered on, and I wept in her arms.

As soon as we got back to the Roses' house, Mr. Rose called the airlines and reserved me a seat to Baltimore early in the morning.

I called Abba's. "I'm coming home," I told my mother. She wrote down the flight information and put my father on.

"Ruth among the alien corn," he said.

"No," I told him. "No. I'm coming home."

I spent the night in the Roses' guest room. As I was falling asleep, I heard the doorknob turn and the soft, sticky, padding sound of footprints entering my room. "Debby," Kevin whispered. "Debby." He couldn't seem to remember that I hated that name. I lay still. "Debby." I took a deep breath, considered embellishing it with a snore, and decided just to exhale noisily. He couldn't have me. Nobody could have me.

. . .

Kevin drove me to the airport. On the plane I sat by the window, lightheaded from fasting, and watched the landscape turn gradually greener as we headed south. My mother was waiting for me at the gate, not dressed for shul; of course she wouldn't be. She hugged me shyly; in just over a week, I had already changed. I felt brave and strong. We drove through Baltimore along the familiar concrete roads that crashed across the city's decrepit downtown. The streets were empty in the late morning; we stopped needlessly at the garlands of red lights decorating bleak intersections and blocks of crumbling buildings. Through the opened windows, warm, dusty wind swirled and teased the hem of my dress.

"I'm so glad you're here," my mother said.

"I am, too."

We pulled up at the side door of the shul on Chauncey Avenue. "Darling," said my mother, "you're sure you don't want to stop at Abba's for a minute?"

I shook my head. "Come with me," I offered, knowing that she couldn't. This place took nerve, more than she dared; I was beginning to see that. I kissed my mother and got out of the car, and from the sidewalk I heard the singing bursting from the building. The windows in the choir loft were open. I recognized each voice: Freddie's, low and gruff; Marty Oberman's lighter bass; Paul and Marty, the tenors; my father's loud, rich baritone. Over them trumpeted Abba, pulling them recklessly toward untried pitches.

I climbed the dusty, dark brown steps to the first floor and looked into the synagogue through the open door. The air dense with dust gleamed white and translucent in shafts of sunlight. Like bolts of lightning, cracks shot through the plaster in the walls above the bimah. The clock on the balcony had stopped. But there were more people than I expected.

Abba stood at his lectern, old and splendid in his white cambric robe. His white hair billowed out from under his onion dome hat; his white mustache arched over his open mouth, his pale eyes, pouched and hooded, glared at the ark's white curtain. He stood on the threadbare carpet in the cloth shoes he wore only on Yom Kippur. They had just begun Musaf. He was singing "Michalkel chaim," one of the eighteen prayers that form the core of every service. "Michalkel chaim: You sustain the living through your kindness, You bring life to the dead through your great mercies." He had written that melody in 1915, when he was a soldier in the trenches in Italy, when he was the young man in the watercolor with the blond mustache listening to his radio. When my father was three years old. Abba had composed it in the night before a dawn assault; he had written it in the front lines.

The prayer ended, and Abba looked up and saw me standing at the doorway. He interrupted his singing, crossed the bimah, in front of God and the congregation, and he kissed me. "*Bleib gesunt,*" he whispered. Be well.

Buoyant, I ran upstairs to the choir loft. Despite the open windows, it was stuffy. In the antechamber a folded newspaper on the arm of the old school chair fluttered in the breeze. My father saw me, and his face lit with precious recognition. I embraced him, clasped his substantial body and breathed the familiar scent of his shaving lotion. Jonny patted my arm. I hugged Uncle Freddie. "Doll, you look gorgeous. The college girl. Have you had lunch? We'll send out for a cheeseburger."

"Mannheimer's is closed," I said, wise now, answering back.

"Freddie, shhh! For Christ's sake, cut it out," hissed my father as he passed out music.

Half of the curtain across the front of the choir loft had torn loose, but it didn't matter who saw me. I picked up a prayer book, and, as I always did, found my place by matching the patterns that the blocks of teardrop letters made on the page of Abba's big prayer book on his lectern. Here. I was in time. It was just beginning, the most beautiful part. Abba sang Hineni, Here I am, God. Here I was; I had to hear this music; I could not imagine myself without it.

The choir joined for the next prayer, the Unesane tokef; the medieval German poem. The curtain of the ark was opened. My father blew on his pitch pipe. Abba sang, in his own key, his own realm, of this day of awe and terror; he sang of God's pity and kindness. My father, in his key, the key in which the piece was written, sang of God's truth. "*You open the book of memories,*" the choir sang.

Abba trumpeted: "*The great shofar is sounded.*"

The choir answered: "*A still, small voice is heard.*"

"*And all the creatures of the earth pass before you like a flock of sheep,*" Freddie sang his solo.

"*Like a flock of sheep.*"

I shivered and closed my eyes. Like my father, I could not stay away. I never tried to stay away again; for more than thirty years I have come back to this singing. I was expected to be silent, but this was where I was going to have to wrestle with my voice. I was going to claim this music. Here is where I would have to make myself heard. But being here was enough, now. It was a beginning.

That afternoon I perched on the dusty marble ledge, as glorious a throne as any princess ever possessed. I was home. The joyful noise washed over me.

Thirteen

A Voice

Abba had moved into an apartment on Eutaw Place across the street from the shul. It had once been a fine apartment, almost as large as the house on Chauncey Avenue. Elaborate woodwork decorated its airy rooms, but its owners had emigrated to the suburbs, and the building, like the synagogue, was rundown. Abba's windows over-looked Druid Hill Park and the reservoir and the shul. He was still its cantor, but he no longer crossed the street; he no longer knew what day it was; he no longer recognized most faces. This Yom Kippur afternoon, Abba sat in his bathrobe, facing the television, oblivious to its babble. His head drooped, his hands lay listless on the arms of his chair. The nurse sitting beside him watched a game show.

It was 1973. My parents and I were in Baltimore for the High Holy Days. Jonny had stayed in California. He had always intended to be-come a lawyer like Freddie, and now that he had finished law school, he clerked for a judge in San Francisco. I lived outside of Boston, in Concord, in a house very much like the one where Louisa May Alcott had grown up. I had married as soon as I finished college, anxious to separate from my family and to take another name. My husband was an older man, worldly and wealthy. I stayed away from my parents to prove how little I needed them, but still I came to Baltimore.

This year for the first time my father acted as cantor; he took Abba's part. He arranged the members of the choir on the bimah so that he could conduct them, too. Marty Oberman was the only bass; in the summer of 1969, after I was married, Freddie had moved his family to Israel. He had represented Rap Brown after the riots in Cambridge, Maryland, and he had grown disillusioned with the civil rights movement, unable to condone its increasing violence and extremism.

I stood in the first row of pews in the grand and shabby synagogue. I was resplendent, as finely dressed as any of the ladies who used to occupy these seats. I spent a great deal of money on material things. My suit was new, and more outfits, with their price tags still dangling from little safety pins, were hanging in the closet in our hotel room. Abba's apartment did not suit the man I had married. My husband hated Yom Kippur, but he disliked being alone more. I traveled with him wherever he went, and he came with me to Baltimore, but then retreated to the hotel to eat and make phone calls. I had brought food on the plane from Boston: challah I had made myself, round for a full year, and quiche, milky food that was kosher, to break the fast. Even now, Abba loved my cooking; it had eased his mind to see that I had become the good wife of a rich man.

My father stood at Abba's lectern, facing the holy ark, facing God. He wore a gray suit and a standard-issue yarmulke. He would not put on Abba's white cambric robe or his white velvet onion dome hat, and he skipped Hineni, the cantor's prayer. My father was sixty-one. I listened to his beautiful voice with mixed joy and sorrow. Loss resonated in his singing; distilled in his voice were the voices of generations that had been silenced. Here was the last, fragile connection. I hated myself for being unable to sing. Now that he was taking Abba's place, my father observed the decorum and refused to leave the synagogue even for an hour in the afternoon, even to stroll around the reservoir.

I had a headache, from fasting I said, but it was as much from the pain of self-definition: the difficulty of being with my family and maintaining the division between my present self and the girl I had been not so long ago. I went back to Abba's apartment and stretched out on the sofa. My mother tried to get me to eat something. I refused. I wished my brother had come; then we could have stood together in shul and repeated Freddie's jokes to each other; Jonny had studied them the way I had studied Hebrew. But Jonny would have been on the bimah with the choir.

When it was time for Ne'ilah, the closing service, I bent down and kissed Abba goodbye. "Deborah!" he said in his gruff and guttural voice. "Deborah! Where are you going?" Still, logistics concerned him.

"I'm going to shul."

"What day is today?" He was agitated; he tried to lift himself out of his chair.

"It's Thursday," I said, as if it were an ordinary Thursday.

"No! What day is it?" he demanded. "What day is it?"

"It's Yom Kippur."

"I have to get dressed. I have to go! Get me up!" He was shouting. The effort to act made him tremble.

"Calm down, Reverend Weisgal," the nurse began. "Just calm down."

"Shut up!" he thundered. He managed to stand; he swayed, uncertain; he did not remember where to go. He felt his tangled hair and tried to smooth it. Tears welled in his eyes. "I have to get dressed! I have to go to shul!"

Helpless, the nurse turned to me.

"Please, get him dressed," I said. "I'll take him to shul."

"Can you?"

"I think so."

She led him into his bedroom. He emerged wearing his tan double-breasted suit, its gabardine shiny with age, and a yellowed shirt. His tie was askew. I straightened it as best I could.

"Take me to shul!" he ordered and took my arm.

"Abba, I'm taking you. We're going now."

He paused at the closet where his hat and cane were stored. I retrieved them. We took the elevator down, and I walked him through the lobby. The doorman stood in surprise when he saw us coming. "Reverend Weisgal, I'm glad to see you," he said, and he hurried outside and stopped traffic on Eutaw Place as, step by slow step, we crossed the street. Abba held on to the tarnished brass railing beside the synagogue's front stairs, and we climbed to the three sets of oak doors at the front of the shul. They stood ajar. My father was singing. Ne'ilah had begun. The ark was open, and the silver crowns and breastplates of the scrolls of the Torah gleamed in the last golden afternoon light. My father stood in that light. His deep rich voice filled the synagogue and echoed in the open dome. Abba pulled a yarmulke out of the pocket of his suit; he let me support him down the center aisle. I was much taller than he was; he had condensed with age. The nurse had brushed his white hair sleek. He looked straight ahead, determined, bound.

We turned left in front of the rabbi's lectern and headed toward the broad marble stairs leading to the bimah. I started to help him up, but he shook me off, roughly, angrily, and mounted the steps alone. I waited there in the aisle, watching him, but he didn't need me. He stood by himself on the bimah listening as my father chanted the murmuring, exalting Ne'ilah melodies.

Daylight dimmed; the breeze from the opened doors cooled; the evening deepened. "*The gates are closing,*" my father and the choir sang. "*Our Father, our King, seal us in the book of forgiveness.*" Surosky removed the shofar from its silk envelope. My father gripped the side of the lectern and threw back his head, preparing for the final proclamations. But before he could begin, Abba crossed the bimah and pushed his son aside. My father yielded his place.

Abba straightened; he grew tall. "*Shema Yisrael!*" His voice rang out: clear, loud, without vibrato, an ancient call. "*Shema Yisrael!*" the choir and the congregation repeated. "*Baruch shem kavod malchuso l'olam va'ed!*" Three times. Abba proclaimed and we answered: "*Blessed be His rule until the end of the world!*" Abba sang: "*The Lord, He is God!*" His voice blared magnificent and startling as a shofar. I kept count on my fingers; my father kept count on his. Abba needed no help. Seven times. For the last time in his shul, he sang.

. . .

As long as Abba lived, we continued to celebrate the High Holy Days in Baltimore, and my father led the services. Jonny came home from

California and joined a law firm in Washington. When he got married, in 1979, Abba could not be at his wedding. For Abba, the present had vanished. My father and mother had closed his apartment and moved him into the Hebrew Home for the Aged in suburban Baltimore.

Abba remembered no words during the last years of his life. When we visited him in the Hebrew Home for the Aged, Jonny and my father sat beside his wheelchair and sang to him, and he recognized them from their voices and sang with them. He always recognized me by sight, and he gazed at me with despair; there was nothing he could remember to say. I leaned against the doorway while the men sang melodies from synagogue services, the tunes his father and grandfather and great-grandfather had sung and written: their noise carried down the overheated, ammonia-smelling halls of the nursing home. The attendants shut his door to keep from disturbing the other patients. They could not hush the old man while we were with him. His voice remained piercing and clear. All his life he sang to God, and surely God listened.

I listened, too, still wishing I knew how to sing with them. Tell your son: that injunction linked those three men in a chain that barred me. But my own constricted throat also shut me off. I did not trust myself to sing, but I had found a voice in silence. Despite my father's declaration that at seventeen I was too old to become a poet, or perhaps because of it, I had written poetry and published it. My father set several of my poems to music, and he worked on them with me. "What about shortening these lines?" he suggested. I shifted words, altered the shape of a verse, marveled at his intuition. "Say it out loud. Does it work? What do you think?" He spoke to me like a colleague. I published journalism. I was becoming a writer. I traveled alone, and when I came home to Concord, I did not talk about my work. I had no children.

. . .

Abba died in December 1981, a week before his ninety-seventh birthday. "Where should the funeral be?" my father wept over the phone.

"In the shul," I said from Boston. "It has to be in the shul."

"But nobody will come. Nobody remembers him."

"They'll come."

The house was sold out. On the bimah, the choir sang, and Abba's sons sat silent in the audience. Afterward at a friend's house, Freddie played jazz variations on the "Yigdal" that Abba had written, and my brother and his wife told us that they were having a baby: Abba's first great-grandchild. I went into the bathroom and burst into tears for the children I did not have, who would never know the beauty of this music, and I sobbed for the marriage I had, which could not make room for a child.

"What are you going to do for the High Holy Days?" I asked my father the following August. I did not dare a "we." It turned out that he had arranged a reprieve. He had gone to the president of the little synagogue in Rockland, Maine, a town on the coast about twelve miles south of our summer house. "I'm Hugo Weisgall," he announced, "and I'm going to lead your High Holy Day services." The president had no idea who my father was, but he found out. In the past, the congregation had relied on cantorial students to chant the services; when they discovered that the co-founder of the Cantors Institute himself was offering to sing, they agreed to let him.

The synagogue was housed in a converted Baptist church a block from the waterfront. In an east wind, the smell of the fish-processing plant wafted in through the open windows. The maples had turned; the blueberry barrens burned red. On that first Rosh Hashanah, my father stood at the cantor's lectern facing the ark, and Jonny and I stood on either side of him, in front of an audience of strangers. Some members of the congregation objected to my presence—a woman's presence—on the bimah, so my father found me a yarmulke and I put it on. My brother and I tried to be the choir. Jonny's voice was like Freddie's, deep and rough, and he made up what he didn't know. To my astonishment, I knew every word of every prayer; I remembered the music, every note.

I could hear the harmonies in my head, but I did not understand how to make them come out of my mouth. Those echoes, the powerful voices of the old choir, resonated too painfully. My father and brother sang as loud as they could, and they drowned my meager voice.

After a few years, Jonny and his family stopped coming regularly to Maine for the holidays. It was a long trip; he had a busy and prosperous legal practice in Washington that demanded a lot of travel, and now, if he wanted to sing our music, he could go to Baltimore. Freddie and Jeanne had returned from Israel. A new congregation had formed in the old shul on Eutaw Place, led by the children of the people who had moved the synagogue to the suburbs. A choir was singing, led by one of the original members, and the new cantor had learned Abba's music.

But my father stayed in Maine, and I showed up faithfully from Boston to stand beside him at his lectern. The congregation began to grow. People came to hear the music. A rabbi who had retired from his congregation in Portland began to lead services with my father, and, whispering across the lectern while the synagogue's president made her announcements, we taught the rabbi Freddie's commentary on the prayers. "The Lord shall reign forever and ever—and that's why the ball game was canceled." His lines had become as immutable as scripture. Over time, many of those strangers became friends; they were doctors, lawyers, merchants, lobstermen. Sometimes, they complimented me on my singing, but I knew I wasn't very good.

Every year, every service, my father improvised and left me dangling in some impossible key, as his own father had done to him. Without warning, he skipped over whole sections the choir used to sing, silencing them with a quick, improvised line. I was terrified of forgetting. My father carried his folders of music to shul in a cardboard box decorated with garlands of flowers, packaging for a china casserole. In it were all the lost choral parts, all the passages he omitted. The noise of the choir grew fainter.

. . .

I met the man who became my new husband in Maine; he was studying composition with my father. I had been hearing about him for several years before I encountered him. And he had cut out and saved some of my magazine pieces, not realizing that their author—I wrote under my married name—was Hugo's daughter. I came alone to Maine one summer and rented a house.

"Don't fall in love with my daughter," my father warned his student before we were introduced, as if I embodied all his wicked women: The Mistress in *The Stronger,* the Stepdaughter in *Six Characters,* the Mother in *Purgatory.*

I was not thinking about falling in love. We became friends. Almost every day we swam at Lake Megunticook. Afterward we talked about music, about the fugues and inventions he wrote every week, and he revealed some of the secrets of harmony and counterpoint he had been learning from my father. We talked about writing and about solitude; we were both alone and unsure. He was deciding whether or not to continue to study music; I was deciding to take back my name, to start myself over again.

We were married in December 1987; my father recovered from his disappointment at losing a disciple. Our daughter, whom we named Charlotte, was born in March of 1989, after a night of snow and thunderstorms. We took her to shul beginning when she was six months old, so that she would have something, however diminished, to remember.

. . .

In the summer of 1991, when he was seventy-one, Freddie died in his sleep. His funeral was held at the old shul in Baltimore; Margit asked me if I would speak. I had not been back there since Abba's funeral. The building had been painted, the marble cleaned. For the first time in my life, I sat on that bimah. Nervously, I awaited my turn. When I stood at the rabbi's marble lectern and saw the crowd, black faces, white faces, Jews and non-Jews, I changed my opening lines:

"If Freddie were here, I know what he would have done," I began. "He would have looked at everybody here and nodded with satisfaction, and he would have said, 'The house is sold out.'" I told stories about that obstreperous man who hated injustice. My brother called me a few days later to say that an article in the *Baltimore Sun* reported that my talk left the audience in tears. A voice, finally: "Maybe I should have been a rabbi," I said.

Fourteen

Still Waters

My brother, my parents, and I were driving south from Berlin across
the bleak Prussian plain, toward the border between East Germany
and Czechoslovakia. We were heading for Prague. For my mother's
seventieth birthday, in November of 1991, the four of us were going
to Prague. My brother had arranged the trip. A tireless tourist like
my mother, he believed in piling on the sights. Prague was not so
far from Berlin and Vienna. We could drive, revising our childhood
trek—now with Jonny and me in the front seat, our parents in back—
down Europe's spine.

I had not wanted to go. I was reluctant to leave my husband and
two-year-old Charlotte. I was wary of my family, wary of their tangling leashes of love, their persistent drama. The drama of *Six Characters* and *Purgatory* had turned on the hell of repeating pattern. I
feared those patterns in my family; I doubted my strength to resist
their strangling tug even for five days.

I was uneasy about Prague, too. Enchanted city: Mozart's city,
the city he preferred to Vienna, the city in which the Holy Roman
Emperor Rudolf II established his strange court at the end of the
fifteenth century, Jewish city, the city of Rabbi Loewe and his Golem,
city of Dr. Faustus and Kafka, who once lived on the street where
Rudolf's alchemists labored. I would have preferred to keep Prague
an idea, to accumulate its enchantments and contemplate its locked-
away beauty in a *kunstkammer* of my mind. I feared that it would be
ugly. I did not want to find that I had been born in a city left drab

and silent after fifty years of communism. More than that: I was afraid to find that I had no connection to Prague, that my having been born there was, as my father had once insisted, only an accident.

"I can't go," I told my brother when he announced his plan.

"It's less than a week; you can't not go." My brother, accumulator of frequent-flyer miles, sent me tickets. Arriving in Berlin, I caught the city's nervous excitement. A strip of new black asphalt paved the site of the demolished wall. At the head of its empty parade ground, the Reichstag rose black and decaying, like a mold-covered cake, and our taxi driver drove us past a colonnade of marble busts: a monument to the generals who had won the war, he explained proudly in his growling East German accent. My father translated. What war had Germany won? The Franco-Prussian War, I figured out finally; these statues had been erected more than a century earlier. That first night, we went to the opera; it wasn't very good, and my father and I left after intermission, while my mother and brother, eager for event, stayed. Where should we go tomorrow, Dresden or Leipzig? Music or art? It was Nathalie's birthday. Art. Dresden, Hugo and I decided.

In the rest of Europe, almost half a century had passed since the end of the war, but here, in the formerly communist countries, time had stopped. These places had been cursed, kept silent. Some parts of the Springer, the Saxon dukes' palace, had been rebuilt. Their rococo decorations lay like a gorgeous border of dark lace against the gray November sky. Other palaces still lay in ruins. We stood in the square in front of the Dresden opera house; they were performing *Meistersinger* that night. "This is where Wagner conducted," my father said. I felt like a child again, counting castles, marveling at fairy tales come alive. Now, though, I took no comfort from fairy tales. I had found the old books my father had given me; I wanted them to read to my daughter. The evil they described, cruel deeds and brutal punishments, these things were not fantastic; in this landscape there were no happy endings.

As we approached the Czech border, we dipped into valleys and climbed steep hills through sober, culled forest. Standing trees had been trimmed of lower branches, underbrush cut down. Here and there we passed a house, steep-gabled with carved wooden eaves, as if it were laden with gingerbread, the kind of house a witch would use as bait to lure children.

We crossed the border into devastation. Along the road, for miles, felled logs lay like abandoned bodies. Dead, matted grass covered the ground. In Teplice, in the industrial Sudetenland, the territory that Hitler invaded after the Munich Pact signed on my parents' living room rug, the buildings' stucco skin had crumbled, as if it was being eaten away. In mid-afternoon the streets were empty, the town smothered by acrid, greasy fog.

I had been driving, but the fog caused my eyes to tear so badly that I could not see. Jonny took over. Approaching headlights appeared faint as failing flashlights. My mother and father sat in the back seat. We crawled along, barely able to see the hood of our own car. I unfolded the road map and saw the name.

Terezin. By the map; we were less than sixty kilometers away from it. I had no idea it was here, on the road to Prague. If I had known, I would have made us take another route. I would have chosen to drive through Leipzig, not Dresden. There was so much to see in newly opened Europe. We could have visited the church where Johann Sebastian Bach served as Kapelmeister, instead of the half-restored palaces of the Dukes of Saxony. I read Terezin on the map but said nothing; I was afraid to speak that word out loud.

"How are we doing?" my brother asked. "What's the next big town?"

"I don't know."

"Look on the map, then."

I pretended to look. "Terezin," I said, choking on the word. "The road goes through Terezin."

"What? I can't hear you!" my mother called from the back seat.

"The road," I shouted. "This road goes through Terezin."

"We should stop there," my brother said. "We have time."

Nobody answered him. This was supposed to be a birthday trip, a celebration. This was no time for Terezin. We followed a Czech Lada that groaned and roared like an outboard motor. It was only four in the afternoon, and already it was growing dark; the air was turning a curdled, opaque, darkening blue. I glimpsed a road sign: Terezin. We were coming closer. We could drive right through; in this polluted fog I hoped we would never even see the town. And I thought that surely the camp and the town were not synonymous; the camp could not have been right on the main road; it had to have been hidden somewhere in the countryside, camouflaged.

My brother saw it, too. "Is it off the road?" my brother asked. "Do we have to make a turn?"

"I don't know," I said. "It looks like the road goes through the town, but I'm not really sure. Maybe you have to turn off somewhere. It's too late."

"I've been there," my father pleaded. "I don't want to go."

I turned around. My father shrank into the back seat. His expression was piteous. He was looking again at what he had seen on a bright spring day when he had been driven the hour north from Prague to accompany American soldiers liberating a concentration camp. He was looking at what I had seen for the first time thirty years earlier in black-and-white photographs—images familiar now and labeled Holocaust—photographs that he had not quite hidden in Abba's house. I had never admitted to finding them; I had never known where they came from. Now, from father's face, I knew. They had been taken in Terezin.

"I don't want to go," he repeated.

"I think we have to go through the town to get to Prague," I said.

My brother was implacable. He would leave nothing unvisited. "We'll find the camp," he said.

"Why?" I asked. "What is there to see? Barracks? Ovens?"

He thought he saw an arrow pointing off the highway, and he veered onto a tiny road that withered into a dirt track. We turned around. We drove on for another few kilometers. Mossy walls loomed in the fog on both sides of the road, hemming us in. Terezin, *Teresienstadt* in German, had been a fortress town built to garrison soldiers of the Hapsburg army. The walls were two hundred years old, gentled by time. Then, an arrow-shaped blue sign, supernaturally legible in the blue haze, pointed to the right: Krematorium. My brother yanked the car through the opening in the wall.

We parked on a gravel apron. My pulse pounded in my head. I was sweating in the freezing damp. Ahead of us, through high, ornamental, wrought-iron gates, a path sloped downhill. From behind the gate, we heard laughter and a dog barking. It was right there, right off the road, in the middle of town. There was no reason to conceal it; the Germans had moved the townspeople out, all except for those who worked at the camp. A freshly painted yellow stucco villa stood behind us, with a makeshift sign leaning against a sawhorse beside the door. Museum, it announced, museum of the art of the inmates of Terezin. We went in. An old man stood at the door; his wife stood at the ticket counter, and their muzzled German shepherd dozed under the stairs. "We close in a few minutes," he said, in German.

My father said: "We have come from America. Where is the camp?"

The guard pointed through the gate. "It is too late to see that now."

Thank God, I thought.

"But you can look through the museum." The guard switched on the lights in the stairwell.

We could take this; we'd seen this stuff in books. Terezin, the model camp, the school, the orchestra, the art, the inspections by the Red Cross, the caged children awaiting the ovens.

"Is this new?" my father said.

Yes, it was, the guard answered. Brand new. The museum had opened only thirty days earlier. The building used to house a school; it had been a boys' school for the forty years under the communists. During those years, there was never any mention of what had happened next door, in the park with its abandoned barracks: no memory. The guard pointed into the fog. Nothing had happened here, until a few months ago.

We all climbed the stairs, keeping a distance between us, as if this was a normal museum and we were each in search of what interested us most. In the first room, there hung a large, expressionistic painting of a string quartet. Four men played their instruments with skeletal fingers. I stared at the black lines of their gaunt cheekbones, the bones of their legs under loose pajama trousers, their flimsy music stands. I heard the music they played: Haydn, Mozart, Beethoven, Schubert, Brahms. Their German culture, their faith. My father's faith, mine. The *Grosse Fuge*. Death and the Maiden.

The next room held the pictures the children had made. My father and I approached opposite walls. I chose one drawing at random. The label gave the age of the boy who drew the picture: ten in 1943. It gave his place of death: Auschwitz. His date of death: 1944. It was a pencil drawing, a portrait, maybe a self-portrait. The child's head was a skull, his eyes big as the bony sockets. I saw the unevenness of the pencil line across the rough texture of the paper. The child stood in front of shelves. No: they were beds with stick figures collapsed on them, staring out at him. I could sense the boy's hand trying to hold steady, his eye concentrating, trying to get the perspective right.

That child could have been me; that child could have been my father or his cousin or his best friend; it could have been my little daughter, who already loved to draw. That child knew his ending, and, regardless, he drew with all his energy. He looked, he saw, he worked to get it right.

I could hear his absorbed breath as he concentrated on his drawing, and then I could hear and see nothing more. I was weeping, sobbing out loud. The drawings flooded together in a blur, but I could see my father standing across the room from me, sobbing with me. His shoulders shook; his body shook. His hands hung at his sides. Tears streamed down his face.

We walked downstairs. My mother and brother had gone ahead of us. I noticed a Plexiglas box on a stand; the box was stuffed with dollar bills. The guard watched us with sorrow. He had a creased face and white hair; he was my parents' age. He had seen all of this. What had he done? He unlatched the door for us and let us out into the bitter fog.

. . .

In the darkness, purple fog reflected our headlights back into our eyes. For an hour, we drove without talking. It had been necessary to stop, to recognize those—those Jews—who had haunted Berlin and Dresden and the straight autobahn aimed at the Sudetenland, to face what remained of them. Remember, the Haggadah commands, remember as if you, yourself, had been redeemed. Or not redeemed. Remembering was a physical act; we were exhausted.

Then magically the fog dissipated and we dropped into the clear valley of the Moldau. We could breathe again. The words of the psalm came into my head: Yea, though I walk through the valley of the shadow of death, I will fear no evil. From Terezin, the drive had taken an hour.

"We're here," my mother said.

The empty road crossed and recrossed the river, a black serpentine through dim and sulfurous city lights. Icy drizzle shimmered on the highway's cracked paving. The four of us shivered; excitement rippled like repeating, rising chromatic scales, like the gathering currents at the beginning of *The Moldau*, streaming into melody. Smetana's barcarole rushed through my head, washing away reluctance and wariness, death and despair, carrying me into Prague.

Jonny drove slowly; my parents began to recognize buildings. "There's the opera house!" my father exclaimed. The baroque nineteenth-century pile backed onto the river; its bronze chariot and rearing teams of horses were illuminated like a national monument. "That's where I conducted *Traviata* for the first time."

"When Joshka and Maria had better seats than I did," my mother added.

My father was seventy-nine; he had diminished in height and weight and was shaped like a gentle egg. He buckled his pants high over his midsection. His skin was white and webbed with shadowy wrinkles. My daughter could make him smile. In the last decade, he had received honors for his work, as many honors as a fierce, beleaguered champion of the obsolete concept of high art and culture could expect to receive. My mother had acquired my father's bulk. She was tireless, she looked ten years younger than her age, and her dark eyes glowed bright and wounded in her broad face.

We got off the highway and drove through badly lit streets, past blocks of solid buildings. Even in the dim light we could see that black coal dust grimed their elaborately carved stone. There were hardly any signs, no stores, there appeared to be no commerce. The street climbed a steep hill and descended into bright light and enormous space. "Wenceslaus Square!" my mother said. Wenceslaus Square, the heart of Prague, the arena of national heartbreak: German tanks, Russian tanks. The Russians, after the Velvet Revolution, had departed only a year earlier. We drove slowly, as if the paving still bore the laddered scars of steel treads. Cafés and restaurants lined the square; their Art Nouveau facades were lit, sinuous and beautiful and shabby. Everywhere there was effusive ornament: an iron balcony railing wrought in the shape of lilies, carved panels under windowsills. The city seemed like Sleeping Beauty, awakening from stopped time, raw and bruised and tender.

In the morning, a thin layer of snow coated the soot, turning Prague into a woodcut, cleansing for a moment its buildings blackened with pollution, softening its overlay of communist concrete. My mother laughed. "I told you. It snows from November to April here. In Prague, I've never been so cold in my life."

. . .

"We'll never find it," my father said. "Everything's different."

"Jonny, drive past the stadium," my mother insisted. "Drive slowly. I think I know where we are. Just a minute. Stop. Turn right. What's the street name? Hrebenkách? Yes. Here!"

We were driving along a ridge. My brother steered onto a road that sloped steeply downhill. Neat houses protected behind gates lined the street, solid, prosperous houses built in the years just after the First World War.

"There it is. That's it, I'm sure! Deborah, can you read the number?" My mother leaned forward in her seat and banged me on the shoulder. "I don't need the number. That's it. That's our house!"

A red Range Rover with a British license plate was parked in the space beside the gate. Behind the gate, a long flight of steps led up to the brown stucco house. The snow was melting on the pachysandra that covered the slope beside the stairs.

"Let's go in," I said.

"We can't do that," my mother objected. "People are living there."

"I'll tell them I was born here. They'll let us in. Anyway, they're British. At least they'll speak English." I started to get out of the car.

"Are you sure you should?"

"Mother! You've come all the way to Prague, and you don't want to try? Of course I'm sure."

My father sulked in the back seat, more afraid of lost connection than I had suspected.

The couple was attached to the British embassy. They welcomed us. My father reluctantly climbed the steps to the front door. He and my mother, the same size now, each bundled into a long coat, each wearing a beret, walked back into their first house. "It hasn't changed!" my mother exclaimed. She stood at the door to the living room, her mouth open in wonder, her eyes as bright and eager as they must have been the first time she saw these square rooms, all hers. "That's where the piano was. And, Deborah, that's where we put the big desk! The secretary, you know, the one where I keep our papers."

"I don't think she ever thought she'd see this house again," I said to the woman who was living there now.

My mother turned; she heard what she wanted to hear. "You're right. I never thought I would live this long."

On the upstairs landing, my mother turned right. "Deborah's room was at the end of the hall, in the front of the house."

That was the room that belonged to the couple's daughter, too, when she was home from boarding school. A huge, stuffed, toy bear waited in a corner. I looked out the windows at the view: the towers of St. Vitus's cathedral and the castle walls. "I always thought I was born there, on the Hradčany," I said to my mother. "I thought you told me that's where I was born."

"Deborah, I did not! I never said that. You don't remember anything, do you?"

"I guess not," I said. Her own memory shifted events around to make a better story, and she did not like to be caught. It didn't matter. If I was not born in that castle, I had been born, like most babies of Prague, within sight of it, and I was, therefore, susceptible to its spell.

Behind the house, the hill continued its steep rise. A curved stone wall surrounded a little, drained, ornamental pool, and steps led to a terrace close to the crest of the hill. Patches of snow clung to the branches of low evergreens. This was the set for the photographs: my mother with her glamorous, wavy hair and her open-toed shoes; my father, round and smooth in voluminous pleated pants; and me, brand new and swaddled in white eyelet.

. . .

Prague was everywhere familiar, as if I had always lived there. I already knew its music. Beethoven had dedicated his *Waldstein* piano sonata to a member of the family whose palace lay across the Charles Bridge over the Moldau, the bridge on the cover of my mother's photograph album. Lobkowicz princes commissioned string quartets from Haydn, and the manuscripts were still kept in their castles. We crossed the Moldau into the old city and drove past a pair of half-naked bronze girls swooning against the doorposts of an Art Nouveau apartment building, their bold and newly polished breasts gleaming in the gray morning. We passed painted facades, some hundreds of years old, some dating from the exuberant beginnings of this century, and Renaissance facades in black and white *sgrafito*, delicate incised carvings, like images traced on Prague's gray winter sky.

We parked at the edge of the ghetto. Crowds waited in line outside the Alte Neue Synagogue, the Old New Synagogue, and at the gate to the Jewish cemetery, crowds of teenagers, eastern European from the look of their badly made clothes and the blaring colors of their hair, their pasty complexions and bright golden teeth. Many were speaking German. They trampled to slush the paths between the gravestones in the cemetery, past the tomb of the great cabalist and mystic Rabbi Löw carved with his lion. The Nazis feared the Golem, my father had once told me; that was why they left Prague's Jewish quarter intact. And Prague was to have been the site of the Reich's museum of the extinct Jews. Something had to remain to memorialize the feat of their extinction. The faces of the teenagers were grim as they marched past the relics of the people who had been destroyed; this history was new to them, freshly revealed and horrible. My father watched these children march.

I wore a flamboyant scarf, gold and blue. Look, our bright clothes proclaimed, look at us; we are here because this is who we are. Americans. Jews. This is where we come from; these sites are not the artifacts of a vanished people. I understood the Hebrew letters on the jumbled tombstones; I spoke the language of their carved symbols; I could read the sorrow in every stone; I knew the names of the dead with no graves. We walked through the bare gothic interior of the Old New Synagogue. It had been built in the thirteenth century, replacing an older one; Jews had lived in Prague since the city was founded. One of the earliest mentions of a settlement on the banks of the Moldau appears in the chronicles of a Jewish merchant who remarked upon the rich, cosmopolitan marketplace in that settlement and the sturdy stone-and-mortar construction of its buildings. Rudolf II met with Rabbi Löw at least once; the two men discussed numerology and mystical unities.

Another synagogue housed a museum of Jewish artifacts; the Germans collected thousands from all over Czechoslovakia and sent them to Prague to be inventoried and catalogued by Jewish workers before they themselves were transported east. We found the breast-plate from a scroll of the Torah; it had come from Ivančice, the label said. Abba could have carried it, Lady could have touched it as Abba passed by her seat. Quietly, we gazed at it. In Smetana's tone poem the rolling Moldau theme smoothes for a few measures into a shimmering, tranquil melody. The current slows; the river lingers, peaceful and still.

In the seventeenth-century Maisels synagogue, named for Rudolf II's minister of finance, delicate painted arabesques orna-mented the walls. Its space was empty of pews, empty of Torah scrolls and prayer books. The women's gallery stretched across the back of the synagogue like a balcony in a theater. We could have been there before, sixty years ago, a hundred years ago. From the balcony I, bored with services, could have studied the congregation, the men downstairs and the women surrounding me on a hot September day, overheated in furs and silks, their High Holy Day finery. My grand-father, dapper and worldly, could have dwelled in that shul, my grandfather, a man who sang lieder and Ne'ilah during that brief time in central Europe when such a thing was possible with the same Jewish breath. I felt Prague's Jews crowding around me in that light and airy building, to pray, to gossip, to mark a year of prosperity, or a year of despair.

I knew what music had inhabited these spaces, what music ech-oed there still; I knew the prayers that had been sung, the harmo-nies that resonated against the ancient stone vaults and the baroque ceilings. My father still sang them; my brother and I sang with him. If the dead were to come back and take up their worship, their sup-plications and hallelujahs, mourner's kaddish and psalms, we could join their choir. We had every note by heart.

. . .

"I want to see the theater where the premiere of *Don Giovanni* was held," I said.

"It's closed, nobody uses it," my father told me. "It's been closed since the war."

"But it's Mozart's bicentennial. They can't miss a chance like this. What's its name?"

"The Mozart theater, I don't know."

"Where is it?"

"Somewhere around here. Not far."

It was just after one; we had watched the Astronomical Clock on the side of the Old Town Hall strike the hour with its procession of mechanical figures: all twelve Apostles, a miser, an infidel Turk followed closely by skeleton Death wielding his scythe. My brother took my parents to a coffee house; I said I would catch up with them in a few minutes. I wondered if the soles of my shoes would stick to the freezing pavement the way wet hands stick to ice. I wandered out of the Old Town Square toward the river and after two blocks came to a smaller square. Facing me there was a building, lime green, clean and saucy, startling against the surrounding grime. The gilt lace capitals of its columns and pilasters flounced seductive as a negligée. Posters in its vitrines announced performances of plays by Václav Havel. I tried the front doors, but they were shut tight. I decided to try the stage entrance.

In *Don Giovanni* were the precursors to the unhappy characters in my father's operas. Zerlina, the tempted beauty; Masetto, her scorned lover; Donna Elvira, cruelly used by Don Giovanni; Leporello, the Commendatore: the mistresses, the unhappy wives and vengeful fathers. And then there was Don Giovanni himself, an unrepentant man who used women badly and sang the most beautiful music, and Prague loved him. I loved him.

As I turned the corner, a procession of people carrying instrument cases crossed the cobblestone square. I sprinted and caught up with a violinist. He was lanky and middle-aged. "Excuse me! What are you rehearsing?" I called in English, though I knew the answer.

The violinist scanned my bright scarf, my chic Western haircut, my eager face; his own face registered confusion at first, then curiosity. "*Don Giovanni.*"

I laughed. "I thought so."

"Why?" He spoke a bit of English. His name was Antonin Rozmajzl; he introduced his wife to me; he had a brother, he told me, who lived in Akron, which he pronounced with a long "a" like "acorn."

"Can I see the theater? I've come all the way from America to see the theater."

"It is closed now." He looked at his wife; she shrugged. "Are you alone?"

At the moment, I was alone. I nodded.

"Then come," he said.

We entered through the stage door. I followed him past a ballet practice room, through a black metal fire door, as yet unscuffed by instrument cases or props or scenery or frustrated singers, into a short corridor, an improvised dressing room. A black cloak hung on a hook. The building smelled of new paint and varnish. Mr. Rozmajzl pushed open a small door and ushered me through. I stood in the wings, thrilling to an old excitement: spying on the mechanics of enchantment. I almost tripped over the Commendatore's monument; he was flat, less than life-size, an image painted on plywood, a thin, spry, avenging statue. The stage was small, deep, and steeply raked.

Mr. Rozmajzl urged me forward. I stepped onto the boards and walked downstage. Tarpaulins half covered the seats, rococo armchairs with blue velvet, delicate, arched backs like little legato marks. The boxes rose in tiers, five rings to the ceiling, their facades decorated with gilded lozenges in which carved putti played. It was marvelous, intimate, built for delight; if I could open my mouth and sing, my voice without effort would touch the highest seat.

"Look here." Mr. Rozmajzl pointed to a white chalk circle drawn on the black painted floor of the orchestra pit. "That was where Mozart stood to conduct *Don Giovanni*."

I came down off the stage, and the three of us wandered through the theater, up to its satin-lined boxes, into its brocaded lobbies, all waiting for men in powdered wigs and ladies in silk hoop skirts. Mrs. Rozmajzl whispered to her husband, and he asked me to excuse them; their family was waiting.

Mine was, too, I told them, and asked when the next rehearsal was going to be.

"Tonight, at six. With a different orchestra; there are two orchestras and two casts, one international and one Czech. Tonight is the international cast."

"I wish I could hear it."

"Go," he smiled. "Why not?"

"How? How could I get in?"

Antonin Rozmajzl regarded me mischievously. "Go," he repeated. "Ask anybody. Do with them what you did with me."

. . .

"Where have you been?" My family was furious when I showed up at the coffee house an hour later.

"To the Mozart theater."

"It's closed," said my father.

"Actually, it's open. I went inside. I saw it. And, they're working on *Don Giovanni*, of course." I flaunted my discovery. "They'll perform it in December, for Mozart's death. There was a rehearsal this morning, and there's going to be another one tonight. Charles Mackerras is conducting. I'm going; we should all go. You have to see it; it's the most beautiful theater I've ever seen."

"Deborah, there you go with your statements." My mother laughed.

"Trust me," I said.

"I do trust you."

"We can't go to the rehearsal," said my reasonable brother. "We've got tickets for the National Theater."

"To see what?"

"*Pagliacci* and *Cavalleria Rusticana*."

"You want to see those operas when you can see a rehearsal of the first opera performed in the Mozart theater in more than fifty years, and the opera they're doing is *Don Giovanni* with an international cast?"

"International? But are they any good?" my father asked.

"The violinist told me they are."

"And he's an expert."

"I have an idea," I said. "I'll go to the rehearsal, and you go to the National Opera, and we'll compare notes."

"What about me?" asked Nathalie. "I'd rather see *Don Giovanni*."

In the end, they all came with me. We sat in the blue velvet *fauteuils* halfway back in the orchestra. My father chatted with Mackerras; we talked to the singers. Donna Anna and Donna Elvira were Australian, Leporello was Czech, and Zerlina, American. Don Giovanni was a young Ukrainian baritone with a cold.

The house lights dimmed halfway. The overture began, the attack a bit ragged. Don Giovanni swaggered onstage in white high-top sneakers and the cloak I had seen that afternoon hanging in the hall. Mackerras stopped the orchestra. Don Giovanni halted, turned, and loped back into the wings. The orchestra began again, and Don Giovanni reemerged. He was tall and slender, his skin pale; his hair arched back from his high forehead; his nose was aquiline, his jaw narrow and square. He grew immense; he filled the stage. The raked stage forced its own exaggerated perspective. It was an illusion, a trick, the magic of the theater and its perfect size: made for transformation. The drama played out close to us. The small proscenium framed the singers; it enlarged them and pulled them out of themselves; they hovered between reality and fiction across the stage's sublime, ambivalent demarcation. They could see every face in the audience, read each reaction; we could see their faces, their breathing, their eyes. Their voices danced in the theater. The music possessed them, and it possessed us; the characters became more vivid and more alive than my brother and my father sitting on either side of me.

Don Giovanni and Zerlina began "*La, ci darem la mano.*" He had been singing quietly, almost speaking, to protect his voice. "*Give me your hand,*" he sang. "*Let's go away together.*"

"*I want to,*" she answered and hesitated in the same breath. "*But I don't want to.*"

Go with him, I thought. Go! He's a beautiful man, a beautiful Don Giovanni. Just for the moment, listen to your own voice. You have enchanted him, too. You won't lose your virtue, you won't destroy your pleasure. You will have had him and his songs, and you will use them to make your own.

Don Giovanni stepped behind Zerlina and touched her shoulders. She shuddered. *"Come,"* he urged, and, forgetting to save his voice, he sang full out, in love, seduced by Mozart, or by the young American's soprano. And when they had sung the duet through, the few people in the audience applauded, the orchestra's string players tapped their bows on their music stands, and Don Giovanni and Zerlina took each other's hands, glanced into the orchestra pit and Mozart's white circle chalked on the floor, where he had stood at his cembalo in his powdered wig, mouthing their words, improvising accompaniments to their recitatives, and they sang their duet all over again.

. . .

Ivančice, where my father came from. There it was: Ivančice, real as a road sign pointing to an exit on the highway that led east from Prague to Vienna. As we climbed the mountains that ranged between Prague and Brno, the sun came out and glinted on a foot of snow. On the mountains' gentler eastern sides the snow was melting. By the time we turned off the highway, about two hours from Prague, the sun shone on meadows whose grass was still green. We were only sixty miles north of Vienna. The country road climbed up and down low, rolling hills planted on their southern slopes with orchards and vineyards. We followed a slow river overhung with willows whose not-yet-fallen leaves hung in bright amber curtains that turned the water gold. The stream meandered through a shallow valley, through Ivančice. My father leaned forward in his seat. "I used to play by that river," he said.

The sky was bright blue. Ivančice's buildings were buff-colored stucco, and red tiles covered their roofs. A few late flowers still bloomed in dooryards. We parked in the main square, opposite the church, with its restrained Renaissance facade and onion-domed bell tower. From the fifteenth century, Ivančice, my father had told me, had been one of the Hapsburg Empire's designated Jewish towns, a community where Jews were free to settle. My father stood still for a few minutes, getting his bearings.

"This way, I think," he said and pointed to the far corner of the square. We followed him along the cobblestone streets. He paused at the first corner and looked up at the house, a three-story stucco building. "That was where the Goldmanns lived. Above the grocery store, the Jewish grocery store. It was on the first floor."

"Where did you live?" I asked. "Where was your house?"

He shrugged. "I don't know." His voice sounded forlorn and lost.

"How can you not know?"

My father glared at me. The road climbed slightly uphill. A hundred yards farther along, on the right, stood the synagogue. Astonished, we all stopped, even my father, as if we had come upon a miracle. The synagogue was large and square, built of blocks of golden limestone. It was glorious; it was nothing like what I had imagined. Across the length of its facade ran an inscription in large bronze Hebrew letters. I deciphered the words: "Come before His gates with thanks, and His courtyards with praise." It was a verse from the hundredth psalm, which begins: "Make a joyful noise unto the Lord." This was a synagogue for cantors.

Through the windows we saw rows of clocks hanging on pegboard, cheap electric clocks. A loading ramp had been built extending out from the front of the building, and a short flight of iron-grillwork stairs led to the side door. How could the Nazis have used the shul for a stable, I wondered. Surely the horses couldn't climb stairs.

Just inside the door, in a tiny lobby, three middle-aged women sat on wooden chairs under a photograph of Havel. They wore flowered cotton smocks over their shabby dresses. "We would like to look inside," my father explained in a mixture of Czech and German. The women considered us and consulted among themselves. "Wait a moment," one of them said to my father in Czech. She pulled on her overcoat and bustled out of the building.

My father remembered enough Czech to understand that the building was a warehouse and distribution center now for an East German manufacturer of electric clocks. The room was close and hot from an electric space heater. Every few moments, the two remaining women reassured us that somebody would be coming soon. We went outside into the cool day and stood on the loading platform in front of the synagogue's sealed main door. We saw the third woman hurrying up the street, bringing with her another woman, who, like her companion, appeared to be in her sixties. But she was better dressed, and she had combed her hair and put on lipstick. She greeted us in German. She could show us around, if we wanted.

Memory had returned to Ivančice. German could be spoken. Jews could be remembered, and my father could remember, too. He stood, deep in conversation, asking questions; I understood names: Goldmann, Loewensohn. Loewensohn had been Uncle Baci's name. The woman nodded. "*Ja,*" she said. "*Ja.*" She remembered their names, remembered them. We crossed the cobblestone street. "Where did you live?" I asked my father again. A three-story building stood opposite the synagogue.

"There," my father said. "I lived there. That was our house. On the top floor. This was the first apartment building in Ivančice. It was very grand. And Uncle Baci and Rosa Neni lived around the corner."

The woman ushered us inside the front door of the apartment building to the entrance hall, narrow and decrepit now. A child's bicycle was propped against a flaking wall. We went through to a paved courtyard. Stucco had chipped from the walls, and weeds flourished between the paving stones. Laundry hung from some of the windows, and on the second story, somebody had added a makeshift balcony, whose patched, corrugated-iron sides clung to the building. My father tilted his head back and pointed to the corner above the balcony. "Those were our windows. My mother would send me downstairs to play here. This is where we kept our goose." I could almost see Lady, with her severe bun and her bleak eyes, gazing down at my father from her window.

He pointed to a corner of the courtyard. "We had a little pen for the goose. I let it out and played with it. When my father came home from the war, my mother had it killed, and my nurse plucked its feathers. I wept. I didn't recognize my father. He walked into the house; he still wore his uniform. He was a stranger with a big mustache, and my mother ordered me to kiss him: 'Go kiss your papa!'"

"What did you do?"

"I ran away. To Uncle Baci."

Our guide had turned to talk to a woman who had come outside to see what was going on. She came back and spoke with my father.

"What did she say?" my brother asked.

"She said that here, in this courtyard . . ." He took a breath and swallowed. "Here. This is where the Germans rounded up the Jews. This is where they collected them and kept them before they loaded them on the train to Terezin."

The woman led us farther up the hill. The road continued past the edge of the town and into the countryside, where it ended at a high wrought-iron gate beside a ruined chapel with weathered oak doors: the Jewish cemetery. Dead grass and vines climbed over the stone steps to the chapel doors. The woman had keys with her, and she unlocked the padlock securing the gate. The cemetery had been mowed, gravestones had been righted, and brambles cut away. Sunlight dappled the grass. Almost nothing had changed since 1938, the last time my father saw his cousins in Ivančice.

A man who had escaped to South Africa had that summer donated money to maintain the cemetery, the woman told my father. They had just begun. She laughed and jingled her keys. She was becoming the unofficial caretaker of the Jewish community, she said, because she spoke German. She added: it was an honor. Hay was strewn on the chapel floor; perhaps this was where the Nazis had installed their horses. A marble plaque inside the chapel entrance, dated 1902, commemorated its donors. My father read the names:

Sinaiberger, Goldmann, Schallinger. He knew them all. We walked faint, ancient paths through the cemetery. It covered the southern slope of a hill, and it was planted with tall spreading trees, oak and linden, that provided cool shade in summertime, while in winter mourners were protected from the north wind.

"There are gravestones here dating from the fifteenth century," my father told us. We followed him; he knew where he was going. He stopped by a red granite marker on which was carved a broken branch—fallen for his country—and the name "Viktor Loewensohn."

"That is my cousin's grave," my father said, telling the old story. "But Rosa Neni never saw it. She refused to visit it. She always believed that one day her son would come home to her."

We strolled back down the road to the shul as if we had done so many times before. A floor of corrugated metal bisected the open space of the synagogue. From the entrance hall we clanged up a flight of metal stairs to shelves and shelves of East German electric clocks. "This was the women's gallery," my father said. "It was in back, like a balcony. My mother always sat in the front row. To keep an eye on me, I think."

The walls of the synagogue held traces of what had been. Stains in the plaster outlined the arch of the carved wooden ark that held the scrolls of the Torah. The proscenium of the box where the choir stood had been boarded up. The chain for the eternal light, the ner tamid, dangled empty over what had been the bimah. My father walked slowly, unsteady on the slippery metal surface. His face was light, his eyes wide and receptive like a child's; he searched for evidence.

I saw my father, a little boy singing in the choir, his thin soprano flailing against his father's big, bright tenor and his Uncle Baci's sweet baritone. Music hadn't been easy for him, either. Nobody had taught him. He had struggled to claim his place. I saw Abba, young and handsome, his fair hair luxuriant under his cantor's hat, singing the music his own father sang, mixing it with the music he had learned in Vienna, and daring to add his own melodies to those of generations. He came back from war with songs. He sang them, and hid his doubts as to their worthiness behind his blue, confident eyes.

I felt my father's anxiety that he would never know the songs and that his voice would never be strong enough to be heard. I saw him leaning over the edge of the choir loft, following the prayers in the rabbi's prayer book. He ducked out from under the implacable gaze of his stern and dangerous mother. I saw his life on this safe and Jewish street: his travels back and forth between shul and his mother's house and his Uncle Baci's; his hours in Hebrew school, his hours practicing the piano; free time on long summer evenings for the low hills and the slow river. Time on long summer evenings to sing Schubert and Mozart and Brahms, and to sit on Uncle Baci's lap and listen to "The Elder Tree Woman." In the twilight, he could imagine an old lady growing in the branches of the elderberry bush outside the window. Here, no evil could ever harm him. He must have hated being transplanted to Baltimore. He had passed his childhood in a garden, among vineyards and willows.

He laughed. "I remember Mrs. Goldmann in the choir. My friend's mother. I was terrified of her. She used to hit me if I was out of tune."

"*Mrs.* Goldmann?" I asked.

"Oh, yes. Women sang in our choir."

Oh, yes. "And not at Chizuk Amuno?"

"In Baltimore they were very strict."

We climbed back downstairs. Racks of clocks, cartons of clocks, clocks were piled everywhere. None of them was ticking. My father walked carefully, watching where he stepped. The wide wooden floorboards were painted crimson. My father stared at the red floor, startled at first, then his face lit up, bright as a child returning home. "I remember the color," he said softly.

Epilogue

One evening in August 1994, my family was having dinner at my parents' house in Maine: I was there with my husband and Charlotte, my brother and his wife and their three children, my mother and father. Just before dessert, my brother got up from the table.

"We have to leave now if we're going to make it," he said to my father.

"Where are you going?" I asked.

"To a choir rehearsal," my brother answered. He paused. "Didn't you know?"

"Know what?"

"The synagogue has formed a choir," my father said.

A member of the congregation, a pediatrician with perfect pitch, had copied my father's music, the pages of choral parts that had been silent for fifteen years. The choir had been practicing since winter, and they were going to sing for the High Holy Days.

"Why didn't you tell me?"

My father shrugged. "Didn't I?"

Before I could ask to go with them, they were out the door. I was furious; they had excluded me again. And I did not have to be left out; women sang in this choir. That year, I sang from my seat. The music sounded as beautiful as I remembered. It had never died; it was just waiting to be sung. I was moved and exalted, grateful and deeply angry.

The following summer, I asked to join the choir. The director was delighted. I took Charlotte with me to my first rehearsal. Most of the members belonged to the congregation, and then there were a few ringers, a few non-Jews. Charlotte and I walked my father to the front of the synagogue. I held my father's arm; he held Charlotte's hand. I carried his cardboard box of music and placed it on his lectern and went to join the choir in the balcony.

"Why don't you play downstairs in the basement room?" I asked Charlotte.

"No," she said. "I don't want to."

"But other kids are down there."

"I want to hear the choir. I'm coming with you!"

"She's grown so much," the choir members exclaimed. "She looks just like you." The Jewish community of Rockland, Maine, I realized, was about the same size as the community in Ivančice had been.

The late summer wind blew the smell of the fish-processing plant in through the open windows. Golden evening light shone on the bimah. My father leaned against the bimah railing. He was eighty-two; when he stood, he tilted dangerously left and seemed about to fall. A few weeks earlier, we had tried to get him up the trail to Maiden's Cliff, but he could not walk more than a few yards without stopping for breath. Just at the point where, always, I checked to see if a mountain lion was lurking, he had asked to turn back.

But he continued working. The New York City Opera was rehearsing his opera *Esther* for its premiere in October. He was writing a Friday evening service that would be, it turned out, the last piece he finished. Abba's tunes, his grandfather's melodies: all had found their way into my father's music, into his operas and songs, and finally into this service. He resisted them, asking how he could use such tunes in the world today, tunes that failed, by their very beauty, to acknowledge the terrible deaths of those who had sung them. He took them apart and disguised the melodies, but they remained his faith. No matter where he was, all his life he returned to sing his father's songs, he returned to the music of his childhood.

He took off his beret and shuffled through his sheets of music. When he was ready, he looked up impatiently. He saw Charlotte standing beside me, and he smiled. My father's smile was Schubertian, I thought; when Schubert shifted into a major key, his music broke your heart.

Dana Goldsmith, the doctor who conducted the choir, gave my father his pitch. But my father, as had his father before him, began wherever he wanted. He sang the beautiful, recurring High Holy Day motif that opens the prayers. His voice emerged rich and clear as a young man's. He beamed, pleased and astonished at his own sound.

"Let me try that again," he said, and began anew, in a different key. Dana Goldsmith, infuriated, rolled his eyes, but the choir found the note. We followed with the Shehecheyanu, the prayer at the beginning of every holiday thanking God for bringing us to this season of celebration.

A soprano sang the haunting, ornamented solo, a melody sung only on the High Holy Days. In memory Abba sang it, but it was as beautiful when a woman sang its long, supple line. "Listen," I whispered to Charlotte, "listen, my sweet girl. This is your music. It belongs to you." But she was already transfixed.

After the rehearsal, I drove my father home. We followed the coast to Camden and headed inland. Maples on the sides of Mt. Megunticook were beginning to turn red.

"This time of year makes me so sad," Hugo said.

"It always has, hasn't it?"

He nodded.

"But you love it, too."

He looked at me balefully. "That depends on what you mean by love."

"I suppose it does." I smiled.

We passed the lake; the last traces of purple shimmered on trailing clouds above the black silhouettes of the low mountains, and a thin band of white light followed the line of their ridges. The mountains, the purple, and the edge of light reflected peace in the still lake.

Charlotte sat in the back seat, singing. Like me, like her father, like her grandfather, she did not have perfect pitch, but she sang that Shehecheyanu, its ornaments and arpeggios, in her own gleeful, noisy, wandering way, in her own shifting keys. All the way home, she sang that prayer while my father and I listened. *Shehecheyanu:* You have kept us alive.

Acknowledgments

I wish to thank those steadfast friends who read and discussed various versions of these words: Katharine Davis, who always understood the underlying emotion, Sue Zesiger, who deflected doubts and provided diversions. And from the beginning, Ellen Hume's grace, honesty, faith, and good sense sustained me in every way as I searched for the right key.

I can only offer Jill Kneerim—exacting editor, dear friend, wise and enthusiastic agent whose practical sense of possibility is what gave this book its shape—a perennial garden of thank-yous. Ira Silverberg brought me to Grove/Atlantic; I am deeply grateful to Elisabeth Schmitz, who edited this book with delicacy and care and with an unerring instinct for story and language and truth.

My mother, Nathalie Weisgall, confirmed many of my guesses and has offered unwavering support. My brother, Jonathan Weisgall, patiently researched questions ranging from Verdi's arias to batting averages; he also spent hours searching for photographs and documents. This story, however, tells only what I remember. They, I am sure, recall those years differently, and I hope that in this account they will find some points of correspondence with their own memories.

Throop Wilder has given boundless love and provided a wild ride. Anne St. Goar prescribed walks, rows down the river, and large doses of friendship. As my deadline approached, the mothers of

Lincoln, especially Nancy Fleming, Katie Walker, Jackie Lenth, and Terry Perlmutter, were always generous and willing to invite my daughter to their houses after school. And I imagine that one day Charlotte will write about what it was like to have her own mother spend so many hours in a silent room.